#24-92 BK Bud May 92

NORTH CARO 〈√〉 **P9-DCY-187**

STATE BOARD OF COMMUNITY COLLEGES
LIBRARIES
SOUTHEASTERN COMMUNITY COLLEGE

SOUTHEASTERN COMMUNITY
COLLEGE LIBRARY
WHITEVILLE, NC 28472

TRADE

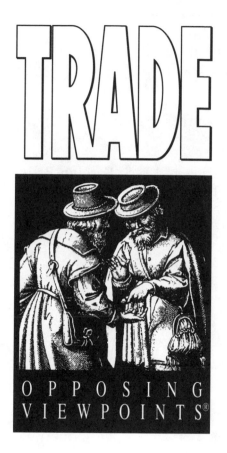

OPPOSING
VIEWPOINTS®

Other Books of Related Interest in the Opposing Viewpoints Series:

HF
1455
.T644
1991

TRADE

OPPOSING
VIEWPOINTS®

David L. Bender & Bruno Leone, *Series Editors*

William Dudley, *Book Editor*

SOUTHEASTERN COMMUNITY
COLLEGE LIBRARY
WHITEVILLE, NC 28472

OPPOSING VIEWPOINTS SERIES ®

Greenhaven Press, Inc.   PO Box 289009   San Diego, CA 92198-0009

No part of this book may be reproduced or used in any form or by any means, electrical, mechanical, or otherwise, including, but not limited to, photocopy, recording, or any information storage and retrieval system, without prior written permission from the publisher.

Library of Congress Cataloging-in-Publication Data

Trade : opposing viewpoints / William Dudley, book editor.
    p.   cm. — (Opposing viewpoints series)
  Includes bibliographical references and index.
  ISBN 0-89908-151-7 (pbk.). — ISBN 0-89908-176-2 (lib. bdg.)
  1. United States—Commercial policy. 2. Free trade.
  3. Protectionism. 4. Balance of trade—United States.
  5. International trade. I. Dudley, William, 1964-   . II. Series:
  Opposing viewpoints series (Unnumbered)
  HF1455.T644   1991
  382'.3'0973—dc20   90-24087

Copyright © 1991 by Greenhaven Press, Inc.

"Congress shall make no law . . .
abridging the freedom of speech,
or of the press."

First Amendment to the U.S. Constitution

The basic foundation of our democracy is the first amendment
guarantee of freedom of expression. The Opposing Viewpoints
Series is dedicated to the concept of this basic freedom and the
idea that it is more important to practice it than to enshrine it.

Contents

Chapter 5: What Is the Future of the World Trading System?

Why Consider Opposing Viewpoints?

"It is better to debate a question without settling it than to settle a question without debating it."

Joseph Joubert (1754-1824)

The Importance of Examining Opposing Viewpoints

The purpose of the Opposing Viewpoints Series, and this book in particular, is to present balanced, and often difficult to find, opposing points of view on complex and sensitive issues.

Probably the best way to become informed is to analyze the positions of those who are regarded as experts and well studied on issues. It is important to consider every variety of opinion in an attempt to determine the truth. Opinions from the mainstream of society should be examined. But also important are opinions that are considered radical, reactionary, or minority as well as those stigmatized by some other uncomplimentary label. An important lesson of history is the eventual acceptance of many unpopular and even despised opinions. The ideas of Socrates, Jesus, and Galileo are good examples of this.

Readers will approach this book with their own opinions on the issues debated within it. However, to have a good grasp of one's own viewpoint, it is necessary to understand the arguments of those with whom one disagrees. It can be said that those who do not completely understand their adversary's point of view do not fully understand their own.

A persuasive case for considering opposing viewpoints has been presented by John Stuart Mill in his work *On Liberty*. When examining controversial issues it may be helpful to reflect on this suggestion:

The only way in which a human being can make some approach to knowing the whole of a subject, is by hearing what can be said about it by persons of every variety of opinion, and studying all modes in which it can be looked at by every character of mind. No wise man ever acquired his wisdom in any mode but this.

Analyzing Sources of Information

The Opposing Viewpoints Series includes diverse materials taken from magazines, journals, books, and newspapers, as well as statements and position papers from a wide range of individuals, organizations, and governments. This broad spectrum of sources helps to develop patterns of thinking which are open to the consideration of a variety of opinions.

Pitfalls to Avoid

A pitfall to avoid in considering opposing points of view is that of regarding one's own opinion as being common sense and the most rational stance, and the point of view of others as being only opinion and naturally wrong. It may be that another's opinion is correct and one's own is in error.

Another pitfall to avoid is that of closing one's mind to the opinions of those with whom one disagrees. The best way to approach a dialogue is to make one's primary purpose that of understanding the mind and arguments of the other person and not that of enlightening him or her with one's own solutions. More can be learned by listening than speaking.

It is my hope that after reading this book the reader will have a deeper understanding of the issues debated and will appreciate the complexity of even seemingly simple issues on which good and honest people disagree. This awareness is particularly important in a democratic society such as ours where people enter into public debate to determine the common good. Those with whom one disagrees should not necessarily be regarded as enemies, but perhaps simply as people who suggest different paths to a common goal.

Developing Basic Reading and Thinking Skills

In this book, carefully edited opposing viewpoints are purposely placed back to back to create a running debate; each viewpoint is preceded by a short quotation that best expresses the author's main argument. This format instantly plunges the reader into the midst of a controversial issue and greatly aids that reader in mastering the basic skill of recognizing an author's point of view.

A number of basic skills for critical thinking are practiced in the activities that appear throughout the books in the series. Some of the skills are:

Evaluating Sources of Information. The ability to choose from among alternative sources the most reliable and accurate source in relation to a given subject.

Separating Fact from Opinion. The ability to make the basic distinction between factual statements (those that can be demonstrated or verified empirically) and statements of opinion (those that are beliefs or attitudes that cannot be proved).

Identifying Stereotypes. The ability to identify oversimplified, exaggerated descriptions (favorable or unfavorable) about people and insulting statements about racial, religious, or national groups, based upon misinformation or lack of information.

Recognizing Ethnocentrism. The ability to recognize attitudes or opinions that express the view that one's own race, culture, or group is inherently superior, or those attitudes that judge another culture or group in terms of one's own.

It is important to consider opposing viewpoints and equally important to be able to critically analyze those viewpoints. The activities in this book are designed to help the reader master these thinking skills. Statements are taken from the book's viewpoints and the reader is asked to analyze them. This technique aids the reader in developing skills that not only can be applied to the viewpoints in this book, but also to situations where opinionated spokespersons comment on controversial issues. Although the activities are helpful to the solitary reader, they are most useful when the reader can benefit from the interaction of group discussion.

Using this book and others in the series should help readers develop basic reading and thinking skills. These skills should improve the reader's ability to understand what is read. Readers should be better able to separate fact from opinion, substance from rhetoric, and become better consumers of information in our media-centered culture.

This volume of the Opposing Viewpoints Series does not advocate a particular point of view. Quite the contrary! The very nature of the book leaves it to the reader to formulate the opinions he or she finds most suitable. My purpose as publisher is to see that this is made possible by offering a wide range of viewpoints that are fairly presented.

David L. Bender
Publisher

Introduction

"Few measures. . .would do more to promote the cause of freedom at home and abroad than complete free trade."

Milton and Rose Friedman

"Our blind allegiance to free trade threatens our national standard of living and our future."

John M. Culbertson

International trade plays an increasingly important role in the world economy. Facilitated by technological advances in transportation and communication, traffic in world trade has exploded in this century. As recently as 1957 the total volume of goods and services traded across national borders was $57 billion. In 1989 that amount had risen to $2.9 trillion.

The United States has been at the forefront of the world trade explosion. The U.S. engages in more trade than any other single nation. In 1989, for example, the U.S. traded $364 billion in exports and $473 billion in imports. These statistics are evidence that the large and relatively open U.S. market has encouraged many countries to export to the U.S., often with great success. As trade attorney Brink Lindsey comments in an analysis of the trade practices of Japan, Korea, Singapore, and other East Asian nations, "For all the major exporters in the region, the U.S. is still the largest single market."

Ironically, it is the economic success of countries such as Japan that has caused many people to question the benefit of U.S. free trade. Critics of U.S. trade policy focus on several related concerns. One of these is the U.S. trade deficit, which in the 1980s reached over $100 billion a year. Another worry is that U.S. industries may decline as they lose sales to foreign competitors. Many observers cite as an example the fact that in 1970, nearly all of the home electronic items used in America were produced by U.S. firms, while in 1990 less than 5 percent were manufactured in the U.S. They argue that U.S. free trade allows other countries to build their industries by trading goods in the American market at the expense of U.S. companies and jobs. As Tennessee representative James H. Quillen states, "We are sentencing ourselves and our children to a bleak future of fewer competitive business enterprises, fewer good jobs, less economic opportunity, and a lower standard of living. As we are now practicing the theology of so-called free trade, we are producing profoundly destructive results for this country." Quillen and others argue for tough trade restrictions to limit the number of foreign products that enter the U.S.

Yet many others, including economist William H. Peterson, argue that efforts to restrict or manage trade will cause more harm than good. "Whatever label it may carry," Peterson writes, "[trade] protection spells destruction." Economist and former presidential adviser William A. Niskanen worries that if the U.S. begins to rely on trade sanctions and restrictions against other countries to improve its own economic situation, it may become the bully of world trade and endanger the whole world trading system.

Whether the U.S. should support and promote free trade in the world is a central issue underlying *Trade: Opposing Viewpoints*. Questions debated are: Is Free Trade the Best Trading System? Is the U.S. the Victim of Other Nations' Unfair Trade Practices? Should Trade Be Restricted? How Critical Is the U.S. Trade Deficit? What Is the Future of the World Trading System? These issues are sure to continue to rise in importance as the Cold War between the U.S. and the Soviet Union begins to fade.

CHAPTER 1

Is Free Trade the Best Trading System?

Chapter Preface

Free trade is the policy of allowing people of one country to buy and sell from other countries without restrictions. Adam Smith (1723-1790), British economist and philosopher, is considered the originator of the free trade idea. One of Smith's central arguments was that while people could conceivably avoid trade by producing all of their own goods and services, most people would not choose such a Robinson Crusoe-like existence. Instead, people are more likely to specialize in certain tasks and trade for others. This is much more efficient and beneficial to everyone, he contended. Smith believed that this principle should apply to nations as well—specialization and trade, rather than complete self-reliance, is best.

Smith's arguments for free trade became one of the foundations of modern economics and, specifically, of U.S. trade policy. Many economists, however, question whether Smith's ideas remain valid for the U.S. today. William R. Hawkins, for example, argues that many nations can and do make policies that undermine free trade in order to obtain certain advantages, such as industrial development and domestic jobs. Unless the U.S. begins to do the same, he asserts, it faces the loss of key industries, forfeiture of world technological leadership, and decline in living standards.

These differences in philosophy underlie many of the issues about trade. The viewpoints in the following chapter consider whether free trade is beneficial for the U.S. and the world.

"International free trade is a way to bind the world together and elevate it to a new vista of world peace and prosperity."

Free Trade Is the Best Trading System

William H. Peterson

Many economists strongly support free trade not only as an efficient use of resources, but as a way to promote international cooperation. In the following viewpoint, William H. Peterson argues that trade, unhampered by government restrictions, is the system that best promotes the just and efficient use of economic resources. He asserts that U.S. support for international free trade following World War II has led to unprecedented peace and prosperity for the world. Peterson holds the Lundy Chair of Business Philosophy at Campbell University in Buies Creek, North Carolina.

As you read, consider the following questions:

1. Why is free trade under attack, according to Peterson?
2. What lessons concerning trade and warfare does the author draw from the past?
3. Why does Peterson believe free trade is a morally just system?

Reprinted from "What Is a Just International Economic Order?" by William H. Peterson, *The Freeman*, January 1986.

We are under attack, both at home and abroad. The target is the rather open—and I think, rather moral—international trading and investment system that has prevailed, evolved, and expanded since the end of the Second World War.

Here in America the attack is now put in the context of the United States having suffered a record foreign trade deficit of $123.3 billion in 1984. . . as a flood of U.S. imports swamps modest increases in U.S. exports. . . .

These skyrocketing deficits are leading to growing political pressure for further stifling our nation's imports and thereby, however inadvertently, setting back economic development throughout the world, especially the Third World. In Washington the political pressure springs from industries suffering the most from foreign competition, such as steel, autos, and textiles. Friends of these industries in Congress are legion. Congressmen and lobbyists claim that millions of jobs have been lost, that more millions of jobs are at stake, and that only further protection will preclude disaster. Imports of everything from cameras to footwear, from copper to copiers, from garments to autos, from Italian wine to Danish silver, are under veiled or open attack. A prominent businessman promotes a 20 per cent manufactured-goods surcharge on all imports (phased out over three years) as a means of "attacking" the big U.S. trade deficit.

The very word attack has military as well as moral overtones, and I don't believe it is unwarranted for me to say that over the longer run world peace, apart from world prosperity, hangs in the balance. A growing system of international cooperation, of freedom and free enterprise—for these are the roots of a just international economic order—is at bay.

Permit me, then, to recall in this regard the slogan of IBM, one of the world's great trading corporations, "World Peace Through World Trade." The remarkable 19th-century French economist Frederic Bastiat made this similar observation, "When goods can't cross frontiers, armies will."

In other words, I believe that the present international economic order is indeed a just one or at least an increasingly just one, despite the incursions of the Soviet Union and other aggressive states such as Libya, Iran, and Vietnam. But the growing forces of protectionism at home and abroad are inadvertently threatening that order and are asking for retaliation. They are playing with fire.

Why Trade?

Do I exaggerate? Historical evidence abounds on the disruptive power of protectionism, on the correlation between free trade and world peace. In the 17th and 18th centuries, protectionism was, of course, a factor leading to the American Revolution. The American Revolution was triggered by such Parliamentary acts as the Sugar Act of 1764 and the Stamp Act of 1765. The Sugar Act imposed a duty of three pence a gallon on "foreign"—i.e., non-British—molasses, a duty which the New England rum manufacturers insisted would ruin them. The Stamp Act hit lawyers, publishers, and traders, requiring all legal documents to be affixed with royal stamps.

But as Adam Smith noted in his *Wealth of Nations*, the fundamental economic issue of the American colonists was larger than duties and stamps. It was the central problem of mercantilism, of protectionist Britain putting down the American colonies, regarding them as but a source of raw materials and a market for its wares, with Britain as the master manufacturer, banker, merchant, and shipper.

Protectionism was also a factor in causing the Civil War, with the protectionist forces of the industrial North goading the agricultural South. When Congress passed the so-called Tariff of Abominations of 1828 and succeeded it with an even higher tariff in 1832, for example, John Calhoun led a state convention of South Carolina to issue an Ordinance of Nullification, the idea that the U.S. Constitution, correctly interpreted, empowered a state to nullify Federal laws inimical to its interests. The tariff issue became embodied in the question of states' rights leading right up to the question of secession and the Civil War.

Lessons from History

Again, the McKinley Tariff of 1890 and the Dingley Tariff of 1897 pushed protectionist walls to the highest levels in the history of America and contributed to the international frictions and retaliations culminating in the First World War. If there was a lesson on the counterproductivity of protectionism to world peace and prosperity, it wasn't learned after that war. For in 1930 came the giant Smoot-Hawley Tariff, approved by President Herbert Hoover. Not only did Smoot-Hawley worsen the tensions that precipitated World War II but it held back in America the recovery that characterized most of the industrial world by the early 1930s.

After World War II, America, to its great credit, extended a program of reciprocal trade agreements, and helped to organize the General Agreement on Tariffs and Trade (GATT) aimed at reciprocally reducing trade barriers around the globe. Postwar historical barriers to world trade indeed have been breaking down the world over, and it is worth noting that since World War II no big international war has occurred. Moreover, a good example of the freer trade movement in action happened in the early 1960s when the Kennedy round of tariff reductions produced a pronounced lessening of protectionism and a speed-up

19

of international development, especially in the Third World.

Against this backdrop, however, is a growing return of the philosophy of protectionism. The job of economic education of people everywhere remains unfinished. We must set forth the case for a system of individual private property rights (without which no other human rights are possible), of open international trade and investment—the things which are the basis for a just international economic order. We should get down to the very basis of society: social cooperation, mutual help, mutual production, and mutual trade. The answer lies in the idea of freedom, free enterprise, and limited—repeat, limited—government.

The Law of Scarcity

Is not trade a kind of glue that holds society together? As a teaser, let me remind you of the dozens of English family names that reveal an occupation of generations past. Consider family names like Archer, Smith, Clark, Cook, Banker, Butcher, Fisher, Farmer, Carpenter, Sawyer, Wheeler, Baker, Cooper, Binder, Mason, Hammer, Saddler, Hunter, Teacher, Brewer, and so on. The phenomenon also applies to foreign tongues. Eisenhower, for example, translates to "iron-maker."

Man trades because of the primordial law of scarcity, the very underpinning of economics, the idea that man must work and produce the means of his survival, or he will perish. Or, as the Lord Jehovah thundered down on disobedient Adam and Eve as they passed through the gates of Paradise: "In the sweat of thy face shalt thou eat bread."

Work overcomes scarcity, but how effectively? To what extent? Because of the principle of what Adam Smith called division of labor (the idea of particularized work skills, of specialization by occupations to bring about greater productivity), work became more meaningful and far more productive. Men and women over time have sought out different walks of life, different trades, different occupations, different professions, different callings.

Yet specialization or division of labor, of lands as well as people, presupposes the market mandate of barter, of trade, of swapping one's surplus goods for someone else's surplus goods, as did Robinson Crusoe and Friday to such salubrious effect. So let me invoke another great principle of basic economic law—the principle of comparative advantage. This principle maintains that total economic well-being is furthered as each person, region, and nation specializes in the creation of those goods and services which can be produced, in relative terms, most efficiently. In this manner the great bugaboo of scarcity—so universal, so ubiquitous—can be better overcome, with that delightful spinoff, as I noted earlier, of greater international peace. In other words, we can hardly expect a supplier in one country to go around and shoot his customers in other countries.

To be sure, the vehicles for world trade are overwhelmingly multinational corporations. And these MNCs are, of course, greedy, imperialistic, profit-hungry, uncaring, exploitative, and suffering from every other evil invective known to man.

Reprinted with permission from *Reason* magazine. Copyright © 1985 by the Reason Foundation, Box 40105, Santa Barbara, CA 93140.

I've invoked the concept of profit, the drive behind the multi-nationals, the drive which I equate with self-interest. How can we defend what appears to me so basic and inescapable a part of human nature? This is not to denigrate altruism and the qual-ities of faith, hope, and charity. But it is to assert the essentially individualistic self-motivated nature of human action, of man ever scouting and weighing options on how to survive, on how to overcome scarcity. And hence the worldwide social need of trade, including international trade, and the universal social need to recognize the innate self-interest side of human nature. In this regard, let me resort to that eminent professor of moral philosophy—for that was his title—Adam Smith, who declared in his *Wealth of Nations*: "It is not from the benevolence of the butcher, the brewer, or the baker that we expect our dinner, but from their regard to their own interest. We address ourselves not to their humanity but to their self-love and never talk to them of our own necessities but of their advantages."

Self-interest—the profit motive—mightily serves the public interest, the common good. But, in truth, it is not an unalloyed good. The mugger in Central Park, for example, is pursuing his self-interest. Hence, trade must itself be subject to ethical considerations, to the absence of fraud, force, and moral turpitude.

A Two-Way Street

Third World nations must realize, I think, that trade is a two-way street. Profit is mutual and without transfer of capital and technology their peoples will languish in poverty and squalor. Yes, MNCs in pursuit of profits will seek out areas of low wages and natural resources as well as areas of high wages and hence high demand. But is it a crime to seek out low wages (and thereby drive them higher)?

Let me remind you that a century and a half ago the U.S. was itself a developing nation, and MNCs, especially those from England and France, invested heavily in our country, most notably in our railroads which bound our fledgling nation together, North and South, East and West. So, too, have MNCs greatly helped write the success stories of "the Gang of Four" in the Pacific Basin—South Korea, Hong Kong, Taiwan, and Singapore. I also want to take note of how French, British, German, Japanese, and American multinational corporations figured in the successful development of the West African nation in which in the early 1960s I served as an economic consultant—the Republic of the Ivory Coast.

Now, is such an international economic order, as I have described, just? Justice is not the easiest word to define. Aristotle said it is a matter of equal rewards for equals and unequal rewards for unequals. The important black American economist, Walter Williams of George Mason University, defines social justice as a matter of "I get to keep what I earn and you get to keep what you earn." I connect justice with ethical choices—rewards for good choices, retribution for bad ones. At any rate, I believe the word "exploitation," in or out of the Third World, is largely in the eye of the beholder whenever choice abounds in a free society.

The key to understanding the relationship between a buyer and seller, employee and employer, saver and investor, producer and consumer is freedom—i.e., voluntarism, the absence of coercion, the ability to shop around for the best offers and the best bids. Such freedom for the individual tends to lead to strong and vigorous economic development as well as to individual well-being.

As a model of such economic development let me offer the case of Hong Kong. Hong Kong is not without problems, but it has prospered without much, if any, government planning and

22

with minimum taxation and regulation. This British Crown Colony, which reverts to Chinese Communist control in 1997, stands as a monument to the remarkable creativity of free trade.

Hong Kong is a city with a population of 5.5 million, mostly refugees from Mainland China, occupying an area of 400 square miles at the tip of South China. Among other things, it is:

- the world's largest exporter of garments, toys and games;
- the world's major supplier of light consumer items including clocks and watches, plastic and artificial flowers, batteries, watchbands, candles, electric fans, and so on;
- the second busiest container port in volume in the world after Rotterdam;
- the second largest shipowning center in the world;
- the third largest international banking and financial center in the world.

On top of the above, Hong Kong has:

- a GNP [gross national product] per capita only lower than that of Japan in Asia;
- the second highest per capita consumption of electricity in Asia;
- on a per capita basis, more bank branches or representative offices than any other territory in the world;
- the highest telephone density in South-East Asia;
- the highest vehicle density in the world next to Monaco.

Having said all this, I am hopeful that you see that the push for protectionism and the assault on multinationals are destined, for the most part inadvertently, to hurt the very people that the purveyors of these ideas say they wish to help—namely, the consumers at home and abroad, including the consumers in the Third World. Protectionism, you see, crushes choice. It denies competition. It depresses living standards. It robs the consumer of one of his most precious possessions—his sovereignty. Where has the consumer fared best, for example, in Ghana where for the most part MNCs have fled, or in its next-door neighbor, the Republic of the Ivory Coast where MNCs proliferate and average per capita income is around three times greater than in Ghana?. . .

The Need for Economic Education

Economic educators have the considerable job of making clear:

- that tariffs don't protect jobs (actually they destroy jobs),
- that the rich hardly become richer by exploiting the poor (actually they get rich in a market economy by enriching the poor, and by raising living standards through capital formation),
- that if we don't buy Japanese cars and copiers the Japanese won't be able to buy our airplanes and soybeans,

23

- that if we don't buy Mexican cotton and Brazilian sugar the Mexicans and Brazilians won't be able to repay their huge debts to American banks.

The Advantage of Trade

The taylor does not attempt to make his own shoes, but buys them of the shoemaker. The shoemaker does not attempt to make his own clothes, but employs a taylor. The farmer attempts to make neither the one nor the other, but employs those different artificers. All of them find it for their interest to employ their whole industry in a way in which they have some advantage over their neighbours, and to purchase with a part of its produce, or what is the same thing, with the price of a part of it, whatever else they have occasion for.

What is prudence in the conduct of every private family, can scarce be folly in that of a great kingdom. If a foreign country can supply us with a commodity cheaper than we ourselves can make it, better buy it of them with some part of the produce of our own industry, employed in a way in which we have some advantage. The general industry of the country, being always in proportion to the capital which employs it, will not thereby be diminished, no more than that of the above-mentioned artificers; but only left to find out the way in which it can be employed with the greatest advantage.

Adam Smith, *The Wealth of Nations*, 1776.

In a free society choice is critical. The sovereign consumer has every producer, big and little, by the jugular, as Ludwig von Mises pointed out. In the market the consumer is King or Queen Customer.

A Moral System

The market system is a moral system, a system of voluntary social cooperation. What is more, it is the Golden Rule in action. As you know, the Golden Rule says, "Do unto others as you would have others do unto you." What does the market say? It says, in the words of Adam Smith in his *Wealth of Nations*: "Give me that which I want and you shall have this which you want." The market, in other words, says, let's cooperate, let's work for each other, let me help you so you can help me. . . .

Let us, then, educate on the case for unhampered world commerce as a key way to help each other at home and abroad. International free trade is a way to bind the world together and elevate it to a new vista of world peace and prosperity, of world respect and understanding.

"Free trade as it is preached today nurtures and reinforces many of our worst problems."

Free Trade Is Harmful

David Morris

David Morris is a writer and director of the Institute for Local Self-Reliance, an organization in Washington D.C. which provides technical assistance and information to communities on issues of urban development. In the following viewpoint, he writes that free trade is a harmful doctrine which promotes economic development at all costs. Morris complains that unlimited free trade results in poverty, hunger, and pollution. He asserts we need to reexamine the values that underlie free trade.

As you read, consider the following questions:

1. Why does the author think that free trade has been harmful?
2. Why is the law of comparative advantage less relevant to today's situation, according to the author?
3. What alternative world economy does Morris propose?

David Morris, "Free Trade: The Great Destroyer." Excerpted, with permission, from the September/October 1990 issue of *The Ecologist*, Station Road, Sturminster Newton, Dorset, UK, DT10 1BB.

Free trade is the religion of our age. In its name, every nation has now become enmeshed in a planetary economy in which the transport of capital, materials, goods and people takes precedence over the autonomy, the sovereignty, and ultimately, the culture, of our communities.

The planetary economy merges nations. Yoshitaka Sajima, vice-president of Mitsui and Company (USA), asserts: "The US and Japan are not just trading with each other anymore—they've become part of each other.". . .

Planetism commands our attention and our resources. The principal tasks before our leaders, we are told, is to nurture, extend and manage emerging global systems. . . . Trade talks are on the top of every leader's agenda, from Mikhail Gorbachev to George Bush. Political leaders meet to develop stable systems for global financial markets and exchange rates to allow the greatest flow of resources among nations with the least instability. . . .

The Doctrine Falters

Yet at this very moment in history when the doctrines of free trade and globalism are so dominant, we find more and more people raising doubts. Two hundred years ago, Benjamin Franklin warned: "The man who would trade independence for security deserves to wind up with neither." Willfully and consciously, we have made that trade.

The absurdities of globalism are becoming ever more evident. Consider the case of the toothpick and the chopstick. A few years ago, I was eating at a restaurant in Saint Paul, Minnesota. After lunch, I picked up a toothpick wrapped in plastic. On the plastic was the word 'Japan'. Now Japan has little wood and no oil. Yet in our global economy, it is deemed efficient to send little pieces of wood and some barrels of oil to Japan, wrap the one in the other and send them back to Minnesota. This toothpick may embody 50,000 miles of travel. Meanwhile, in 1987, a Minnesota factory began producing millions of disposable chopsticks a year for sale in Japan. In my mind's eye, I see two ships passing one another in the northern Pacific. One carries little pieces of Minnesota wood bound for Japan; the other carries little pieces of wood from Japan bound for Minnesota. Such is the logic of free trade.

Two centuries of trade has not evened up disparities in world living standards but exacerbated them. According to Swiss economist Paul Bairoch, per capita GNP [gross national product] in 1750 was approximately the same in the developed countries as in the undeveloped ones. In 1930, the ratio was about 4 to 1 in favour of the developed. Today it is 8 to 1.

Consider the plight of the Third World. Developing nations borrowed enormous sums of money to create the infrastructure to specialize in what they do best and to expand their export capacity. To repay the loans, these countries had to increase their exports even more to earn internationally acceptable currencies. One result has been a dramatic shift in their agricultural resources from producing food for internal consumption to producing food for export. Economists point to increased exports of wheat and soybeans from the developing world as evidence of their progress. But take the case of Brazil. Brazilian per capita production of basic food stuffs (rice, blackbeans, manioc and potatoes) fell 13 per cent from 1977 to 1984. Per capita output of exportable foodstuffs (soybeans, oranges, cotton, peanuts and tobacco) jumped 15 per cent. Today some 50 per cent of Brazil suffers malnutrition. Yet one leading Brazilian agronomist still calls export promotion, "a matter of national survival". In the global village, a nation survives by starving its people.

Trade and Exploitation

The world has never had a genuinely free and fair trading system. Ever since people argued whether trade follows the flag or the flag follows trade, trade has been based on domination and dependency, and has been an instrument of them. The ideology of free trade has been used, as ideologies often are, to justify the strong in taking advantage of the weak and to persuade the weak that it is neither conceptually respectable nor in their own best long-term interest to protect themselves.

James Robertson, *Future Wealth*, 1990.

Even in the United States, the most developed of all nations, free trade has not prevented living standards from declining over the last 15 years. Americans work almost half a day longer today for lower real wages than in 1970. Less leisure time, less time with the family and community. If the present trend continues, we may have less leisure time in the 1990s than we had in the 1970s.

Rethinking Values

Clearly, it is time to re-examine the doctrine of free trade and its corollary, the planetary economy. We can begin by discussing values. Albert Einstein once noted, "Perfection of means and confusion of ends seems to characterize our age". Fifteen years ago, the New York *Village Voice* dubbed our generation, 'Consumers of change'. But we should not confuse change with progress. Bertrand Russell described change as 'inevitable' and progress as 'problematic'. We must decide what values we hold most dear and then design an economic system that reinforces those values.

27

For advocates of free trade, competition is both necessary and healthy, spurring innovation, raising productivity and above all lowering prices. The more competition, the better. The consumer is held to be 'king', ultimately deciding which product and company survives in a vigorous and unregulated marketplace.

Price and Cost

If price is to be our guide for buying, selling and investing, then price should tell us something about efficiency. Efficiency should refer to the amount of real resources used per amount of useful product manufactured. We might measure efficiency in natural resource terms, that is, by measuring the amount of waste produced in converting a raw material into a consumer or industrial product. Or we might measure efficiency in human terms, that is, by measuring the amount of hours it takes for a person to make a product. . . .

But price is no measure of efficiency. In fact price is arguably no reliable measure of anything. The prices of raw materials, labour, capital, transportation and waste disposal are all heavily subsidized. In Taiwan, for example, strikes are illegal. In South Korea, until recently, unions could not be organized without government permission. To all intents and purposes, South Africa uses slave labour. Many developing nations have no maximum hours, minimum wage or environmental legislation. As the American economist Howard Wachtel notes:

> "Differences in product cost . . . that are due to totalitarian political institutions or restrictions on economic rights reflect no natural or entrepreneurial advantage. . . . Free trade has nothing to do with incomparable political-economic institutions that protect individual rights in one country and deny them in another."

Goods from developed nations may carry a higher price because their workers are paid a decent wage. But their prices are usually lower than they would otherwise be because of other kinds of subsidies. For example, we build interstate highways and levy taxes on heavy trucks that do not cover the damage done to the roads by their passage. We provide water to California farms at public expense, charging farmers as little as five per cent of the going market-rate of water, and give huge direct subsidies to corporate farmers. We allow the costs of agricultural pollution to be picked up by society as a whole. And then we are told that it is cheaper to grow a tomato in California and ship it to Massachusetts because of California's climatic advantages. If we withdrew all the subsidies, it might very well be cheaper to raise produce near the point of sale.

Indeed, across the economy, there is an enormous disparity

between the price of a product or service to an individual and the cost of that same product or service to the society as a whole. . . .

The Delusion of Free Trade

In touting free trade to other nations, the United States has not only invited its own economic destruction but also misled other countries in their expectations from international trade. It is time for America to reject this false god and accept the blame for preaching an unrealistic doctrine. We must repudiate the notion that the rest of the world can achieve economic growth by unbalanced sales to the U.S. market. . . .

The delusion that free trade is the road to worldwide affluence has influenced many countries; the delusion will hurt many of them. We need to escape from this belief and build a new system of international trade—one that rests on realism and mutual benefit for all nations.

John M. Culbertson, *Harvard Business Review,* September/October 1986.

If price is no real guide to costs and efficiency, the second main pillar of free trade—the law of comparative advantage—is also questionable. There are two kinds of comparative advantage: absolute and relative. Absolute comparative advantage is the easiest to understand. Differences in climate and natural resources suggest that Guatemala can do some things better than Minnesota and vice versa. Guatemala should raise bananas and Minnesota should raise Walleye pike.

Relative comparative advantage is a somewhat less intuitive, but ultimately much more powerful, concept. As David Ricardo, a principal architect of the doctrine of the free trade movement, explained:

"Two men can both make shoes and hats and one is superior to the other in both employments; but in making hats he can only exceed his competitor by one fifth or 20 per cent, and in making shoes he can exceed him by one third or 33 per cent—will it not be for the interest of both that the superior man should employ himself exclusively in making shoes and the inferior man in making hats?"

Thus even if one community can make every product more efficiently than another, it should specialize only in those items that it produces most efficiently in relative terms and trade for the others. Each community, and ultimately each nation, should specialize in what it does best.

Yet, in an age of increasing mechanization, the theory of com-

29

parative advantage is fast losing its credibility. Even a half century ago, John Maynard Keynes could comment, "A considerable degree of international specialization is necessary in a rational world in all cases where it is dictated by wide differences of climate, natural resources, native aptitudes, level of culture and density of population . . . (but) experience accumulates to prove that most modern processes of mass production can be performed in most countries and climates with almost equal efficiency."

Time was when technology spread slowly. In northern Italy, in the 17th century, stealing or disclosing the secrets of silk-spinning machinery was a crime punishable by death. At the height of the industrial revolution, Britain protected its supremacy in textile manufacturing through laws banning both exports of machines and emigration of men who knew how to build and run them. A young British apprentice, Samuel Slater, brought the industrial revolution to the US by memorizing the design of the spinning frame. Today technology transfer is simple. According to Dataquest, a market research firm, it takes only three weeks after a new US-made product is introduced before it is copied, manufactured and shipped back to the US from Asia.

Economies of Scale

According to advocates of free trade, bigger production units are necessary to keep the costs of production as low as possible. No one would or could deny that there are economies of scale. There is no question that when I move production out of my basement and into a factory, the cost per item produced declines dramatically. But when the factory multiplies output a 100-fold, production costs do not tend to decline much further. The vast majority of the cost decreases are captured at fairly modest production levels.

For farming, the USDA [United States Department of Agriculture] studied field crops and concluded, "Above about $40-50,000 in gross sales—the size that is at the bottom of the end of medium sized sales category—there are no greater efficiencies of scale." Another USDA report agreed, "Medium sized family farms are as efficient as the large farms."

In production, Harvard Professor Joseph Bain's pioneering investigations in the 1950s found the minimum efficient factory was often far smaller than the average plant. And the factory could be significantly reduced in size without suffering major price increases. In other words, we might be able to produce shoes for a region rather than for the nation at about the same price per shoe. And if we were to withdraw our subsidies to the transportation system, locally produced and marketed shoes might actually be cheaper than those brought in from abroad. . . .

Let me now explore the possibilities and strategies for a new kind of world economy, one whose metaphor would be a globe of villages, not a global village. This would be a planetary economy that emphasizes community and self-reliance. Such self-reliance would not be the same as self-sufficiency. As biologist Russell Anderson suggests, self-reliance is "the capacity for self-sufficiency, not self-sufficiency itself." It gives us the capacity to survive if cut off from suppliers by natural or man-made intervention. It encourages us to maintain a diversity of skills within our societies and to localize and regionalize productive assets. It is a strategy that welcomes 'foreign' capital, but not at the expense of local ownership; that promotes competition but also encourages cooperation; and that recognizes the value of the voluntary sector as a vital underpinning of civil society. It is a strategy that emphasizes prevention rather than treatment and that looks towards a society which promotes satisfaction rather than consumption.

Once dismissed as 'Utopian', the paradigm of a globe of villages is already beginning to help solve pressing national and local problems. . . .

Time for Change

The challenge, then, is to move away from the paradigm of the planetary economy and to create in its place an economy that allows us to produce most of what we need from our own local human, natural and capital resources on a sustainable basis. In that respect, I agree with John Maynard Keynes when he wrote:

"I sympathise with those who would minimize, rather than with those who would maximize, economic entanglement among nations. Ideas, knowledge, science, hospitality, travel—these are the things which should of their nature be international. But let goods be homespun whenever it is reasonably and conveniently possible and, above all, let finance be primarily national."

Goods should be homespun to maintain a productive capacity and the skills associated with producers. When we abandon our ability to produce for ourselves, when we separate authority from responsibility, when those affected by our decisions are not those who make the decisions, when the cost and the benefit of doing things are not part of the same equation, when price and cost are no longer in harmony, we jeopardize our security and our future. . . .

We also undermine democracy. Thomas Jefferson warned us that democracy depends on the widespread distribution of property. By property, he meant the ownership of productive assets. In his time, the ideal democrat was the yeoman farmer, the multi-skilled and largely self-reliant man and woman. Having the capacity to be self-reliant, such a person would be less willing to sell a vote for hand-outs from a political party. Having the knowledge of how things are made, and how the natural world works, such a person would be an informed participant in the political process.

One may argue that free trade is not the cause of all our ills. Agreed. But free trade as it is preached today nurtures and reinforces many of our worst problems. It is an ideological package that promotes ruinous policies. And most tragically, as we move further down the road to giantism, and planetism and dependence, we make it harder and harder to take another path. If we lose our skills, our productive base, our culture, our traditions, our natural resources, if we erode the bonds of personal and familiar responsibility, it becomes ever-more difficult to re-create community. It is very, very hard to put Humpty Dumpty back together again.

Another Way

Which means we must act now. We need to challenge the postulates of free trade head on, to preach a different philosophy, to embrace a different strategy. There is another way, but to make it the dominant way we must change the rules, indeed, we must change our own behaviour. And to do that requires us not only to challenge the emptiness of free trade but to promote an economics as if community matters.

=====

"Global integration is the best way for all countries—rich and poor, large and small—to become wealthier together."

=====

International Free Trade Benefits All Nations

John C. Whitehead

John C. Whitehead served as deputy secretary of state under the Reagan administration. The following viewpoint is taken from a speech before the Economic Policy Council of the United Nations Association of the U.S.A. In it, Whitehead argues that trade has promoted economic growth and interdependence among nations. Future economic prosperity, he states, depends on the continued growth of free trade.

As you read, consider the following questions:

1. How has global trade been beneficial, according to Whitehead?
2. Why are trade restrictions harmful, according to the author?
3. What world economic problems does Whitehead describe?

John C. Whitehead, address before the Economic Policy Council of the United Nations Association of the U.S.A., September 20, 1988.

I would like to explore the following points:
- The basic forces promoting freer trade and economic integration since World War II;
- The damage national governments do when they try to frustrate economic integration; and
- The current challenges threatening integration and global prosperity.

Finally, I want to say a few words about the relative position of the United States in the world economy.

Understanding Global Economic Integration

The globalization of our daily lives is evident everywhere —from the products we buy and use to the attention paid to exchange rate movements in the morning newspaper. Globalization is not simply a matter of increased trade; we see it also in the worldwide markets for currencies and credit, in the pattern of production, and in the flow of information and technology. At the dawn of the industrial revolution, new ideas took decades to filter even across Europe; now they spread around the world at the speed of light.

[Economist] Joseph Schumpeter viewed economic growth as a process of "creative destruction," with new technologies and products constantly replacing the old and outmoded. Today, as such changes come more quickly than ever, we hear calls for protectionism and economic nationalism. But history shows that it would be wrong to heed those calls. Globalization and rapid economic advance are linked. Global integration is the best way for all countries—rich and poor, large and small—to become wealthier together.

The distinguished men who shaped our international economic policy in the 1940s—people like Cordell Hull, Harry White, William Clayton, and George Marshall—were guided by a fine sense of history and, above all, by the bitter lessons of the interwar years. The international economy, which had flourished in the decades before 1914, was largely destroyed in subsequent war and revolution. Efforts to rebuild the system after 1918 were only partially successful, and the world economy almost disintegrated in the Great Depression.

The Sorry Legacy of the 1930s

As country after country resorted to "beggar-thy-neighbor" policies, trade shriveled, and employment and output plunged. The United States contributed to the sorry legacy of the 1930s through the Smoot-Hawley tariff and by scuttling the London economic conference.

Fortunately, after the Second World War, we rejected isolationism and economic nationalism. Instead, in the spirit of Bretton

Woods and the Marshall Plan, we opened our markets and allowed others to follow at their own pace. In Europe, men of vision—Robert Schuman, Jean Monnet, and Ludwig Erhard —guided the reconstruction of a war-torn continent. Economic integration replaced ancient rivalries; prosperity became a joint pursuit.

Trade Minimizes Conflict

To minimize conflicts in the future we should aim to create a world in which people are free to buy what they want, live and work where they choose, and invest and produce where conditions seem most propitious. There should be unlimited freedom for individuals to trade within and across national borders, widespread international division of labor, and worldwide economic interdependence. Would-be traders should encounter no restrictions or barriers to trade, enacted out of a misguided belief in economic nationalism and the supposed advantages of economic self-sufficiency. Friendships among individuals living in different parts of the world would then be reinforced daily through the benefits they reap from buying and selling with one another. Thus a sound basis for peaceful international relations would be encouraged.

Bettina Bien Greaves, *Free Trade: The Necessary Foundation for World Peace*, 1986.

Aided by timely Marshall Plan aid, the countries of Western Europe achieved remarkable economic growth during the 1950s and 1960s. Japan did even better. In less spectacular fashion, Canada and the United States also prospered.

These were years of rapid decolonialization as many former colonies became new countries. Whereas the IMF [International Monetary Fund] and World Bank had 31 members initially, they had 151 members in 1988.

In the postwar period, growing output and living standards were promoted by a progressive freeing-up of trade and investment flows. Widespread exchange controls were phased out; tariffs were cut; capital controls were eased; and a variety of regional free trade arrangements—most notably the EEC [European Economic Community] were introduced, encouraging further flows of goods, services, investment, and manpower among member countries.

Unsung Millions

While enlightened government policies established a more open, market-oriented framework for postwar recovery and growth, the real heroes of the story were the unsung millions of individuals on every continent whose creativity and hard work made possible an unprecedented era of prosperity.

Increasingly, the world economy has become a single stage with leading roles played by multinational companies. Citicorp raises capital, obtains deposits, extends loans, and trades currencies all around the world. General Motors buys and produces components in scores of countries, assembles them in strategic locations, and markets its finished vehicles on every continent. And, of course, not all multinationals are headquartered in America—consider such names as Siemens, Philips, Thomsen, Mitsubishi, Honda, Hyundai, and Daewoo.

Global economic integration is driven by continuing advances in science and technology. Columbus took 3 months to cross the Atlantic. By 1850, a clipper ship could make the trip in 15 days. Some 70 years later, Lindbergh's daring flight took 33 hours. Today, the Concorde gets us there in 3 hours and 20 minutes. For much of today's commerce, physical distance is irrelevant: modern telecommunications links us by voice, visual image, and documentation in less than a second.

Nation States and the Gains from Trade

National governments can impede or promote global economic integration. Trade is, of course, the standard example. Import-competing producers often seek protection from competitors abroad. Such protection widens their profit margins, but it limits choice and raises prices to domestic consumers. And it harms domestic exporters and those domestic firms which receive less protection against imports.

Governments also often choose to limit incoming foreign direct investments. Such constraints benefit domestic firms that would face additional competition. But they hurt domestic consumers and those domestic residents who might supply goods and labor services to the incoming foreign-owned concerns.

Although a free trade policy benefits some domestic residents and hurts others, the gainers generally gain more than the losers lose. Conversely, protection usually hurts domestic residents on balance. These conclusions hold even without taking account of the dynamic gains from free trade, stemming from heightened competition and the introduction of new products and services.

Aside from their diverse impacts on domestic residents, trade restrictions, of course, usually hurt foreign producers. Japanese quotas hurt U.S. rice growers; U.S. quotas hurt New Zealand lamb producers. In light of these considerations, [the Reagan] Administration—albeit with some important slippages—has sought to encourage open trade policies both at home and abroad.

During the past several years, however, economic integration has come under pressure as the world economy has been buffeted by extreme inflation and disinflation.

We have cut inflation, but the legacy of the struggle remains: heavily indebted developing countries, low commodity prices, high unemployment in Europe, and large trade imbalances. These dislocations have prompted a host of dire forecasts. But do they reflect reality?

Trade and Technology

With Americans in the lead, entrepreneurs have created a global electronic ganglion of information and capital markets on line 24 hours a day. This planetary utility has transformed the business environment. Modern telecom does not only transfer money in real time; it also transfers some of the most important products of the information age, such as software packages, chip designs, computer schematics, telecom architectures, manufacturing control programs, and industrial formulas. Relatively small firms now face rivals and pursue opportunities around the world. . . .

The new fabric of global interdependence is a precious and unprecedented achievement of the current era. It represents an enduring triumph of capitalism. It would be nothing short of a tragedy to throw it away in an effort to restore the mercantilist zero-sum games that have produced a grim global history of war and poverty.

George Gilder, *Policy Review*, Spring 1988.

Consider the record. Since 1982, the United States has enjoyed a robust economic expansion and markedly lower inflation. Assisted by lower taxes and significant deregulation—and prodded by foreign competition—our output has risen since 1982 at an annual rate of 3.8%; our manufacturing productivity has risen by almost 5% per annum; and our unemployment rate has fallen from over 10% in early 1983 to less than 5.5% in 1988. . . .

Recent strong U.S. economic growth has been accompanied by even stronger growth in Japan, Britain, Canada, and Asia. . . .

But, of course, problems remain—in particular, an overhang of Third World debt, creeping protectionism, and a big U.S. trade deficit. A few words on each:

The Debt Problem

Since 1982, the creditor banks in the industrial countries have bolstered their ability to absorb defaults by adding to capital and reserves. Nonetheless, a serious confrontation between the debtor countries and the banks would still threaten the international financial system.

[The Reagan] Administration has sought to avoid that confrontation—encouraging the banks to lend new money and the debtor countries to reform their policies with IMF assistance. The process has proceeded case by case. To strengthen their trade balances, the debtor countries have had to endure severe economic austerity. Is there a better way?

Numerous "global solutions" have been proposed. But these schemes all fail to reflect important differences among the debtor countries; they would tend to reward poor policies; and they would require backstop insurance by creditor-country taxpayers. I believe that the case-by-case approach will work *provided:*

First, that we can lower barriers to debtor-country exports; and

Second, that the debtor countries revamp their economies.

These countries have spawned numerous state-owned enterprises. (In Mexico, for example, state-owned firms rose from 86 in 1970 to 1,155 in 1982.) Inefficient and overstaffed, these concerns often require massive state subsidies. They should be cut back, closed down, or privatized.

Debtor countries have also tended to fix exchange rates, interest rates, and other key prices at levels that lead either to shortages or to gluts. They need less price fixing and more reliance on market forces. For their part, creditors must realize that a large external debt imposes "a marginal tax on reform." Unless both sides work together to reduce this tax, reforms may never occur.

To prevent LDC [less developed country] debts from burdening the international economy in the 1990s, will require cooperation and goodwill. . . .

Creeping Protectionism

Alas, the free-trading ideal of [the Reagan] Administration differs from the "warts-and-all" real world. In country after country, narrow domestic interests have persuaded all-too-willing governments to impose restrictions on imports. True, tariffs have been cut substantially. But all too often, they have been replaced with even more damaging nontariff barriers designed to evade GATT's [General Agreement on Tariffs and Trade] jurisdiction.

The GATT needs refurbishing. It needs a quicker-acting, binding mechanism for settling disputes and a routine procedure for monitoring trade policies. It needs to cover services as well as goods and agricultural products as well as manufactures. And it needs to cover intellectual property rights. We hope to persuade our trading partners to accept these changes. . . .

The U.S. trade balance can strengthen only if our domestic savings rise relative to our domestic investment spending. Assuming further growth in investment spending, we need to achieve some combination of smaller budget deficits and greater personal and business saving. If Gramm-Rudman-Hollings sticks, our budget deficits will fall; and if the recent changes in consumer spending and corporate profits persist, private savings will also rise. . . .

Our Relative Economic Strength

Let me conclude with a few words about the place of the United States in the world economy.

At the end of World War II, the United States dominated the world economy. In 1950, we accounted for two-thirds of the total output of the G-7 countries and over one-third of total G-7 exports. [The Group of 7 includes Canada, France, Italy, Japan, the United Kingdom, the United States, and West Germany.] Our real wages and worker productivity were well above levels in other countries.

Now, some four decades later, we remain the world's leading industrial power, but other free-world countries have gained enormously in relative wealth, output, and productivity. Some say that this development represents a failure of our national will and leadership. Not at all. It was inevitable—and highly desirable—that the war-torn economies of Japan and Western Europe regain their prewar capabilities. Indeed, that was the explicit purpose of the Marshall Plan. It was also natural for their economies to benefit from a technological catchup. As these countries have prospered, they have become stronger markets for our exports and low-cost suppliers of many desirable goods and services.

French wines, Japanese automobiles, Italian suits, British woolens, and German machine tools—these foreign-made products, and many more, enhance our living standards and stimulate innovation by our own producers.

Despite the debt crisis, the developing countries, as a group, have achieved an even more impressive rate of growth than our OECD [Organization for Economic Cooperation and Development] trading partners since the end of World War II. This, too, was natural. Starting from a much lower economic base, they had even greater scope for borrowing (and adapting) advanced technology than did Japan or Western Europe.

Nowhere have these gains been more impressive than in the newly industrializing economies of the Pacific rim. South Korea, Taiwan, Singapore, and Hong Kong—and, to a lesser extent, Malaysia, Thailand, Indonesia, and the Philippines—have become important producers and exporters of manufactures. Indeed, their successes are forcing painful adjustments in competing sectors in all of the older industrial countries.

Since 1983, trade across the Pacific has exceeded trade across the Atlantic. Nonetheless, the Pacific rim countries can benefit materially from greater cooperation. . . . We need to undertake joint discussions and cooperative actions in the areas of transportation, telecommunications, education, and natural resources.

Trade and Communism

More interesting than a comparison of the United States against its major trading partners is a comparison of the free-market NATO [North Atlantic Treaty Organization] countries against the countries of the Warsaw Pact. In 1960, the combined gross national products of the NATO countries exceeded those of the Warsaw Pact by some $2.5 trillion (in 1986 dollars). By 1986, the gap had more than doubled to $5.5 trillion.

Far from burying the Western economies, the communist command economies have fallen increasingly behind. Recognizing that central planning just doesn't deliver the goods, the leaders of the two largest communist countries—China and the Soviet Union—have sought to inject large elements of capitalism into their systems.

These evolving actions—together with *glasnost* and *perestroika* —have momentous implications for the peoples of the free world as well as for the peoples of China, the Soviet Union, and the Soviet satellites. Is it possible that the Russian bear will become the Russian lamb—and a neocapitalist free-trading lamb, at that? Time will tell.

"There are some pretty good reasons to favor a nationalist policy that reduces free trade, entanglements and interdependence among nations."

International Free Trade Exploits Poor Nations

Herman Daly and John Cobb Jr.

Herman Daly is an economist and author whose works include *Steady-State Economics.* John Cobb Jr. is professor emeritus at Claremont School of Theology in Claremont, California. The following viewpoint is taken from their book, *For the Common Good.* Daly and Cobb argue that global trade enables rich and powerful nations and corporations to exploit the world's people and environment. The authors call for measures to restrict world trade and global interdependence.

As you read, consider the following questions:

1. Why do Daly and Cobb assert that there is no such thing as a global community?
2. What principles should govern trade, according to the authors?
3. According to Daly and Cobb how would U.S. economic self-sufficiency benefit Third World nations?

Reprinted, with permission, from an excerpt of *For the Common Good* by Herman Daly and John Cobb Jr., as the excerpt appeared in *New Options* magazine, December 26, 1989.

It's nice to talk about a world community. It's nice to talk about a global community. But it doesn't exist.

There is such a thing as a national community. And if we value community, then surely we have to protect it where it exists.

In today's world you hear a great deal of discussion about free trade and the global economy, and "integration into the world economy." And this is usually put forward as a good thing —helping to build an international community, being neighbors with everyone in the world, and so forth.

Both of us have always been internationalists. It's only recently and through a certain amount of painful re-thinking that we've come to see that free trade is a bad idea. We've come to see that, in today's world, there are some pretty good reasons to favor a nationalist policy that reduces free trade, entanglements and interdependence among nations.

Death of Affluence

To appreciate the enormous breach of community implicit in modern free trade, consider what the U.S. capitalists are, in effect, telling the U.S. laborers. They are saying that labor has to compete in the world market against the poor masses in the overpopulated Third World countries such as Mexico, Brazil, and so on.

No longer will U.S. labor have the advantage of superior technology or management, because those attributes move with capital. Furthermore, an enormous reservoir of cheap labor in India and China, almost half the world's population, has previously not competed in the world's labor market, and is about to enter.

By making the world of separate national communities into a single common, overpopulated labor pool in the name of free trade, the U.S. would compete away the high standard of living of the majority of its citizens!

A high standard of living is not the only good thing that depends on community. Once community is devalued in the name of free trade, there will be a generalized competing away of community standards.

A Lowering of Standards

Social security, medicare, and unemployment benefits all raise the cost of production just like high wages, and they too will not survive a general standards-lowering competition. Likewise, the environmental protection and conservation standards of the community also raise costs of production and will be competed down to the level that rules in overpopulated Third World countries.

It may be argued that the downward pressure on wages toward subsistence will eventually turn around, and that the rapid industrialism made possible by free trade will involve the vast labor force of the world in productive work. The expectation is that the Gross World Product will be enormous, and all will enjoy together a hitherto undreamed of prosperity.

Huck/*People's Daily World.* Reprinted with permission.

But there are hundreds of millions of unemployed people today, and many more are underemployed. The size of the work force is growing very rapidly in most Third World countries. The method of capitalist economic growth requires ever fewer workers in relation to production. It is hard to share the expectation that this increasingly automated industry will absorb this vast work force.

Environmental Considerations

The likelihood that this problem will be solved by growth seems even more remote when the process of industrialization is placed in the context of what is known about the environment. The quantity of resources required and the quantity of waste produced in this scenario stagger the imagination. Certainly global warming and the melting of the ice caps will be accelerated—to the extent that societies will have to cope with massive physical dislocations.

World community at least at present is an abstract vision. Real community now exists only at national and subnational levels. Free traders, having freed themselves from the restraints of community at the national level and having moved into the cosmopolitan world, *which is not a community*, have effectively freed themselves of all community obligations.

We believe it is folly to sacrifice existing institutions of community at the national level in the supposed service of nonexistent institutions of community at the world level. Better to build and strengthen the weakening bonds of national community first, and then expand community by federation into larger trading blocs among national communities that have similar standards regarding wages, welfare, population control and environmental protection.

Balance Trade

By what principles, then, should international trade be governed, if not by free trade and comparative advantage?

The first of these principles is that trade should be balanced.

Perhaps the simplest way to balance trade is to limit imports to rough equality with expected exports. One way that can be done is by issuing import quota licenses, and auctioning them to competing import firms.

If we have balanced trade, then there is no need for international lending and borrowing.

The consequence of free international finance—a necessary complement to free trade—has been the running up of unrepayable debts. Banks pumped money (the trade surpluses of oil-exporting countries) into Third World countries at a rate much greater than the ability of those governments to build wisely or to administer honestly.

Does elimination of international lending mean that developing countries could no longer import needed capital equipment from the U.S.? By no means. Brazil could still import tractors and computers and pay for them with coffee and shoes. Brazil simply could not borrow in order to import tractors and computers *faster* than it could export coffee and shoes. Nor of course could the U.S. borrow by importing products and services faster than it could pay for them with other products and services.

Elimination of all international lending and borrowing is admittedly extreme. Is there not room for permitting some international transfer on capital account along with the compensatory imbalance on trade account? We believe there could be—if the money were to be spent on clearly beneficial and productive projects as judged from the perspective of both national communities. This is an area for further reflection and research.

According to establishment economist Lester Thurow, "Tariff protection and subsidies imprison us in a low productivity area.

44

If we cannot learn to disinvest, we cannot compete in the modern growth race."

Thurow is correct. If the U.S. is committed to competing in the great international growth race, then it should impose no tariffs. It should cease producing whatever can be produced more efficiently (that is, cheaply) elsewhere. It will, of course, cease to be even remotely self-sufficient, since the growth race encourages specialization.

Trade Should Decline

As a basis for a new international trading regime in the 21st century, we need to start from the following principle:

The total volume of international trade—as a proportion of total world economic activity—should fall, as nations and localities everywhere move towards greater economic self-reliance and more conserving economies. . . .

The emphasis must now shift toward meeting a greater proportion of national needs from national work, national production and national resources, with import substitution generally taking priority over export promotion, at least for the foreseeable future.

James Robertson, *Future Wealth,* 1990.

But we see no reason to hold competition in the modern growth race as sacrosanct. There are other means of meeting human needs that induce less suffering and are far less costly to the planet.

We would opt out of the international growth race and all the disinvestment that entails in order to rebuild a self-sufficient national economy. The simplest, most effective policy instrument for doing that is the tariff.

Tariffs would protect now-endangered industries from further erosion and allow them to begin to recover lost ground. Tariffs would also encourage new enterprise in areas where the U.S. has become dependent on imports. With the assurance that these industries could be profitable while paying suitable wages, capital would flow to them.

The operation of the free market—within national boundaries reinforced by tariffs—would lead to the industrial self-sufficiency that would make possible truly free trade, that is, trade in which the nation is free to engage or not.

A system of tariffs is not without its economic costs, as any economist will quickly point out. It is designed to raise the price of goods—and that will have a negative effect on the purchasing power of consumers.

But there is also no question that in one way or another the American standard of living will be reduced. A correction for America's vast international debt and profligate spending these past years cannot be avoided.

We do not argue that our version of a tariff system will work better in terms of the increase in GNP [gross national product]. By that standard it may well be worse. We argue that it will work better in terms of a true index of economic welfare, and much better in terms of what are considered noneconomic goals.

Third World Fallout

Third World countries will suffer in having tariffs imposed on their exports to us. Equally threatening to these countries would be the reduction of capital that would be invested in their industrialization.

A moral argument can be made that the U.S. should do nothing to slow down the industrialization of the poorer nations. This argument has force only to the extent that industrialization actually benefits poor people in poor countries and not just the elite. This is frequently not the case.

The only industrialization that would help the masses would be based on "appropriate" technology—one that enhances the ability of ordinary people to deal with their problems. But this is not what is of interest to foreign investors. International capital introduces techniques and methods that render Third World countries more dependent on the First World.

The U.S. has two basic choices. It can remain in the free trade system, paying a high price in the standard of living of its workers and its future economic power. In this way, it can for some time export capital and scatter factories around the world. This would help Third World elites.

Alternately, the U.S. can seek self-sufficiency and control over its own economic life. If it does that, it will have a strong moral responsibility to assist many Third World nations in becoming self-sufficient again . . . since the U.S. bears major responsibility for having persuaded them to abandon relative self-sufficiency for the international trading system.

Assuming that the nation chooses the path of balanced trade through tariffs for the sake of self-sufficiency, a major problem would be that of retaining incentives for efficiency in production.

The whole purpose of the tariff is to reduce foreign competition. Yet healthy competition is essential to the market system.

To insure healthy competition in the national market would require policies designed to prevent consolidation of economic power in a few hands. A policy that handicaps imports must be accompanied by others that would intensify competition at home.

Every effort should be made to reverse the trend toward merg-

46

ers and takeovers, friendly and unfriendly, and to increase the number of smaller businesspeople and manufacturers.

Tax laws can be written to discourage mergers and encourage spin-offs. Government can also use economic incentives to encourage the decentralization and breakup of conglomerates. All of this can be supplemented by enforcing antitrust laws already on the books and passing new ones as needed.

Regionalization

The single greatest factor leading to the deindustrialization of America has been capital mobility across national lines. But a second problem, almost as serious, is capital mobility within the country.

The goal of our economics, an economics for community, is to restore to communities the power to determine their own affairs. That requires a regionalization of economic power and activity that would attach capital to regions. This would be a deep reversal of recent trends.

What policies will encourage such a reversal? Four suggestions:

• Before plants are closed, efforts should be made to buy them locally. Sales to workers are an ideal solution.

• Whenever a plant is about to change hands, workers or other local interests should be given an option to bid against the proposed purchaser.

• Educational programs about how the community gains from buying community-made products can begin to counter national advertising which seeks to promote name brands. A growing demand for locally made products will stimulate new businesses.

• A city could form a council to which such groups as business, labor, the professions, and religious institutions would elect representatives. Although the council would have no formal power, it would be understood that no important policies would be adopted by the mayor and elected city council without consultation. Participation in such councils would tend to build community and deepen roots in such a way as to reduce mobility.

Supporters and Opponents

It is important to consider who can be enlisted on the side of a self-sufficient national economy.

One group is those deeply concerned for national security. Even when this is viewed in the narrowly military sense, no one can be indifferent to the ability of the nation to produce its own arms.

Another group is all those businesspeople who are already seeking trade protection. This group is growing all the time.

The most important constituency for rethinking national economic policy is labor. But as long as it accepts the free trade ideology that is destroying it, its ability to resist the consequences of that ideology is slight.

There are dangers in alliances with each of these groups. So we count on a fourth group whose support is less tied to economic self-interest: a network of persons whose consciousness has been changed by participation in feminist and environmental movements, who have never lost an appreciation for the virtues of thrift and self-reliance, who have all along wanted to keep power closer to the people.

Without the leadership of this group, a political coalition of special interest groups cannot succeed.

There is still another group whose support we covet. This is that rather small group of persons who have a deep and knowledgeable concern for the Third World, and are convinced that the U.S. should foster self-sufficiency—not dependency—in the Third World. We have a practical need for their moral authority because of the charge of immorality that will be directed against the move to a self-sufficient national economy.

It is important to consider also who will be against this change. First and foremost, it will be opposed by the financial community. It will also be opposed by economic ideologues and special interest groups, especially importers and retailers.

Mass support for the free trade view will come from those who identify themselves primarily as the economist's traditional "economic man," the rational consumer. Goods manufactured by workers earning U.S. wages will cost more than those that have been imported duty-free. Also, the quality of many U.S. products is inferior, and this situation is likely to continue until more of our best scientists are freed from military research and until labor and management become more of a community working together to improve their products.

Exposing the Fallacies of Free Trade

The current affluence, however illusory, suggests that this may not be the right time to press for change. It is a good time to expose the fallacies of free trade as applied to the situation today. But people will be more willing to consider change when the weakness of the economy is more publicly visible. That time will come again.

"Imports have given Americans a better standard of living."

Free Trade Benefits the U.S.

Brink Lindsey

Brink Lindsey is a trade attorney in Washington, D.C. In the following viewpoint, he argues that the U.S. has gained much from free trade. U.S. consumers benefit from foreign goods, he writes, and U.S. industries benefit from foreign markets and competition. He argues that a growing number of countries have adopted free-trade policies, and concludes that the U.S. should remove its own protectionist barriers and continue to make free trade a cornerstone of its economic policy.

As you read, consider the following questions:

1. What two important trends does Lindsey see in world trade?
2. What five developments contributed to the global trade boom, according to the author?
3. Why has the U.S. not lived up to its free-trade ideals, according to Lindsey?

Brink Lindsey, "Trade Secret." Reprinted, with permission, from the Winter 1990 issue of *Policy Review*, the flagship publication of The Heritage Foundation, 214 Massachusetts Ave. NE, Washington, DC 20002.

America may be winning the Cold War, but according to a now fashionable line of thinking, it is already in danger of losing the peace. The era of military confrontation with the Soviet Union is ending, to be replaced, so the argument goes, by a period of *economic* confrontation with our erstwhile allies—most notably, Europe and Japan. The emergence of the new dispensation is supposedly well underway. In this scenario, the old multilateral free trade system, anchored by a dominant United States, is coming unglued; at the same time, rival protectionist blocs are beginning to coalesce.

The United States, meanwhile, is purportedly vulnerable in this new era because of its continued and anachronistic attachment to free trade. The fear is that by maintaining open markets while the rest of the world hides behind protectionist barriers, the United States is committing the economic equivalent of unilateral disarmament. If America is to survive as a great power, say these "economic nationalists," it must learn to play by new rules: in other words, industrial policy at home, and "managed trade" (that is, import and export quotas) abroad.

This picture, for all its drama, rests on a gross misreading of recent international developments. From all the alarmist rhetoric pouring out of Congress and the press, one would think that the great expansion of international trade during the '50s and '60s is now in full reverse, that protectionist barriers are being thrown up all over the world, and that the flow of goods and services across national borders is drying up.

A Trade Boom

In fact, the opposite is true. During the past years—while Japan-bashing and obsessing over the trade deficit have become national pastimes—the world has been experiencing a sustained trade boom that rivals any in the postwar era. Contrary to the conventional wisdom, import barriers during this time have been falling in many parts of the world, including, of all places, Japan. . . . From 1986 to 1988, import growth was several times faster for many of America's leading trading partners than it was for the U.S. Even in absolute dollar terms, the import rises in Japan and West Germany were almost as large as in America.

Moreover, initiatives at the national, regional, and global levels are making prospects look bright for further and dramatic liberalization of trade, extending the free trade principle to sectors of the world economy never before covered. These trends are well known in the business and financial worlds, but in political circles they remain all but ignored.

From 1983 to 1988, the volume of world trade in merchandise grew 34 percent, or an average of 6.1 percent a year—up from a sluggish annual pace of 2.8 percent from 1973 to 1983, but in line with growth rates of 6.1 percent from 1953 to 1963 and 8.9 percent from 1973 to 1983. ("Volume" figures in this article come mainly from the General Agreement on Tariffs and Trade, or GATT, which adjusts the value of world trade in dollars to take account of both inflation and currency fluctuations.) Far from slowing down or going into reverse, world trade has thus returned to the pattern of robust expansion during most of the period after World War II. The total value of world trade in merchandise in 1988 was estimated at $2.88 trillion, of which approximately $730 billion were attributable to growth after 1983.

Jim Morin. Reprinted with special permission of King Features Syndicate, Inc.

This expansion in world trade is running far ahead of growth in the world economy generally. Since the 1982 recession, world output has been growing at an annual rate of around 3.75 percent; trade volumes have been expanding half again as quickly. This fact signifies two important trends. First, it suggests that the trade boom—with its resulting increases in competition, specialization, and economies of scale—is leading the worldwide economic expansion. Second, it means that the international component of world economic activity is growing; in other words, markets are truly becoming global in scope.

What drove the '80s trade boom? Five contributing factors stand out: in the United States, brisk increases in both imports and exports; the Japanese export boom, now accompanied by a flood of new imports, particularly manufactured products, coming into Japan; a phenomenal trade expansion in the rest of East Asia; dynamic trade growth in the European Community (EC), particularly at the intraregional level; and rapid growth in services trade.

Yankee Expansion

Everyone is familiar with the American appetite for imports. The volume of U.S. imports in 1987 was 64 percent higher than it was in 1980. In the mercantilist mind-set, this looks like some sort of catastrophe. The simple truth, though, is that these imports have given Americans a better standard of living. VCRs, Walkmans, stereos, high-performance automobiles, microwave ovens, low-priced fabric, clothing, and shoes—these are among the benefits of America's open markets. Moreover, these imports are doing more than simply feeding a consumption binge; between 1986 and 1988, imports of capital goods accounted for nearly two-thirds of the growth in U.S. import volumes. Finally, the excess of imports over exports during this decade has a flip side, namely net inflows of foreign capital. This capital has built new plants, created jobs, and helped to fuel America's longest-running peacetime expansion.

Turning to the other side of the balance of payments ledger, the United States has also experienced an export surge since the dollar began its fall in 1985. From 1986 to 1988 the volume of U.S. exports increased at an annual average rate of 14 percent. By contrast, import volume increases averaged 8.5 percent during the same period.

Import Craze in Japan

The trends in U.S. imports and exports are well known, if frequently misunderstood. Japan, on the other hand, has made sweeping changes in its trading practices that have gone almost completely unnoticed here at home. For many years, Japanese policy has been to encourage export industries as the key to economic growth generally. The policy has been undeniably successful: Japan's share of world exports has climbed from 6.4 percent in 1973 to 9.2 percent in 1988 (third behind West Germany and the United States), while in overall output this small and resource-poor nation has attained the rank of an economic superpower. In particular, from 1980 to 1985, exports from Japan increased in volume by 42 percent. Since the yen began to strengthen in 1985, though, Japan has been restructuring its economy toward a greater reliance on domestic demand (as opposed to export performance) as an engine of growth. The result has been a massive infusion of imports.

With the endless tirades against Japanese protectionism and "unfair trade" practices that dominate discussions of our trade deficit, one can be excused for imagining that Japanese markets remain impenetrable, or that any liberalization undertaken under pressure has been more or less cosmetic. Although Japan's merchandise surplus is still in the neighborhood of $80 billion, the volume (currency-adjusted) of Japanese imports jumped almost 40 percent from 1985 to 1988, while export volume rose by only 5 percent. With manufactured goods, the numbers are even more dramatic: the volume of imports shot up 80 percent between 1985 and 1988. . . .

Dragons' Leap

Although American exports to Japan have been on the rise, the main sources of Japan's import surge have been the "Newly Industrializing Economies" or NIEs—South Korea, Taiwan, Hong Kong, and Singapore (more colorfully known as the "Four Dragons")—and such emerging Southeast Asian nations as Thailand and Malaysia. . . .

The trade boom emerging in these East Asian countries is truly phenomenal. Exports have been skyrocketing: in 1987 alone, annual export volume grew 24 percent for South Korea, 14.5 percent for Taiwan, 32 percent for Hong Kong, 19 percent for Singapore, 17.5 percent for Thailand, and a "mere" 8.5 percent for Malaysia. The Four Dragons' share of total world exports was over two-and-a-half times greater in 1988 than in 1973. And increasingly these exports are destined for other countries in the region rather than the United States or Europe. For example, the U.S. accounted for 24.8 percent of Hong Kong's total exports in 1988, down from 33.2 percent in 1984. During the same period, Hong Kong's exports to the rest of Asia rose from 33.6 percent of total exports to 41.6 percent. Among the Four Dragons, exports to other "dragons" generally grew faster in 1988 than exports to the rest of the world. . . .

Good-bye Eurosclerosis

Although East Asian trade is rising fast, the European Community remains the world's premier trading region. Total exports of the 12 EC members in 1988 accounted for approximately 40 percent of world exports. Intra-EC trade was the largest component of this picture, amounting to about 60 percent of total EC exports, or 23 percent of world exports. . . .

Trade outside the region, though, remains extremely important to the EC. Exports from EC members to third countries in 1988 constituted 16 percent of world exports, far more than the total exports of either the United States or Japan. In dollar figures, extra-EC imports and exports exceeded $880 billion in 1988. Despite all the talk about the threat of a "Fortress Europe," the EC's stake in keeping trade channels open is enormous. . . .

All told, the old image of "Eurosclerosis" no longer applies. With an investment boom in full swing, real output increasing at over 3 percent a year, and 2 million net new jobs created in 1988 alone. . . . Europe looks positively vital. This growth is pushing and being pushed by the expansion of international trade.

Services Trade

All of the statistics in this article up to now have had to do with merchandise trade, or trade in goods. The other major component of the world trading picture is trade in services, which until recently received little attention and for which reliable figures are still scarce. Despite the sketchy data, though, developments in services trade clearly played a vital role in fueling the '80s boom.

Traditionally, services trade was concerned predominantly with the movement of goods and people across borders—shipping, port services, passenger travel, and tourism. In the past few years, though, technological innovations and changing patterns of production have created trade in services—for example, telecommunications, advertising, insurance, banking, and construction—that formerly were confined within national boundaries. These forms of trade are still so novel that current methods of balance of payments reporting (the best source of data on services trade) continue to lump these services into the catch-all category "other private services and income." Growth in this category has been vigorous and sustained: since 1970, the value of "other private services and income" worldwide has been expanding at the rate of 15 percent a year, outpacing not only other services but merchandise trade as well. This former loose-change category is now the largest single component of the international services sector, accounting for some 40 percent of its overall value.

Services trade as a whole has been estimated at $560 billion for 1988. This figure is almost certainly too low, given that some countries do not report certain service items, and that other services (such as those transmitted electronically, or those between corporate affiliates) often escape detection under current tracking systems. Even so, $560 billion represents approximately 20 percent of the total value of 1988 merchandise trade, or roughly the entire value of world food and fuel exports. . . .

One of the most promising developments involves economies that have struggled during the '80s but are now beginning to open their markets in the hope that this will lead to prosperity. Since 1985, Mexico has reduced its maximum tariff from 40 percent to 20 percent, abolished official import prices and a 5 percent umbrella import tax, and lifted import licensing requirements for 95 percent of tariff items. Mexico's total imports have more than doubled in dollar value since 1986 (imports from the United States are up 250 percent).

Comparative Advantage

Free trade increases the wealth (and employment opportunities) of all nations by allowing them to capitalize on their comparative advantages in production. For example, the U.S. has a comparative advantage in the production of food because of its vast, fertile land and superior agricultural technology and labor. Saudi Arabia, on the other hand, does not have land that is well suited to agriculture. Although Saudi Arabia conceivably could undertake massive irrigation to become self-sufficient in food production, it is more economical for the Saudis to sell what they *do* have a comparative advantage in—oil—and then purchase much of their food from the U.S. and elsewhere. Similarly, the U.S. could become self-sufficient in petroleum by squeezing more oil out of shale rock and tar sands. But that would be much more costly than if the U.S. continued to purchase some of its oil from Saudi Arabia and elsewhere. Trade between the U.S. and Saudi Arabia, or any other two countries, improves the standard of living in each.

Thomas J. DiLorenzo, *The Freeman*, July 1988.

India, although targeted by the United States as an "unfair trader" under the new Super 301 law, has also made important strides toward liberalization. In the past few years India has reduced or eliminated import duties on machinery, and has significantly cut the list of products subject to restrictive import licensing. India's 1988 imports from the United States jumped 70 percent in dollar value over the previous year (total imports increased 19 percent).

Brazil, another "unfair trader," has itself begun to move away from the import substitution model of development in which it has tried to encourage substitution of foreign goods with local products by erecting huge tariff barriers. The average tariff rate has dropped from over 50 percent to around 30 percent, and the list of prohibited imports has been pared down from 4,500 items to about 1,000. Brazil's import numbers remain stagnant, though, in the midst of balance of payment difficulties caused by its foreign debt crisis. . . .

While trade expansion has been impressive during this decade and future liberalization looks promising, there still remains much to be done. Japan clings to an archaic and inefficient distribution system that chokes demand for imports. The EC pours an unbelievable $120 billion a year into agricultural subsidies, and another $50 billion into subsidies for steel production, shipbuilding, and other industries. And in the developing world, import substitution remains the dominant policy.

Rise in U.S. Protectionism

The protectionists are dead wrong, though, when they claim that the United States is the only injured party—that other countries are "unfair traders" while the United States, playing free-trader nice guy, is left to finish last. The unfortunate fact is that our hands are about as dirty as everyone else's. Indeed, while the trend in the rest of the world has been toward increased liberalization, in the United States protectionism has been on the rise: one estimate shows that the share of U.S. imports affected by substantial trade barriers has gone up from 12 percent in 1980 to 23 percent in 1988. We have import limits on textiles and clothing, steel, cars, machine tools, ceramic tiles, cheese and other dairy products, sugar, and peanuts. We subsidize agriculture to the tune of tens of billions a year. We maintain various "Buy American" laws in the field of government procurement. Our antidumping and countervailing duty laws act as de facto protectionist barriers. And now, under the new Super 301 law, we threaten unilateral retaliation against "unfair trader" countries that do what we do but not what we say. The point here is not to bash America, and certainly not to apologize for the misguided policies of other countries, but rather to underscore that an American trade policy based on a holier-than-thou attitude is not only unconstructive, but also unwarranted.

Rather than looking where to fix blame for the problems that remain, we should work to improve what has already been accomplished. After all, world trade is booming and the ongoing trade expansion that has served as a motor of postwar economic growth is continuing to hum. Contrary to the doomsayers' dark prophecies, the world does not appear to be entering a period of neomercantilist trade wars; quite the opposite, economic and political obstacles to international commerce are being eliminated. These trends may be reversed, of course; rhetoric is becoming increasingly poisonous, and misunderstanding abounds. But if the progress made up to now can be built upon, the promise of a global economy that is truly integrated and free may one day be fulfilled.

"The United States notion of 'free trade' as a political and economic panacea . . . [is] a threat to the economic future of the United States."

Free Trade Harms the U.S.

John M. Culbertson

Promoting the expansion of free trade has been official U.S. policy since the end of World War II. In the following viewpoint, John M. Culbertson argues that the U.S. is alone in supporting free trade while other countries use trade to attain national goals. Such a situation, he writes, allows other countries to take advantage of the U.S. and has led to economic decline. Culbertson is a professor of economics at the University of Wisconsin at Madison and has written several books on trade, including *The Dangers of "Free Trade"* and *The Trade Threat and U.S. Trade Policy.*

As you read, consider the following questions:

1. Why is Japan more successful than the U.S., according to Culbertson?
2. In the author's opinion, how has free trade harmed the U.S.?
3. What should be the basis of U.S. trade policy, according to Culbertson?

Excerpted, with permission, from *The Trade Threat and U.S. Trade Policy* by John M. Culbertson. Madison, WI: Twenty-First Century Press, 1989.

Forty years ago, the United States dominated the world economic scene. Other nations seemed doomed to be forever in its shadow. Japan's economic prospects then looked disturbingly grim. It seemed impossible that little, resource-poor, war-damaged Japan could by the 1980s push the United States aside and become in many respects the world's economic Number One. But that is what happened. Why did it happen? What now lies ahead on the road the United States and Japan have been travelling?

Japan's Rise

Japan adopted an activist trade policy and industrial policy like the one England had used in achieving its great rise to world economic leadership in the nineteenth century. Japan managed its foreign trade to achieve its economic advance by gaining for itself the rewarding, skill-building, high-income, success-making industries of the times. It accomplished this by taking over foreign markets for the products of these industries, particularly the uniquely rewarding market of the United States, while protecting from imports its own rewarding industries. Japan exported much more than it imported, particularly in its trade with the United States. Through this one-sided "trade" Japan made a net takeover of desirable U. S. industries and jobs.

Japan's policy was pursued forcefully and with realism, skill, and effective organization. It was extraordinarily successful. Japan's economic rise was meteoric.

The United States followed a very different economic gameplan—to a very different outcome. The United States assigned itself the task of leading other nations into a new era of worldwide "free trade." All nations were to cease their regulation or management of their foreign trade, leaving such trade to be determined by private interests in pursuit of private profit.

U.S. Policy

Thus, the United States "trade policy" was essentially to have no trade policy, and to try to persuade other nations not to have a trade policy either. The United States shifted from its earlier practice of limiting its imports to protect its manufacturing industries to this new goal in the 1930s. This was done on the argument, the questionable argument, that such a deregulation of foreign trade would be favorable to world peace. When *laissez faire* economics and economic deregulation became fashionable in the United States in the 1970s and 1980s, it was argued that the deregulation of foreign trade would improve world economic efficiency and bring benefit to each participating nation.

The claim that the deregulation of foreign trade would raise standards of living and benefit all nations was based on the hypothetical cases of economic theory, not on experience, which seemed to tell a different story. The idea that underlay the economic rise of England from the fifteenth through the nineteenth centuries was that the key to national economic success is specializing in manufacturing and trade, leaving unrewarding agriculture to other nations. If some industries advance a nation, while others hold it back, then a nation's future depends on what goods it produces and exports, and what goods it imports and thus does not produce. In this view, the pattern of a nation's trade can either raise it up, as did the trade of earlier England and recent Japan, or push it down, as did the trade of the recent United States. If this is the case, it is potentially ruinous for a nation to let the pattern of its trade be determined by private interests, and yet worse to let it be determined by the self-serving trade policies of other nations.

© Wicks/Rothco. Reprinted with permission.

If this is the true story of the effects of foreign trade, the United States notion of "free trade" as a political and economic panacea was an unsuitable basis for a foreign-trading system, and a threat to the economic future of the United States. The new policy of making the United States the "point nation" in a

59

crusade for world-wide deregulation of foreign trade thus never had a solid justification in experience or in knowledge of economic processes.

In "setting a good example" for other nations in its quest for world-wide unregulated foreign trade, the United States left its market—by far the world's greatest and most attractive market for the products of the success-making industries—unusually open to take-over by foreign production. With its eye on the visionary goal of a world of *laissez faire* foreign trade—and trusting economists' assurances on the blessings of "free trade"—the United States did not worry about other nations taking over its wide-open market, its desirable industries and jobs, its economic future.

A Sitting Duck

The United States ~~thus~~ has made itself a "sitting duck" for the ~~activist~~ trade policies of Japan and the other nations that copied its approach. These countries ran great trade surpluses with the United States, took over its markets for the products of the ~~attractive~~ making the most money industries, took over its industries and jobs, upgraded the jobs, incomes, training, skills of their people and the capabilities of their firms. The United States ran great trade deficits with these countries, gave up its markets for the products of the attractive industries, gave up its desirable industries and jobs, downgraded the jobs, incomes, training, skills of its people and the capabilities of its firms.

The economic rise of Japan and its copiers and the economic decline of the United States thus were the two sides of the same coin. Japan understood the foreign-trade game, played realistically to win, and won. The United States did not understand the game, based its actions on a utopian crusade for a world governed by *laissez faire* economics, and lost. . . .

To rescue what still can be saved of the economic future of the United States requires prompt adoption of a new kind of trade policy for the nation, one that assumes responsibility to protect the economic future of the people of the United States. This trade policy needs to be based on a realistic, cause-and-effect understanding of the workings and effects of various patterns of foreign trade in today's world. The new policy must be based also on a realistic view of the theories, the attitudes, and the prospective policies of other nations. The vision of the United States as the ideological schoolteacher or righteous preacher of *laissez faire* economics—neglectful of the needs and interests of its own people—is an unsuitable basis for the nation's trade policy and an impediment to progress toward a generally beneficial system of foreign trade. . . .

Achieving a realistic and pragmatic approach to trade policy requires an understanding of some characteristics of today's foreign trade that have not been brought to the attention of most Americans. The following brief statements will raise for consideration the essential points.

Realities of Today's Foreign Trade

Foreign trade operates in a different context now than before the Second World War; it poses a new type of threat to the economies of the high-wage nations. Before recent decades, the scope of foreign trade was limited by the speed and cost of transportation and communications, by national cultural and political factors, and by colonialism, which excluded most of the world's people, and particularly its low-wage nations, from competing with Western nations for markets and for the desirable manufacturing industries. Before recent decades, there was no practical threat that the world's major, high-income nations would suffer a serious decline in standard of living caused by international wage-competition, by one-sided foreign trade that pulled wages everywhere down to a lowest-common-denominator level. Now that threat exists. The economic decline of the United States reflects it.

Despite the fashionability among Americans of internationalism and anti-nationalism, the nation and the national government provide the essential top-level organizing framework of the human world. Unregulated foreign trade that undermines the independence and the effectiveness of nations threatens to undermine the existing organizational structure of human life without providing any workable replacement. The current popularity of "eliminating barriers," of "globalization," of "one-world," of "post-nationalism" carries the false implication that weakening the effectiveness of national governments and national societies will make the world a better place. But no considered interpretation seems to exist as to how post-national mankind would function. As the performance of the United Nations has shown, world government with substantial organizing and problem-solving powers is not now feasible. Recent episodes in many nations illustrate the—to many, surprising—grip on people of ethnic, language, and national associations. Curing human problems by creating "one world" of standardized, deculturized, malleable human beings has been shown not to have the feasibility that past reformers had assumed. Doubtless most Americans, if they were aware of the issue, would fight against the disappearance of the independence of the United States through its "economic integration" into "the world economy."

Civilized human life requires some form of effective governmental organization. Experience has done nothing to support the hopes and expectations of the anarchists. Thus, weakening the nation or making it ineffective is to be expected to bring not the "one world" of the utopian visions, but destructive international competition, inability to maintain civilized standards,

61

degradation, and open conflict.

Unregulated foreign trade in a world of diverse nations is fundamentally anomalous, a cause of destructive competition, in permitting firms to evade national regulations and laws by shifting production to other nations. Trade within a nation is subject to an elaborate framework of laws, regulations, customs, moral and social standards that limit socially destructive activities and maintain civilized ways of life. Nations differ widely in the political and social frameworks of their economic activities. Unregulated foreign trade governed by private profit causes firms to, say, shift production of goods sold in the U.S. market to countries where costs are lower because regulations are few and wage levels are low. Permitting such shifts of production to low-standards nations creates a general system of destructive competition in which production is shifted from high-standards nations to low-standards nations where costs are lower. The nation that is unwilling to give up its protection of worker safety and of the environment cannot reasonably permit the unlimited importation of goods that can undersell its goods because they are produced in nations that do not protect their workers or their environments. In a world of diverse nations, thus, the very notion of permitting unlimited imports from other nations does not make sense.

A Failed Experiment

America is presently undergoing the greatest socioeconomic upheaval since the Great Depression. A vast experiment in untested economic theory has become government policy. We have decided to shut down our factories and give away our manufacturing capability to foreigners, who can operate with cheap labor under working conditions that are illegal in our own country.

Under the banner of "free trade," the giant and most effective industrial democracy the world has ever seen is being dismantled at such an alarming pace that it threatens the very future of America.

George Vargish, *What's Made in the U.S.A.?*, 1988.

An especially important damaging effect of unregulated foreign trade is causing production in low-wage nations to undercut that of high-wage nations, throwing the workers of all nations into wage-cutting competition, and thus acting to bring wage levels throughout the world to a lowest-common-denominator level. The primary factor causing the shifting of desirable U.S. industries to Japan, and later from Japan to South Korea, and then to China and other countries, was the ability of low-wage production to undersell high-wage production in unregulated foreign trade. Given that wage levels in some large nations are severely depressed by excessive and rapidly growing populations, a system of unregulated foreign trade would cause a large decline in the standards of living of the United States and other high-income nations. By permitting capitalists to "shop the world" for cheap labor to combine for their profit with the capital, the technology, the management methods, and the markets that reflect the past achievements of particular national economies, unregulated foreign trade works to make it impossible for any nation by its own achievements to achieve a high standard of living. A world of uniformly low living standards implies the loss not only of luxuries and superfluities, but also of science, knowledge, education, advanced technology, medical care, welfare programs, and the dignity and hopes of ordinary people. It implies moving backward to a lower level of human life. . . .

Misleading Textbooks

The examples used in economics textbooks to depict unregulated foreign trade as automatically increasing economic efficiency without adverse side effects misleadingly present only selected special cases, usually hypothetical cases of balanced or barter trade between the nations (rather than between private parties). Also implicitly assumed is that the trade does not cause the shift of the desirable industries to one of the countries. The case of, for example, a balanced exchange of wheat for wine that assuredly benefits both "England" and "Portugal" would have to be arranged between the governments of the two nations. The trade then would be balanced because the governments arranged for it to be balanced, and would benefit both nations because otherwise both governments would not sign the agreement. "Free," or unregulated, for-private-profit trade ordinarily has none of these characteristics. It ordinarily is out of balance, as is the trade of the United States. No mechanism exists to assure that it is beneficial to either of the nations. That it is profitable to the private traders does not mean it is beneficial to either nation.

The economic success of a nation depends critically on the character of the industries in which it is engaged, which depends on the pattern of its foreign trade, what kind of goods it produces and exports and what kind of goods it imports and thus does not produce. Some industries provide new skills and capabilities, cumulative technical leadership, freedom from low-wage foreign competition and thus ability to provide high incomes to people. Other industries offer none of these benefits. The recent rise of Japan and its copiers depended on their taking over the rewarding industries. This was accomplished by taking over the markets of other nations for these success-making industries, especially the

United States market. Other nations understood how much they gained by taking over U.S. markets for products of the attractive industries, but United States policy-makers have not comprehended that what they gained the United States lost. . . .

U.S. Decline

The pattern of foreign trade that resulted from the failure of the United States to have a trade policy that protected its national interests has put the nation on a road of economic decline because of the net shift of industries and jobs to other nations resulting from the protracted trade deficit of more than $100 billion a year and the take-over of the U.S. market for the success-making industries by other nations, which resulted in the up-grading of their economies and down-grading of the U.S. economy. These two kinds of damage that can be done to a nation by foreign trade have been abundantly illustrated in history, have been understood for centuries, and are understood now by the policy-makers of most nations. The blind-spot of U.S. policy-makers on this matter is a threat to the future of the nation.

Its destructive pattern of foreign trade was the central and decisive cause of the economic decline of the United States. The deindustrialization and job-downgrading of the United States—and the spectacular economic rise of Japan and its copiers that is its counterpart—reflected the interactive and cumulative effects of a number of causal factors, which cannot be precisely disentangled. Some U.S. failings were caused or aggravated by the demoralization and the forced cut-backs of American firms that resulted from the massive take-over of the U.S. market by low-wage foreign production. The great accomplishments and realistic policies of some other nations were an essential part of the picture. So were changes in world economic and political circumstances that in any case would have reduced the dominance the U.S. economy temporarily had after the Second World War.

But, taking account of all these factors, it seems reasonable to judge that (1) if U.S. trade policy had not given away the nation's premiere markets and permitted massive, unbalanced imports but had insisted on *level* and *common* beneficial trade with other nations, the United States would not have experienced a massive loss of desirable jobs, downgrading of its industry and down-jobbing of its people, and (2) given the destructive pattern of foreign trade U.S. policy permitted to occur, nothing American business and workers could have done could have prevented a serious deterioration in the nation's economic situation and prospects. Given the other elements in the picture, the self-destructive U.S. trade policy was a necessary and sufficient condition for the economic decline of the United States.

Distinguishing Between Fact and Opinion

This activity is designed to help develop the basic critical thinking skill of distinguishing between fact and opinion. Consider the following statement: "U.S. unemployment rates fell from more than 10 percent in early 1983 to less than 5.5 percent in 1988." This is a fact which can be checked by looking up U.S. Department of Labor unemployment statistics. But the statement, "Tariffs cause unemployment," is an opinion. Whether tariffs actually destroy jobs is a debatable issue about which many people disagree.

When investigating controversial issues it is important that one be able to distinguish between statements of fact and statements of opinion. It is also important to recognize that not all statements of fact are true. They may appear to be true, but some are based on inaccurate or false information. For this activity, however, we are concerned with understanding the difference between those statements that appear to be factual and those that appear to be based primarily on opinion.

Most of the following statements are taken from the viewpoints in this chapter. Consider each statement carefully. *Mark O for any statement you believe is an opinion or interpretation of facts. Mark F for any statement you believe is a fact. Mark I for any statement you believe is impossible to judge.*

If you are doing this activity as a member of a class or group, compare your answers with those of other class or group members. Be able to defend your answers. You may discover that others come to different conclusions than you do. Listening to the reasons others present for their answers may give you valuable insights into distinguishing between fact and opinion.

O = opinion
F = fact
I = impossible to judge

1. Strikes are illegal in Taiwan.
2. Free trade has been a disastrous policy for the U.S.
3. The city of Hong Kong leads the world in exports of clothes, toys, and games.
4. U.S. protectionist trade policies usually hurt Americans more than foreign competitors.
5. Americans worked almost half a day longer for lower real wages in 1990 than they did in 1970.
6. Free trade promotes policies that will undermine our sense of community and culture.
7. Everyone's economic well-being is promoted when each person, region, and nation specializes in the creation of those goods and services that can be produced most efficiently.
8. The average per capita income is three times greater in the Republic of the Ivory Coast than in Ghana because the Ivory Coast practices free trade.
9. Citicorp Bank raises capital, obtains deposits, extends loans, and trades currencies all around the world.
10. Many developing nations have no maximum working hours, minimum wage, or environmental legislation.
11. In Mexico, the number of state-owned firms rose from 86 in 1970 to 1,155 in 1982.
12. Imports, up 64 percent in 1987 from 1980, have given Americans a better standard of living.
13. Stealing or disclosing the secrets of silk-spinning machinery was a crime punishable by death in seventeenth-century Northern Italy.
14. Japan became the world's foremost economic power by taking over foreign markets and protecting its own industries from imports.
15. India's imports from the United States jumped 70 percent from 1987 to 1988.
16. International free trade is a way to bind the world together and elevate it to a new vista of world peace and prosperity.
17. Social security, Medicare, and unemployment benefits all raise the cost of production, and thus will not survive in a world free-trade market.
18. Tariffs would protect endangered industries from further erosion and allow them to begin to recover lost ground.
19. Many foreign manufacturers operate with cheap labor under working conditions that are illegal in the U.S.
20. Today approximately 50 percent of Brazil's population suffers from malnutrition, even though per capita output of exportable foodstuffs (soybeans, oranges, cotton, peanuts, and tobacco) jumped 15 percent from 1977 to 1984.

Periodical Bibliography

The following articles have been selected to supplement the diverse views presented in this chapter.

Brian Ahlberg	"Trade: Major Political Issue of the 1990s?" *Utne Reader*, November/December 1989.
Patrick J. Buchanan	"Sun Setting on Free Ride for Free Trade," *Los Angeles Times*, November 22, 1990.
Thomas J. DiLorenzo	"The Political Economy of Protectionism," *The Freeman*, July 1988. Available from The Foundation for Economic Education, Irvington-on-Hudson, New York 10533.
Jeff Faux	"Labor in the New Global Economy," *Dissent*, Summer 1990. Available from the Foundation for the Study of Independent Social Ideas, Inc., 521 Fifth Ave., New York, NY 10017.
Eamonn Fingleton	"Eastern Economics," *The Atlantic Monthly*, October 1990.
Richard A. Gephardt	"America and the New Global Economy," *USA Today*, May 1988.
Bennett Harrison	"Global Winners and Losers," *Technology Review*, July 1990.
David R. Henderson	"A Surprising New View of the Economy," *Fortune*, December 31, 1990.
Robert Kuttner	"Economic Nationalism," *The New Republic*, November 21, 1988.
Michael McMenamin	"Trade War," *Reason*, January 1991.
Charles Oliver	"The Ghost of Christmas Presents," *Reason*, January 1990.
Karen Pennar	"The Gospel of Free Trade Is Losing Apostles," *Business Week*, February 27, 1989.
William H. Peterson	"Thinking About Protection: The Hawkins Prescription for Trouble," *The World & I*, October 1989.
Gerald W. Sazama	"Free Trade vs. Protectionism," *Christianity and Crisis*, April 4, 1988.
Juliet Schor	"The Great Trade Debates," *Zeta Magazine*, March 1988. Available from The Institute for Social and Cultural Communications, 116 St. Botolph St., Boston, MA 02115.
Gus Tyler	"The Myth of Free Trade—Is It Part of the 'Moral Law'?" *Dissent*, Spring 1988.

Is the U.S. the Victim of Unfair Trade Practices?

Chapter Preface

A common complaint heard in the U.S. about free trade is that it is a one-way street. As Congressman James H. Quillen argues: "The rest of the world is not playing by our free trade rules. America has opened many of its markets to the world, while most of the world has imposed greater restrictions on imports from us. They are practicing unequal competition." He and others argue that foreign countries take advantage of the open markets of the U.S., promoting their own industries at the expense of U.S. industries and jobs. Author William J. Gill expresses this viewpoint in strong terms: "Virtually every country on earth is waging trade war against America, while our government surrenders one industry after another to imports from abroad."

Others object to the idea that the U.S. is being unfairly victimized by foreign trade. They argue that free trade benefits the U.S. because U.S. consumers benefit from the wider selection of goods and services, and U.S. businesses are strengthened by foreign competition. Economists such as Thomas J. DiLorenzo, for example, believe U.S. trade retaliation against other nations will only bring harm. "If foreign governments are foolish enough to harm their own citizens by erecting trade barriers, it is unfortunate for those citizens," he writes. "But there are no sound reasons why American consumers should be penalized for the ill-conceived trade policies of foreign governments."

The following viewpoints examine the question of whether the U.S. is being victimized by its trading partners, and what the U.S. should do in response.

"Tariffs, quotas, nitpicking customs regulations, licenses, and other import restrictions prevent American products from competing in foreign markets."

The U.S. Is the Victim of Unfair Trade Practices

Don Bonker

Don Bonker, a former Democratic congressman from Washington, has written extensively for magazines and newspapers about trade issues and human rights. The following viewpoint is taken from his book *America's Trade Crisis*. In it, Bonker argues that many foreign countries use unfair trading practices to give their exports advantages over U.S. products, and to restrict imports from the U.S. He describes a variety of foreign trade practices which he believes unfairly harm the U.S.

As you read, consider the following questions:

1. Does Bonker believe the U.S. is innocent of unfair trade practices?
2. How does import dumping harm the U.S., according to the author?
3. What role does financing play in international trade, according to Bonker?

From *America's Trade Crisis* by Rep. Don Bonker. Copyright © 1988 by Congressman Don Bonker. Reprinted by permission of Houghton Mifflin Co.

What is "unfair trade"? Distortions in the world trading system can take many forms. Predatory exporting practices like dumping, subsidies, targeting, or counterfeiting give foreign companies a competitive edge in the United States and in third-country markets. Tariffs, quotas, nitpicking customs regulations, licenses, and other import restrictions prevent American products from competing in foreign markets. The Reagan administration's report defined unfair trade practices as "government laws, regulations, policies or practices intended either to protect domestic producers from foreign competition or artificially stimulate exports of particular domestic products."

To be honest, no country, including the United States, is entirely pure when it comes to protecting domestic interests. In the world of trade, fairness is often in the eyes of the beholder. As Sir Roy Denman, the European Community's ambassador to the United States, wryly notes, "What one does oneself is fair trade, and what the other fellow does is unfair."

Throughout the 1980s, it became obvious that many nations were playing fast and loose with international trade laws. U.S. exporters faced a maze of tariffs, quotas, and Byzantine regulations designed to keep their products out of foreign markets. Closer to home, subsidized imports displaced domestic manufacturers, throwing thousands out of work. U.S. firms won contracts overseas, only to see a competitor steal the deal with the help of a subsidized government loan package. . . .

Import Dumping

The more prominent examples of unfair trade include the following:

Price Leadership
We're Number 1

40% below Intel and AMD
15%-20% below other Japanese suppliers

Win With the 10% Rule
Find AMD and Intel sockets. . .
Quote 10% below their price. . .
If they requote,
Go 10% again . . .
Don't quit till you *win!*

25% Disti Profit Margin
Guaranteed
Hitachi Eproms

This memo, sent to U.S. distributors of Hitachi semiconductors in February 1985, is a classic illustration of dumping—generally, the practice of exporting at a loss in order to drive other producers out of the marketplace or to maintain domestic employment.

As the memo makes clear, Hitachi was instructing its distributors to cut prices to whatever level necessary to gain market share, while guaranteeing them a 25 percent profit margin As one representative of the U.S. industry testified before a Senate subcommittee, "It is clear to us that in our industry international trade lawlessness is the order of the day."

In the early 1980s, Japan aggressively targeted the world semiconductor market, driving prices downward in an effort to capture U.S. market share. Even when semiconductor prices fell below production costs, the Japanese companies absorbed the losses. Japan's enormous semiconductor firms were much better equipped for a battle of attrition than their small U.S. counterparts. As a result, by mid decade, Japanese firms had captured about 90 percent of the U.S. market for certain chips.

Closed Markets

"Protectionism" has been a dirty word in this country at least since the Reciprocal Trade Act of 1934. Other countries, which are delighted to deploy the word to influence our domestic debates, are equally determined to practice the policy when it comes to "protecting" their own industries. We stubbornly insist on the idea that they accept our values, yet the greatest protectionists in the world are some of our closest trading partners.

We will not open markets abroad until we first open minds here at home. We must recognize and react to powerful forces that seek to keep markets closed to our products. The forces are not only legal, but cultural, and they operate at every level, on every product.

Richard A. Gephardt, *The Wall Street Journal*, April 12, 1988.

In response to Japanese dumping, U.S. semiconductor companies filed three separate complaints with the Commerce Department. Commerce confirmed the industry's accusations and negotiated a far-reaching agreement requiring Japan to stop dumping in the U.S. market, dismantle import barriers that blocked U.S. sales in Japan, and stop dumping chips into other markets in order to displace U.S. manufacturers.

In April 1987, less than eight months after the semiconductor pact was reached, it was clear that Japan had failed to abide by the agreement. Citing evidence of continued dumping in other markets and continued barriers to the Japanese market, President Ronald Reagan slapped a $300 million tariff on certain Japanese televisions, computers, and other electronic products. As Japan has taken steps to eliminate market barriers and third-country dumping, the President gradually lifted these sanctions.

The Japanese semiconductor battle is only one example of dumping. Other cases range across the whole spectrum of American industry, from basic chemicals to the most sophisticated high technology.

Congress recognized the dumping problem as far back as 1916, when it passed a law providing a civil course of action for private damages against parties who dumped foreign merchandise in the United States. Five years later, Congress passed the Antidumping Act of 1921, which authorized investigations of alleged dumping practices and the imposition of antidumping duties. Worldwide, most governments have condemned dumping and instituted laws to penalize imports sold below fair market value.

Subsidy

In May 1986, a coalition of U.S. sawmills filed a petition with the U.S. government, accusing the Canadian government of unfairly assisting its lumber manufacturers and demanding retaliatory action. Pointing to the rapid increase in Canadian lumber imports, which had captured over one-third of the entire U.S. market, the American lumber industry accused Canada of selling government-owned timber to its firms at unfairly low prices. Under the U.S. government's competitive bidding system, a given tree might cost $1500, depending on species and quality; under Canada's noncompetitive allocation system, an identical tree might sell for only $150.

After five months of expensive legal efforts on both sides, the U.S. Department of Commerce ruled that Canada's timber pricing system did, in fact, confer an unfair advantage of roughly 15 percent on Canadian lumber imports. As a result, the department imposed an offsetting 15 percent import fee on all lumber from north of the border. Several months later, U.S. and Canadian negotiators agreed on a settlement under which Canada would assess a 15 percent exit tax on all lumber shipments bound for the United States; Canada also pledged to revise its timber pricing system to eliminate any unfair advantage for its sawmills.

The Canadian timber case is a classic example of a subsidy that distorts normal trade flows. An illegal subsidy exists whenever a foreign government offers payments or other economic benefits that reduce an exporting firm's production costs or prices. Laws to impose countervailing duties to penalize foreign subsidies are the oldest U.S. procedures against unfair trade, dating back to 1897.

Subsidies are often hard to determine because governments, as a matter of course, provide many services that contribute to a country's general competitiveness—education, physical infrastructure, research, and so forth. Depending on the specific case, these types of assistance are generally considered an acceptable form of economic development.

When governments provide more direct assistance to specific exporting industries, however, they often cross the threshold into unfair subsidies. These can range from direct cash grants and tax breaks to reductions in utility or transportation rates.

Although many of these practices are considered unfair by international standards, the determination of what constitutes an unfair subsidy has become considerably more difficult in recent years. The variety and sophistication of subsidies has grown much faster than the body of international law governing them.

Targeting

Many foreign governments have begun to participate actively in the promotion of certain industries. This practice, known as "targeting," involves the identification of new and promising sectors, then taking whatever action is necessary to ensure their success.

Foreign government targeting has threatened a number of U.S. industries. Our private firms simply cannot compete with a foreign firm that has the unlimited resources of its government behind it.

In addition to dumping, subsidy, and targeting, a number of sundry practices are considered unfair by U.S. law, including patent infringement, price fixing, false labeling, and trademark infringement. Long before 1980, when the United States had a favorable trade balance, Congress recognized these problems and provided a statutory framework for dealing with them. U.S. trade law provides relief when the activities of foreign governments, firms, or U.S. importers have been responsible for injury to a domestic industry.

In certain cases, our trade law allows temporary import relief even when no unfair foreign practices are alleged. When a rapid surge of imports captures a major share of the U.S. market and threatens the existence of domestic manufacturers, a U.S. industry can petition for temporary relief in the form of tariffs, quotas, or a negotiated restraint agreement. In theory, this provision is designed to give the U.S. industry a brief "breathing space" in which to modernize and become more competitive. After a short time, the import restrictions are lifted, and the U.S. industry must compete head to head with the foreign imports.

[Michael R. Sesit in *The Wall Street Journal* writes]

> Fuji Electric Co. of Japan and other companies were in the final stages of assembling bids to build generators for the proposed $36 million Mae Moh power plant in Thailand. General Electric considered itself the leading candidate: Thai officials had called GE's equipment technically the best. But only 10 hours before the deadline for bids, Japan's export-financing agency offered the Thais subsidized loans and an $8 million grant to help them pay for the project. Not surprisingly, this fi-

nancing package overcame GE's technical superiority. The Fuji consortium won the contract.

GE's loss of the Mae Moh power plant contract illustrates another growing problem in international commerce. Increasingly, foreign governments are winning big-ticket contracts for their firms through the use of "mixed credits"—official export promotion loans combined with foreign aid grants or other bargain-rate credits that make even an inferior bid irresistible to developing nations.

An Undeclared War

The Wall Street Journal noted that the use of mixed credits amounts to an "undeclared trade war" that is intensifying at a time when the United States and our major trading partners "already are in danger of falling into a traditional trade war."

Mixed credits—also known as tied-aid or blended credits—have received less public attention than other unfair trade practices, but they have plagued U.S. companies competing overseas. In earlier times, international sales were financed by the purchaser, either through his own funds or borrowing. After World War I, the amount of individual sales began to rise rapidly, and exporters began to provide credit to purchasers by borrowing themselves. In time, commercial banks were reluctant to extend credit solely on the basis of the supplier's signature, which gave rise to the current system of government export credit guarantees.

Different Rules

In today's world, many countries can copy US products and production methods and undersell US production. They can do it because of labor costs that are only a fraction as high, lower costs of defense programs and taxes, government regulations, interest rates, and subsidies by their governments. Foreign trade reflects international price-cutting competition, with the various nations playing under different rules.

John M. Culbertson, *The Christian Science Monitor,* June 15, 1987.

In the late 1950s, the French began "sweetening" the export-financing pot to help their exporters by offering a type of foreign aid to developing countries that were having trouble financing their imports. French exporters began to rely on mixed credits as a means of beating their foreign competitors in strategic markets. In the 1970s, competition intensified and other nations followed suit.

Increasingly, sales on large-scale contracts are decided not on the quality of the goods but on the financing terms offered by the exporter and his government. Mixed-credit offers have grown from $212 million in 1975 to $2.1 billion in 1980 to $6.5 billion in 1984. Using the rule of thumb that each $1 billion of U.S. exports generates 25,000 jobs, a conservative estimate would be that over 500,000 American jobs have been lost to predatory foreign financing since 1980.

As one frustrated executive, Jack Pierce, vice president of the Boeing Company, said, "The entire world is turning into the O.K. Corral. You've got barter, countertrade, private and multi-currency deals, government, government export credits—everything but the kitchen sink."

The United States was not prepared to deal with this latest assault against free trade. . . .

Tariffs and Quotas

Victor K. Kiam, president of Remington Products, outlined some of his company's problems before a House subcommittee.

> In Venezuela, where we have had access, we started to build a business. We invested in advertising. We exported. . . . Then the door was shut. So not only did we lose the continuing sales of our product in Venezuela, we lost our investment in advertising which occurred over three years, and now we are out of business, and all the money we invested in the advertising is completely lost to us.

When U.S. firms try to export their products, they often face a formidable array of barriers to those markets. The story of Remington's efforts to crack the Venezuelan market is indicative of the obstacles that exist worldwide. Remington shavers encountered stiff tariffs and customs taxes in Venezuela. Then a combination of foreign exchange and price manipulations by the government made imports uncompetitive against domestically produced goods. Remington also faced a complex import licensing system, followed by difficulty in obtaining foreign currency it needed for importing. Finally, as if these restrictions weren't enough, Venezuela does not allow the use of foreign-produced advertising. Mr. Kiam's familiar television commercials had to be produced in Venezuela.

Historically, tariffs or import fees have been the most common barrier to foreign merchandise. Often instituted simply to raise revenue, tariffs are also used to increase the price of imported goods to protect domestic industries.

Since 1947, negotiators have reduced tariffs to an average of less than 10 percent among industrialized countries. In contrast, many developing nations retain very high tariffs to protect domestic industries, although they often export to developed nations at lower rates. . . .

Another pervasive import barrier is the quota, ranging from a total ban on imports to quantitative restrictions on certain products. While quotas are generally illegal under international trade law, there are exceptions. A particularly frustrating case for American exporters is Japan's use of quotas on agricultural products. Japan's rice growers are not only protected from imports; they also receive subsidies. Even wheat imports are controlled to keep prices high and quantities restricted so that consumers do not switch from rice to wheat products.

The Japanese government also protects its beef industry through quotas that ensure that imported beef is not sold at a price lower than the local product. Japanese consumers pay a heavy penalty for these quotas—beef prices in Japan are four to six times the world market average. Small wonder that overall food costs in Tokyo are 70 percent higher than in New York City and more than double those in Los Angeles.

Other Non-Tariff Barriers

In addition to tariffs and quotas, nations employ a myriad of subtler, less tangible barriers to keep imports out and protect domestic interests. Non-tariff barriers include complex licensing requirements, currency restrictions, countertrade requirements, "buy-domestic" government procurement policies, service and investment restrictions, and a variety of fees.

Non-tariff barriers obscure exporters' understanding of how a country's import system works. All too often, these barriers go hand in hand with discrimination, corruption, and substantial financial risk to the potential importer.

While the gradual reduction in tariff rates worldwide in the last half century has helped to promote a more open global economy, the sharp rise in non-tariff barriers has worked in the opposite direction. Non-tariff barriers are particularly common in nations with heavy international debt burdens. By frustrating foreign exporters with a variety of barriers, debtor nations help to generate a positive balance of trade and foreign exchange to meet their debt obligations.

While debt-saddled countries can perhaps be excused for non-tariff barriers designed to restrict nonessential imports, these tactics are inexcusable among countries that arc racking up sizable trade surpluses. Korea and Taiwan have made protectionist tariff and non-tariff barriers a cornerstone of their national economic development strategies. They have maintained high trade barriers long after their industries have become internationally competitive.

"We have radically different definitions of fair trade for Americans and foreigners."

The U.S. Is Not the Victim of Unfair Trade Practices

James Bovard

James Bovard is a journalist specializing in economic issues. He has written for *The New York Times*, *The Wall Street Journal*, and other publications. In the following viewpoint, he argues that complaints about unfair foreign trade practices are unjustified, and often come from people who simply want protection from foreign competition. He argues that U.S. trade laws defining unfair trade practices are vague and need to be reformed.

As you read, consider the following questions:

1. What unwritten premise underlies U.S. trade laws, according to Bovard?
2. What problems does the author find with the concept of dumping?
3. Why does Bovard believe U.S. trade policies are dishonest?

James Bovard, "U.S. Trade Laws Are a National Disgrace." Reprinted from *USA Today* magazine, January copyright 1988 by the Society for the Advancement of Education.

The U.S. Department of Commerce is almost as ingenious at discovering "economic crimes" as was Stalin's Soviet Union. In the kangaroo court system of trade investigations held in the U.S., foreign businesses are almost certain to be convicted of some offense. U.S. laws on fair trade are far more arbitrary and punitive than the fair-trade laws of most of our trading partners. They inevitably result in less competition, higher prices, and increased government interference in the marketplace.

Increase in Cases

Since 1983, the U.S. has brought more unfair-trade cases than any other country in the world. Since 1980, the Commerce Department has found only six percent of the imports it has investigated not guilty of unfair-trade practices. It will investigate almost any import if so requested by a domestic industry. As Gilbert Kaplan, one of the State Department's top trade experts, has stated, "I think the Commerce Department can prove illegal dumping against any import it chooses."

Unfair trade is one of America's biggest growth industries. In the past decade, Congress repeatedly has expanded the definition of unfair practices. Increasingly, what was deemed fair last year is illegal this year, and it demands retaliation. As former International Trade Commission (ITC) chairman William Leonard has observed, "Every time Congress takes another whack at the law, it gets more biased and easier for domestic industry to win a decision." Yet, even though the current trade laws blatantly are biased against foreign businesses, Congress seems resolved to make them even worse—to create a perfect Star Wars trade law capable of shooting down all incoming imports before American consumers can buy them.

Protectionism has become far less honest in recent years. Instead of openly advocating the sacrificing of U.S. consumers to domestic corporations and unions, politicians concoct an endless list of purportedly unfair practices used by foreign firms. Instead of proposing to give up economic efficiency and productivity, members of Congress preach the necessity of retaliating against an endless list of domestic policies of foreign governments. Instead of openly proposing to close U.S. ports and borders, members of Congress proclaim the need for a "level playing field"—which translates into the U.S. government punishing whomever it chooses, for whatever reason.

U.S. Trade Laws

Our trade laws could be described properly as the Foreign Business Excess Profits Program, since the tendency is to require foreign companies to sell their products to Americans at higher prices than they otherwise would, and thus to inflate foreign profits (often while reducing foreign sales volume). In the past 10 years, foreign companies have made billions of dollars in extra profits in the U.S. thanks to trade restrictions. Yet, if a foreign company allegedly loses one percent of its U.S. profits, members of Congress become incensed, claiming that the foreign company is trying to destroy its American competitors through "dumping." Before we allow Congress to crucify American consumers on a cross of "fairness," we should understand the convoluted, contradictory, and perverse idea of fairness that Congress is championing.

How Should We Respond?

If foreign firms are prepared to sell us their goods below costs, we should let them. We can improve our standard of living and economic power by consuming their finished goods, and use their intermediate goods to cut our own production costs. Acts of predation can become opportunities for subsidy, if we are wise enough to take advantage of them.

Alex Huemer, *The Freeman,* April 1989.

Our trade laws are based on the unwritten premise that any foreign company that takes business from a U.S. firm is guilty of damaging the U.S. The Congress, in writing trade laws, often shows a general hostility toward imports by failing to make a distinction between fair and unfair foreign practices. U.S. trade laws have far broader definitions of unfair trade than do those of other countries. Under these laws, there are two major types of trade crime. One is dumping, wherein a foreign product is sold in the U.S. for less than it sells for in its home market or for less than the Commerce Department's "constructed fair value." The other is for a foreign firm selling in the U.S. to be subsidized by its own government; in such cases, the Commerce Department imposes a countervailing duty equal to the alleged amount of the government subsidy.

Although these trade laws may sound reasonable, in practice they rapidly become a bureaucratic nightmare of arbitrariness and uncertainty. What is "less than fair value"? Technically, it means selling a good for less than the price in the foreign home market or for less than its alleged cost of production. However, Commerce Department analyses of foreigners' costs of production are arbitrary and often senseless. U.S. trade laws require that Commerce always assume in its cost-of-production construction that a foreign company makes an eight percent profit. As Deputy Assistant Secretary of Commerce Kaplan, trying to convince Congress that the current laws are effective, told a

Senate subcommittee, "What company, unfamiliar with the antidumping law, could imagine that the United States requires that at least eight percent profit must be included when calculating a constructed value?"

All trade cases that prove that foreign companies are selling below cost of production also assume that the companies are making an eight percent profit. Nobody at Commerce can explain this reasoning. If a foreign company has an actual profit of seven percent, then the company, by U.S. law, is guilty of selling at a loss of one percent. Such laws are intended to convict foreign businesses without rhyme or reason.

We have radically different definitions of fair trade for Americans and foreigners. As Fred Smith of the Competitive Enterprise Institute said, "If our antidumping laws applied to U.S. companies, every after-Christmas sale in the country would be banned."

Fairness in Action?

In 1986, Commerce cited China for a dumping margin of 66.65% on its porcelain-on-steel cookware—meaning that China allegedly was spending $1.67 to secure $1.00 in sales in the U.S. How did Commerce divine 66.65%? Since China does not have a market price system, Commerce looked elsewhere to deduce the cost of Chinese cookware production. It decided that Thailand was "at a level of economic development comparable" to China's, but Thai cookware makers refused to open their files to Commerce—justifiably, since foreign companies that have voluntarily helped Commerce in the past subsequently have been hit with dumping charges themselves.

Commerce then decided to judge China by comparing its cookware prices with those of Dutch, French, and West German cookware. Not surprisingly, Chinese prices were much lower. (Chinese quality was also lower, but Commerce did not adjust for that.) Commerce thus purportedly proved that China unfairly was dumping its pots and pans on America. After Commerce's verdict, the Customs Service imposed a 66.65% surtax on all incoming Chinese porcelain-on-steel cookware.

Using an analysis based on constructed fair value, Commerce proved that Romania was selling tapered roller bearings for 8.7% less than their fair value, claiming that, because Romania was at roughly the same economic level as Portugal, and Portugal could not make tapered roller bearings that cheaply, Romania must be selling at a loss. Commerce also used this Portugal-based proof to show that Hungary was selling the same product at a 7.42% loss.

Commerce made use of all its wizardry in calculating the fair price of tapered roller bearings from China. First, they decided that India was a surrogate economy and then calculated what it would have cost to make this product in India. Raw material prices were pulled from the Steel Authority of India (even though Indian prices differ from Chinese prices), the cost of labor was pulled from International Labor Organization reports (again, even though Chinese and Indian labor costs are different), and 31% was added for employee fringe benefits (again, not a common Chinese practice). Commerce then assumed a 10% overhead rate and an automatic eight percent profit for the imaginary Indian producer, made currency conversions from Indian rupees to U.S. dollars, and compared that total to the U.S. price of the Chinese imports. Through these convoluted calculations, Commerce proved that the Chinese were exporting tapered roller bearings for 0.97% less than their fair value. This is like an authoritarian regime spending weeks torturing a suspect—who finally admits at the end that he once jaywalked.

Bureaucratic Quibbles

The vast majority of trade cases are simply instances of U.S. bureaucrats quibbling about such matters as which expenses of a foreign country to allow, how to calculate foreign costs of production, what adjustments to make for exchange-rate fluctuations, and how to compare prices for arbitrary adjustments for differences in quality, sales volumes, and wholesale versus retail sales figures. In 1984, Italy was convicted of a less-than-fair-value margin of 1.16% on its pads for woodwind instruments —even though Commerce admitted that it did not compare sales of identical products in Italy and the U.S.

In many cases, the alleged dumping margin is less than the deductions Commerce makes for foreign brokerage, foreign inland freight, ocean freight, U.S. customs duty, U.S. brokerage, and freight and marine insurance. In other words, the foreign company is not selling its products for less in the U.S. than in its home market. Rather, the U.S. sales price for the foreign product is not high enough in comparison to the home-market price to please the Commerce Department. . . .

In any trade case determining injury from foreign competition, there is a blatant double standard at work. As former ITC chairman Leonard has noted, "The ITC more or less takes on faith the price and profitability information supplied by domestic industries. But the price information is usually meaningless because it does not show the quantities being sold." Of course, U.S. producers have an incentive to overstate their prices to make it easier to prove that foreigners are unfairly underselling them. No American company ever has been penalized for lying about its prices in an ITC investigation.

If a company does not feel that it is being hurt, then it has no incentive to reply to an ITC price survey. Thus, because the entire system is based only on information from companies claiming to be hurt, it is rigged to produce biased results. As Peter Suchman, a lawyer for the American Association of Exporters and Importers, told a Senate hearing in 1986, "It is notorious among practitioners that the so-called surveys conducted by the Commission are totally unverified and are an open field for domestic companies to say whatever they want to about their prices. And in fact, they have the added incentive in a method such as that which has been proposed of trying to knock their overseas competitors out of the market by rigging that comparison."

A False Premise

The whole point of our trade laws is to prevent foreigners from dumping their products, bankrupting U.S. companies, and then taking over the market and victimizing American consumers. However, these dire consequences never happened, not even before the existing trade laws were enacted. As Judge Robert Bork noted in 1978, "Predation by such [pricing] techniques is very improbable." The Supreme Court stated in 1986, "There is a consensus among commentators that predatory pricing schemes are rarely tried, and even more rarely successful."

The more intense the international competition has become, the less chance any one company or country has had of cornering the world market. As World Bank economist J. Michael Finger observed, "The customer's best defense against predatory pricing is the availability of an alternative supplier." If Japan tries to ratchet up car prices, the South Koreans will soon make mincemeat of Japan Incorporated. If West German breweries try to put the squeeze on American beer drinkers, Belgian, Canadian, and Mexican beer companies will come to the rescue.

The Commerce Department's "trade medicine" is almost guaranteed to be far more harmful than any illness it purports to treat. Our trade laws routinely inflate domestic prices to protect consumers against the one-in-a-million possibility that a foreign company could corner the market and raise prices. With world capital markets being so open and responsive, it is extremely doubtful that a company that did temporarily corner a market could hold on to its monopoly for very long. The most successful cartel of modern times—OPEC [Organization of Petroleum Exporting Countries]—could not have lasted as long as it did without U.S. government laws that discouraged domestic oil production and encouraged excessive domestic oil consumption.

It is far more likely that Commerce errs in its analyses of foreign costs and sales efforts than that foreigners deliberately are losing money so they can bankrupt American businesses. Most violations of our trade laws are crimes without a motive. If foreign companies don't intend to take over the U.S. market, what incentive do they have to sell at a loss? How likely is it that

Kenya, Turkey, or Zimbabwe successfully will bankrupt all their American competition? Most of our trade laws are good only for harassing foreigners and enriching American lawyers.

Dumping

The whole idea of dumping—the idea that it is a crime for companies to sell the same product for two different prices in two different markets 15,000 miles apart—is absurd. There are many reasons that a company would sell a product for different prices in different parts of the world. If a businessman charges higher prices in New York than in Kansas, does that prove he is trying to bankrupt every business in Kansas, to achieve a monopoly, and to take advantage of consumers? If the states regulated interstate trade the way the Commerce Department regulates international trade, our economy would grind to a halt and we would soon be about as prosperous as, say, Yugoslavia.

Dumping in Practice

Dumping is commonly characterized as an international form of predatory pricing. Foreign producers, the theory goes, unload their goods at cut-rate prices in hopes of driving out the U.S. industry and charging inflated monopoly prices later. But the whole concept of predatory pricing is now regarded by most economists with suspicion. Research indicates that predation seldom if ever works—the up-front costs are just too high, and the chances of ultimately prevailing (i.e., enjoying monopoly profits) are too slim and speculative.

In the case of dumping, the likelihood of predatory behavior is even more remote. After all, allegations of dumping usually involve several competing companies from a given foreign country, and often target imports from more than one country. If even domestic predation is farfetched, then international predatory conspiracies border on paranoia.

Brink Lindsey, *The Wall Street Journal*, October 15, 1990.

Congress is the biggest lobby in the world for excessive profits for foreign manufacturers. Almost every trade restriction indirectly forces foreign companies to raise their prices and thereby hurt American consumers. The voluntary restraint agreements that cover foreign autos and steel have added over $5,000,000,000 to the prices and profits of foreign manufacturers. Yet, Congress is unconcerned about huge foreign profits as long as no Japanese company loses 50 cents on a sale and thereby tries to destroy America. It is okay to burden American consumers with artificially high prices, but it is unforgivable to compete with

American businesses through artificially low prices.

In June, 1987, Secretary of Commerce Bruce Smart wrote in a letter to *The Wall Street Journal* that "selling below cost by American producers in the American market is a common—and legal—practice. But selling to Americans by American firms competing with one another does not threaten to transfer wealth and unemployment across international boundaries." This mercantilist view was thoroughly refuted by Adam Smith more than 200 years ago. If foreigners are selling below cost, that means that they are transferring wealth to Americans. Should the U.S. government be so paranoid about foreigners bearing gifts? How can a foreign company give Americans money and at the same time destroy American jobs?

The issue is not whether a foreign company, intentionally or inadvertently, gives a slight subsidy to American consumers. It is whether a foreign company is likely to be able to take over the U.S. market, bankrupt U.S. competitors, and then drive up prices. So-called fair-trade advocates can not produce any examples of this happening.

Dishonest Policies

The worst thing about our trade laws and their pending revision is not that they represent absurd, idiotic, or suicidal economics, but that they are dishonest. As protectionism has become less politically fashionable, Congress has found new names to use to achieve old evils.

For over 100 years, the cry of "fair trade" has been a red herring used to close the borders and sacrifice the welfare of some Americans to the profits of other Americans. Many domestic companies and business organizations would oppose free trade even if every foreign government followed the policies of the U.S. government exactly. The goal is not fair trade, but less competition and higher profits for domestic manufacturers.

If Congress wishes to close our borders and blockade our ports against cheaper, higher-quality foreign goods, it should do so openly. If Congress wants to hold up consumers, it should not hide behind a smoke screen of fairness. If Congress wants a trade war, it should admit that it is launching a first strike on our trading partners—and it should not excuse itself by pointing to some minor border incident to justify a massive retaliation to save the national honor.

"Japan isn't playing fair with the United States."

Japan's Trade Practices with the U.S. Are Unfair

Fred Barnes

Japan is a target of U.S. trade complaints, partially because it consistently sells more goods than it buys from the U.S. In 1989, for instance, its trade surplus with the U.S. was $49 billion. In the following viewpoint, Fred Barnes argues that Japan unfairly restricts imports while taking advantage of the open U.S. market. He argues that the U.S. should pressure Japan to change its trade practices. Barnes is a journalist and senior editor of *The New Republic*, a journal of opinion.

As you read, consider the following questions:

1. What examples of Japanese trade practices does Barnes describe?
2. What caused the collapse of the U.S. semiconductor industry, according to the author?
3. Why does Barnes argue against trade protectionist measures directed at Japan?

Fred Barnes, "The Japan That Won't Play Fair." Reprinted, with permission, from the August 1990 *Reader's Digest*. Copyright © 1990 by The Reader's Digest Association, Inc.

American construction firms, among the best in the world, are all but excluded from Japan's $275-billion-a-year construction market. They've gotten a total of $200 million in contracts, while their Japanese competitors signed contracts worth $2.6 billion for work in the United States in 1988 alone.

At one point, Tokyo bureaucrats sought to bar American skis from Japan. They argued that Japanese snow was "different," that American skis wouldn't work right. Officials also blocked the import of certain U.S.-made medical testing devices—on the ground that U.S. safety-test data were not acceptable.

And though Japan brought the game of baseball from America, the Japanese discouraged the import of American bats for years. They required that each shipment be opened, inspected and tested. Few were approved.

Not Playing Fair

Japan isn't playing fair with the United States. U.S. military might protects Japan and the sea lanes crucial to its survival as an economic superpower, but Japan fiercely resists American entry into its markets. It has also violated trade agreements and promises. When Americans cry foul, Japan then spends millions on Washington lobbyists to stifle complaints.

Meanwhile, easy access to the U.S. market, the world's biggest, allows Japanese companies such as Sony and Honda to grow rich and powerful. As a result, there is increasing pressure in the United States for trade restrictions against Japan—steps sure to harm both nations and the world economy.

American firms confront multiple roadblocks in Japan. Some, such as IBM, Coca-Cola and Procter & Gamble, have overcome official and cultural barriers to thrive in Japan. But other U.S. companies have required the assistance of the American government to be successful. Absent repeated warnings by American officials of cooler U.S.-Japanese relations and tariff retaliations, some U.S. firms have trouble even getting a toehold.

Economic Warfare

The experience of Motorola, the electronics giant, is typical. In 1957, Motorola president Robert Galvin committed his company to doing business in Japan. The reception in Tokyo was chilly. It wasn't until 1966 that Motorola was allowed to establish its first joint venture. It was another 15 years before Nippon Telegraph and Telephone (NTT), Japan's biggest electronics consumer, became a customer.

When NTT agreed to buy portable paging devices from Motorola, Japanese government officials tried to short-circuit the deal by forcing NTT to buy more expensive and less advanced Japanese pagers. Thanks to intervention by U.S. officials, NTT stuck to the deal. In 1987, a year after Motorola won the right to sell cellular phones, Japanese officials insisted there were no frequencies available in Tokyo for the Motorola phones. The market was opened up only after the U.S. government brought heavy pressure.

JAPAN
OH, BOY... A PIECE OF THE TRADE PIE!

Bill DeOre, *The Dallas Morning News*. Reprinted with permission.

Compare Motorola's experience in Japan with that of Japanese firms in the United States. Japanese auto makers have been lured to this country by tax breaks, grants, special loans, job-training programs, transportation links and favorable land deals. Kentucky attracted a Toyota plant in 1985 by offering incentives worth $234 million. In 1986 Indiana got a Subaru-Isuzu plant with 1700 workers on the strength of incentives totaling $90 million. That's more than $50,000 per job.

U.S. More Open

"The U.S. is far more open than Japan," says Motoo Shiina, a former Japanese legislator. He and other Japanese I interviewed in Tokyo concede there's an imbalance in U.S.-Japanese relations. But it's hardly the fault of the Japanese alone. Americans gobble up hightech, high-quality Japanese products. American goods of lesser quality, abysmal business decisions (such as the failure to exploit the market for VCRs) and insufficient funding for research and development have all contributed to a persistent U.S. trade deficit with Japan of nearly $50 billion a year.

To their credit, the Japanese are on America's side on most international issues. With the United States unable to increase its foreign aid, Japan will become the biggest donor nation in 1990. At U.S. urging, Japan now provides debt relief to Latin America. From 1985 to 1987, the Japanese bought U.S. Treasury notes and other dollar securities heavily to keep the dollar strong and interest rates from rising, "rescuing the Reagan Administration and the world economy from currency misalignments and financial crisis," according to international economist David Hale.

Still, Japan undermines the goodwill it creates by practicing what management expert Peter Drucker has called "adversarial trade." Time and again, the Japanese have promised to curtail their one-sided trade policy. But little happens. In late 1980 Japan agreed to buy at least $300 million a year in U.S. auto parts starting in 1981. It took eight years to reach that mark. In 1990, Japan vowed in trade talks to make structural changes in the Japanese economy to increase imports. Within weeks, Japanese officials were trying to wiggle out of some of the promises.

Targeting for Dominance

In 1985 Rep. Marcy Kaptur (D., Ohio) carried with her to Japan Champion spark plugs, which are manufactured in her Toledo district (as well as elsewhere). She was protesting U.S. auto-parts manufacturers' lack of access to Japanese markets. Handing a spark plug to each official she met, Kaptur asked why Japanese auto makers wouldn't buy the plugs, which are original equipment not just in U.S.-made cars but in Volvos, Rolls-Royces and BMWs. When she met Yasuhiro Nakasone, then Japan's prime minister, her reputation preceded her. "Where's my spark plug?" he asked.

Kaptur's campaign yielded results. Champion got a piece of the Japanese auto-parts market. But it wouldn't have if Kaptur, as a U.S. official, hadn't put up a stink. "Increased market access to Japan is greatly enhanced when direct government intervention comes into play," says Michael P. Skarzynski, Assistant Secretary for Trade Development with the U.S. Commerce Department.

In the 1970s U.S. firms held 60 percent of the world's semiconductor market. By 1989, our world share had dipped to 35 percent, while Japan's was 51 percent, nearly double that of only a decade earlier.

The American collapse is all the more distressing because of the key role of integrated circuits, a type of semiconductor. These small silicon or germanium chips on which electric signals can be stored are the essential component in the computer, telecommunication and other industries relying on electronics. The country that controls the semiconductor industry controls the technological future and its rewards.

How did the United States stumble? It was partly our fault, partly Japan's doing. The American semiconductor industry didn't pay enough attention to growth. In 1984 it spent eight percent of sales on research and development and another 18 percent on new plants and equipment. That's twice what other U.S. industries spent, but only half what Japan spent for semiconductor growth. The Japanese targeted this industry for dominance. Their skill in mass-producing chips of extraordinarily high quality played a significant role. And they deliberately sold below cost to gain market share. The strategy worked. By 1987 U.S. semiconductor producers lost a combined $500 million, and many firms left the field.

Having scored a triumph in the semiconductor market, the Japanese are now targeting other industries, including aerospace, biotechnology, supercomputers and computer software.

Hired Guns

The security and economic alliance between the United States and Japan has produced peace and prosperity for both countries. Yet Japan has at times acted more like a threat than an ally. For instance, in 1989 a prominent politician named Shintaro Ishihara raised the prospect of his country's selling critical military technology to the Soviet Union instead of the United States. Ishihara argued that Japan "holds very strong cards in high-technology capabilities." The stakes would be high. For example, exporting to the Soviets the computer chips needed for missile accuracy would upset the entire military balance.

Ishihara's suggestion appeared in his best-selling book, *The Japan That Can Say "No,"* co-authored by Sony chairman Akio Morita. Japanese officials disavowed Ishihara, as did Morita. But the book attracted attention in Washington, particularly in light of an earlier incident.

In the early 1980s the Toshiba Machine Co., a subsidiary of the Japanese electronics giant Toshiba, sold precision milling machines and software to the Soviets. These machines, with the aid of controllers supplied by the Norwegian company Kongsberg, allowed the Soviets to build quieter submarines that are more difficult to detect. Consequently, the United States faced an alarming new threat to its security. Estimates of the cost of developing countermeasures were as high as $8 billion.

90

The Toshiba case bared another troubling aspect of American-Japanese relations: the Japan lobby in Washington. The Senate voted to bar Toshiba sales in the United States for at least three years, which would have cost the company $10 billion. But after Toshiba hired a regiment of U.S. lobbyists, the penalty was reduced in the House to a ban on sales to the U.S. government by the Toshiba subsidiary, a slap on the wrist that cost Toshiba only several hundred million dollars. "In my 15 years in the Senate, I've never seen a lobbying campaign so orchestrated at so many levels," said Sen. Jake Garn (R., Utah).

Keeping U.S. Products Out

Many American products are kept out of Japanese markets or are sold there at high prices. Examples: A pair of blue jeans that sells for $32 in the U.S. costs $55.63 in Japan. A set of American-made golf clubs that costs $420 in the U.S. is priced at $659.15 in Japan. . . .

Secretary of Commerce Robert A. Mosbacher has said bluntly, "When there is a new [American] process, a new industry, a new technology, the Japanese find ways to keep American companies from selling in quantities until they have an opportunity to build a similar item or develop the technology themselves. It's the same pattern with supercomputers, with semiconductors way back, with amorphous metals technology, with satellites and more.

The Washington Spectator, June 15, 1990.

The Japanese spent $43 million on lobbying and related activities in 1989 alone. It is estimated that, along with their American subsidiaries, they spent up to $60 million more for lawyers, publicists and advisers. Over the years these have included some of the best-connected people in Washington: former Democratic national chairman Charles Manatt, former U.S. trade representative William Eberle, former Oklahoma Congressman James R. Jones and former CIA [Central Intelligence Agency] director William Colby.

Of course, there's nothing wrong with representing the Japanese. Virtually every major country hires Washington lobbyists (though the Japanese employ by far the most). But there's nothing comparable in Tokyo. There are far fewer Japanese lawyers or former government officials lobbying for American interests. So Japanese companies have political muscle in Washington that American firms can't match in Tokyo.

Despite appearances, Japan is not buying up America. The net worth of Japan's investment here has soared—from $5 billion in

1980 to $53 billion by 1989. However, it's still relatively small—
just over half the British investment in the United States. Early
in 1990, the Japanese held less than four percent of total U.S.
government debt. As of 1988, they owned less than one-tenth as
much American farmland as the British and Canadians.

Rather than a threat, Japanese investment is an enormous
boon. It finances debt (including the nation's budget deficit),
stimulates productivity, holds down interest rates and retail
prices, and provides tens of thousands of jobs.

Once again, though, Japan does not reciprocate. In 1988 alone,
the Japanese investment in America was $7^{1}/_{2}$ times the U.S. investment in Japan. The Japanese economy is riddled with car-
tels and old-boy networks. Companies and assets are sold
largely among Japanese, with foreigners rarely offered an opportunity to buy. The same is true for real estate. "The bottom
line on investment in Japan is that it's not a natural outlet for
foreigners," says David Smick, publisher of *The International
Economy.*

In 1988 Martha Seger of the Federal Reserve Board voted to
bar the takeover of California First Bank by the Bank of Tokyo.
"U.S. banks are not permitted to make comparable acquisitions
in Japan," she said. Four Japanese securities firms were admitted to the New York Stock Exchange as primary dealers. No government pressure was needed. But it took an act of Congress to
get three American firms admitted to the Tokyo Stock Exchange.

Protectionism Not the Answer

Just as popular fear that the Japanese are buying up America is
mistaken, so are the protectionist solutions many politicians offer. The United States already limits the import of Japanese cars
and imposes a quota on Japanese steel. Erecting further trade
barriers won't help. "They benefit no one," explains Richard
Rahn, chief economist for the U.S. Chamber of Commerce. Rice
farmers are protected by trade restrictions in Japan, causing
Japanese consumers to pay nine times the world price for rice.
"We don't want Americans to pay three times what they should
for TVs," says Rahn.

The Japanese would almost certainly retaliate, further block-
ing U.S. goods and touching off a trade war. This would strangle
the global competition that makes free markets so productive
—and so appealing to nations just emerging from decades of
communist poverty.

The fact is that competition from the Japanese has been good
for this country. In a whole range of industries, it has forced
management and labor to shape up. American cars are better
made today because they faced tough Japanese—and Korean
and West European—competition. Adds economics writer

Robert J. Samuelson: "It's the same story in many industries: steel, machine tools, copiers. By making our companies more efficient and imaginative, the Japanese improve our living standards. In the 1980s, U.S. factory productivity (output per hour) jumped 38 percent. That's the best gain for a decade since World War II."

The Need for Pressure

The problem, again, isn't Japanese purchases and exports. It is that Americans aren't free to sell products in Japan and invest there. To force Japan to play fair, America needs trade negotiators as tough as junkyard dogs, and lots of them.

If pressure is the only thing that gains entry to the Japanese market, more must be exerted by top U.S. officials. Forceful intervention by Commerce Secretary Robert Mosbacher prompted the Japanese to allow the sale of ten times more Jeep Cherokees and to permit Toys R Us to open a Tokyo outlet.

America must convince the Japanese that totally free markets are best for them, for us and for the world. We must make the Japanese realize that it pays to play fair.

"The trade deficit is not prima facie evidence of unfair trade practices by Japan."

Japan's Trade Practices With the U.S. Are Fair

William A. Niskanen

William A. Niskanen is chairman of the Cato Institute, a Washington, D.C. research organization that supports free trade and is against government intervention in the economy. From 1981 to 1985 he was a member of the Council of Economic Advisors to President Reagan. In the following viewpoint, he asserts that U.S. complaints of Japanese unfair trade practices are misguided. Niskanen argues that the U.S. trade deficit does not prove that Japan is an unfair trader. He concludes that U.S. actions to punish Japan for unfair trade practices could harm the global trading system.

As you read, consider the following questions:

1. Why does Niskanen find the actions of the U.S. trade representative in 1989 so disturbing?
2. What evidence does Niskanen use to show that Japan's economy is open to trade with the U.S.?
3. What motivates U.S. trade complaints against Japan, according to the author?

William A. Niskanen, "The Bully of World Trade." Excerpted, with permission, from the Fall 1989 issue of *Orbis: A Journal of World Affairs* published by the Foreign Policy Research Institute.

On May 25, 1989, the U.S. trade representative (USTR) cited three practices of the Japanese government as "significant barriers" to U.S. exports, and demanded negotiations to resolve the dispute thus begun. These charges and demands were lodged against Japan even though the practices in question follow international trading rules and even though they mirror the United States's own trading practices. Moreover, if the controversy is not resolved to Washington's satisfaction, the USTR is authorized by American law to impose punitive tariffs on selected Japanese products.

Such, to date, has been the first use of "Super 301," that section of the 1,000-page Omnibus Trade and Competitiveness Act of 1988 requiring the USTR to identify which countries and practices most limit U.S. exports. In a global context, the action is not economically important—rather like an individual in a large city robbing a local convenience store. What makes the action so troublesome is that the perpetrator is the local bishop: the leading long-time proponent of free trade, the U.S. government, has moved openly to become the bully of the world trading system. This it has done by unilaterally redefining "unfair" trade.

Defining Unfair Trade

Traditionally, "unfair" trade has been defined as any practice that is not consistent with rules to which each affected party has agreed. But the U.S. government now says, in effect, that any practice perceived to harm U.S. interests is unfair, whether or not it is consistent with international trade rules or is similar to practices found in the United States and other countries. By so defining unfair trade, the U.S. government feels free to demand that other governments change their domestic laws, regulations, and business practices to serve American desires. If they fail to do so, Super 301 legislation allows the U.S. government to back up its demand by threatening foreign governments with punitive U.S. tariffs on their countries' products.

Japan has been the special target of this new U.S. trade policy but it is not the only target, and it will probably not be the last. This is the true concern. In the long run, the world trading system may not survive aggressive implementation of the new U.S. approach.

How did this state of affairs come about? Why is Japan a special target of U.S. trade policy? And what are the most likely next steps in trade relations between the United States and Japan?

For nearly forty years, beginning in 1947 with the General Agreement on Tariffs and Trade (GATT), the U.S. government led the effort to develop a world trading system based on the

95

rule of law, a common dispute-settlement procedure, and the mutual reduction of trade barriers. The two most important rules of the system were nondiscrimination in tariffs (the "most favored nation" rule, which specifies that the tariffs on imports from one country be no higher than those on imports from any other country) and the elimination of quantitative limits on nonagricultural imports.

Henry Payne. Reprinted by permission of UFS, Inc.

For the most part, this was a remarkably successful effort. Major rounds of tariff negotiations in the 1960s and 1970s led to considerable reductions in the average tariffs of the member states. Approval of the Generalized System of Preferences in 1971 substantially broadened the number of countries holding membership in GATT. As a result, through about 1980, international trade increased more rapidly than the gross national product (GNP) of most member countries.

To be sure, implicitly and explicitly, both the original Agreement and the bodies established to oversee its implementation have allowed major exceptions to GATT trade rules—the most important exceptions are those involving agriculture, textiles, and steel. Nevertheless, the transition from a pre-war world of economic nationalism to this post-war trading system based on law contributed to an unprecedented period of prosperity in most member states.

Legally, though, GATT has had an anomalous status, right

from the start. In the late 1940s, the U.S. Senate bowed to anti-free-trade sentiment in agriculture and the service industries, and failed to ratify a permanent international trade treaty. This left GATT, which was merely an executive agreement, as the principal vehicle for trade negotiations. Consequently, member countries have felt free to diverge from the agreements reached under GATT, and no country more so than the United States.

Japan a Special Target

Added to this is the U.S. government's long history of making Japan a target of specific restrictions. As early as 1907, popular concern in California about rising immigration from Japan led President Theodore Roosevelt to negotiate an agreement with the Japanese government to limit the number of passports issued to emigrants to the United States. In this way, what might be called a "voluntary emigration restraint" established a precedent for the first major use of "voluntary export restraints" (VERs) as an instrument of U.S. trade policy.

This first major VER took effect in 1937, and again it was Japan that was singled out. A rapid increase in the importation of cotton textiles from Japan in the early 1930s brought about negotiations between representatives of the producers in both countries, apparently with the consent of both governments. An agreement was signed that limited Japanese exports of cotton textiles and selected cotton products to the United States, and this agreement was later extended through 1940.

Although such VERs violate both of GATT's main principles, the United States government renewed the use of this instrument, again with Japan as the target, early in the GATT era. A resurgence of cotton textile imports from Japan in the early 1950s provoked another voluntary export restraint at the request of the U.S. government. Effective from 1957 through 1961, this agreement was later broadened to other countries and other textile and apparel products. In 1968 came the first set of VERs on steel, affecting both Japanese and European exports to the United States. . . .

Unexpected Events

With time, the focus of U.S. pressure shifted from agreements limiting Japanese exports to agreements opening the Japanese domestic market. While Americans got most of what they sought in these agreements, the consequences were often unexpected. Thus, an agreement to open the Japanese capital market was approved in 1984, but one effect was a continued strengthening of the dollar against the yen—the opposite of what the administration had anticipated. In 1985, the two governments instituted "market-opening, sector-specific" negotiations for four product areas: telecommunications, pharmaceuticals, computers and electronics, and forest products. But these efforts did American industry little good. Similarly, the Semiconductor Agreement of 1986 was expected, by American officials, to increase sales of U.S. semiconductors in Japan, but a continuing dispute over the interpretation of this agreement has weakened its effects. Finally, U.S. pressure induced the government of Japan to substitute high (but declining) tariffs for its very restrictive quotas on the importation of beef and citrus, but other countries (such as Australia and Brazil) may be the primary beneficiaries.

Washington also pressured the Japanese government to shift its macroeconomic policy, hoping this would increase Japan's domestic demand and reduce the strength of the dollar against the yen. Such measures were affirmed by the Plaza Accord of 1985 and the Tokyo economic summit in 1986, and they appear to have been strikingly effective from the U.S. perspective. Japanese domestic demand and imports have increased sharply and the dollar/yen exchange rate has declined. Indeed, such macroeconomic measures by both the U.S. and Japanese governments have proven to be far more effective than trade measures in reducing the U.S.-Japanese bilateral trade deficit.

Doubts on Japanese Unfairness

In the context of this history, the Super 301 muscle-flexing of May 1989 was not revolutionary in origin or in scope. The USTR charged that three obscure practices of the Japanese government represent "significant barriers" to U.S. exports. But even a cursory look at these practices must raise doubts about the charge.

First, Japan's governmental entities may not purchase foreign-manufactured *space satellites*, if such a purchase would interfere with Japanese industrial development objectives. Nevertheless, American firms supply a large proportion of the components for Japanese satellites and are members of joint ventures to supply satellites to private purchasers.

Second, the purchase of foreign *supercomputers* by Japan's governmental entities and public universities has been effectively foreclosed to outsiders because Japanese firms offer those institutions deep discounts. Yet U.S. sales to private Japanese purchasers have increased, and the Japanese government recently invited U.S. firms to bid on supplying it with eight supercomputers.

Third, a variety of product standards, building codes, and fire codes reduces the general demand for *wood products*. But there is no reason to believe that these codes discriminate against U.S. or other foreign suppliers; they are just as onerous for Japanese firms.

Several observations about these charges are in order. None of the activities condemned contradicts GATT trading rules or the developing GATT government procurement code. Each of these practices matches similar ones in the United States, such as "Buy America" provisions in government procurement, discounting of computers to universities, and complex building and fire codes. And, in the end, reversing all three of these practices would increase U.S. exports to Japan by only about $2 billion a year.

The real question posed by the Super 301 citations is whether the threat of U.S. trade sanctions is an appropriate way to pressure foreign governments into changing domestic laws, regulations, or business practices that may have the indirect effect of limiting U.S. exports. Congress has decided that such measures are fitting, even though similar behavior by foreign governments would be met with congressional outrage.

Why Pick on Japan?

Why is Japan, today as in the past, so obviously a special target of U.S. trade policy? Japan's formal barriers to imports are now among the lowest in the world; Japanese tariff rates average about 2 percent, compared to about 4 percent in the United States, and the range of products covered by quantitative limits on imports is smaller than in the United States. As U.S. import barriers increased substantially during the 1980s, Japanese barriers fell. The Japanese government accelerated the reduction of tariffs to which it had agreed in the Tokyo Round and, under U.S. pressure, removed some of its quantitative limits on agricultural imports.

Japan's import barriers are also dramatically different from those of the other two countries, Brazil and India, that were designated for Super 301 negotiations. The average tariff rate in Brazil is 37 percent, in India 138 percent, and each of these countries also has a restrictive system of import licensing. One cannot help but wonder what criteria would select these three countries for the initial negotiations.

Moving beyond trade barriers, the government of Japan has also permitted appreciation of the yen against the dollar, allowing it to increase by 71 percent since 1979 and by 86 percent since the dollar's strength peaked in 1985. This rise in the currency's value has pushed down prices of U.S. products in Japan and raised prices of Japanese products in the United States. By comparison, the trade-weighted average of the major currencies (including the yen) has declined about 5 percent since 1979 and increased by 54 percent since the dollar's peak in 1985. Thus, there is no reasonable basis for asserting that the government of Japan has used either formal trade barriers or exchange-rate manipulation for protectionist objectives in the 1980s.

The record also indicates that the Japanese economy is ever more receptive to U.S. exports. From 1979 through 1988, U.S. exports to Japan increased by 114 percent (in current dollars), including a 34 percent jump in 1988 alone. Over the same period, U.S. exports to Japan rose from 9.6 percent to 11.7 percent of total U.S. exports, despite U.S. government restrictions on the export of Alaskan oil and on the export of logs from Western public forests.

Success Breeds Envy

What then about the view. . . that Japanese companies believe in "predatory" competition?

The notion that American companies, by contrast, compete in a benign fashion is faintly romantic and fully foolish. What the Cambridge economist Joan Robinson used to call the "animal spirits" of capitalist entrepreneurs surely are manifest in both countries. The successful always appear more predatory. This was exactly the stereotype of British entrepreneurs during the 19th century and of the "ugly" American in the '50s and '60s. With success, one gets one's share of envy and resentment.

Jagdish Bhagwati, *The Wall Street Journal,* April 26, 1990.

In sum, the large and continuing U.S. trade deficit with Japan ($52 billion in 1988) is not due to slow growth in U.S. exports to Japan but to a rapid growth of U.S. imports from Japan. From 1979 through 1988, U.S. imports from Japan increased 242 percent, despite the widening government blockade to these imports. Certainly, the trade deficit is not prima facie evidence of unfair trade practices by Japan.

What Motivates U.S. Complaints?

Given this record, what motivates the antagonistic U.S. trade stance vis-à-vis Japan? The most obvious answer is that Japan has been a formidable competitor—initially in textiles, later in standard industrial products, more recently in certain high-technology products. For the most part, low prices and high quality, not unfair trade practices, have been the reason for Japan's success. In addition, undoubtedly, the complex web of business and government relations in Japan limits entry by foreign firms—as well as by new Japanese firms. For both reasons, universal trade rules alone do not seem to protect established Western industries, and thus Western governments have implemented one trade measure after another against Japan. Perhaps, too, an element of hostility based on memories of World War II may yet influence politicians in the West.

Ironically, the government of Japan also bears some responsibility for its victimization. The U.S. government targets Japan in part because Tokyo is uniquely responsive to pressure. In 1986, when Washington put pressure on the governments of West Germany, Switzerland, Taiwan, and Japan to establish VERs on machine tools, the two European governments resisted, but Taipei and Tokyo caved in. More recently, the European Community notified U.S. officials that it would not negotiate with the U.S. government in response to a Super 301 charge; but the Japanese were willing. Furthermore, the nature of the Japanese responses—VERs, floor prices on exports, and various changes in domestic practices—undermines the role of law in international trade. The U.S. government did not have the authority to implement these restrictions, yet Tokyo acceded to U.S. pressure in an effort to avoid harsher measures. Such responses are shortsighted: giving in to a bully invites more acts of aggression.

A Big Bully

In the end, though, the bully's actions must be blamed primarily on him, not on his victim. And Washington must face the sad fact that it has become the major bully of the world trading system. This situation can be resolved by a U.S. reaffirmation of its commitment to the rule of law in international trade; or by foreign resistance to U.S. pressure for measures inconsistent with the rule of law. In the near future, the latter is more likely than the former. . . .

A more active resistance to U.S. pressure, especially by the government of Japan, is probably necessary. World trade can survive little bullies, for their actions can be avoided or effectively countered. But it cannot survive a big bully.

"We need to convince foreign countries that it is in their interest to eliminate their trade barriers and to do so promptly."

The U.S. Should Retaliate Against Unfair Trade Partners

Daniel P. Moynihan

How the U.S. should respond to other nation's trade practices is a controversial issue. In 1988 Congress passed new trade laws which gave the president additional direction and authority to charge other countries with unfair trading practices and to retaliate against those countries. In the following viewpoint, Daniel P. Moynihan gives some reasons why such measures are needed. He argues that U.S. trade retaliation is necessary in order to protect U.S. interests and promote free trade. Moynihan is a Democratic senator from New York who previously served as U.S. Ambassador to the United Nations.

As you read, consider the following questions:
1. Why is trade retaliation sometimes necessary, according to the author?
2. Under what circumstances are retaliatory measures justified, according to the author?
3. Is trade retaliation always the best option, according to Moynihan?

Daniel P. Moynihan, statement before the U.S. Senate Finance Committee, March 17, 1987.

Foreign trade barriers to exports of U.S. goods, services and investment present a serious problem for the Unites States. Japan is the nation most frequently cited for such practices, but other countries in the Far East and other areas of the world are also guilty of acts, policies and practices that constitute significant trade barriers. . . .

Our representatives have tried to remove these barriers to U.S. exports through negotiations, but too often to no avail. In part, this reflects the fact that foreign countries have little incentive to reduce their trade barriers because they believe correctly that the U.S. will do nothing in response. . . .The threat of retaliation is useful in making progress in negotiations. Yet as any parent—or game theory specialist—would attest, to be credible the threat must not be seen as empty. However, of the 58 Section 301 cases initiated since the statute was enacted in 1974, there have been only seven instances of retaliation—and these after protracted negotiations.

This has to change. We need to convince foreign countries that it is in their interest to eliminate their trade barriers and to do so promptly.

I believe that limiting those countries' access to our markets can provide the much needed leverage. We should require the President to use his existing authority under Section 301 of the Trade Act of 1974, as amended, to retaliate against countries that persist in maintaining trade barriers—particularly when they have agreed to do otherwise. . . .

The President would be required to use his authority—under Section 301 of the Trade Act of 1974, as amended—to impose retaliatory import restrictions against foreign trade practices that: (1) violate the international legal rights of the United States ("unjustifiable"); and (2) are unfair and inequitable ("unreasonable") or place U.S. companies at a disadvantage ("discriminatory").

The President would be required to retaliate within 15 months of the initiation of an investigation or within 9 months of a favorable GATT [General Agreement on Tariffs and Trade] ruling. The deadline could be extended by the President for two 60 day periods if he certified to Congress that resolution of the dispute appeared imminent.

Retaliation against an *unjustifiable* practice would not be required if : (1) the GATT finds the practice is not unjustifiable; or (2) a settlement is reached that offsets or eliminates the unfair foreign practice. In addition, retaliation against an *unreasonable* or discriminatory practice would not be required if the President certifies to Congress that satisfactory resolution of the dispute appears impossible and that retaliation would harm "the national economic interest."

The President would be authorized to terminate or modify the retaliation—and, if necessary, provide compensation—if the GATT subsequently finds the retaliation to have been a violation of U.S. obligations or the industry agrees that the foreign practice has been eliminated or reduced.

The United States Trade Representative would be required to estimate the value of additional U.S. goods and services that would be exported if each unfair trade practice identified in the annual survey (National Trade Estimates) was eliminated. He would be required to initiate cases : (1) against all foreign trade practices that are "unjustifiable" and constitute a "significant" barrier to, or distortion of, U.S. trade; and (2) against those "unreasonable" foreign trade practices the elimination of which would create the greatest expansion in U.S. exports.

U.S. Leverage

Ironically, the massive trade deficit that compels the United States to reform its trade policies also generates enormous negotiating leverage; America is the largest market for dozens of nations. The threat to close U.S. markets to nations unwilling to open their markets to American goods, services, and investment is the best—perhaps the only—negotiating chip the U.S. possesses. Any meaningful, self-interested U.S. trade policy must use this tool to expand market access for nations that do negotiate trade expansion agreements and limit market access for nations that do not.

America must not succumb to the lure of old-fashioned protectionism: there will always be those who would rather erect barriers to foreign goods and services than improve their own ability to compete. At the same time, U.S. policymakers must be sophisticated enough to discern the difference between closing U.S. markets to avoid foreign competition and threatening to close them as a device to open foreign markets. The former shrinks trade, the latter expands it. Our national interests lie with expanded trade. But in a more complex world of competing economic systems, a sophisticated negotiating strategy must recognize that the path to our ultimate goal is rarely straight. In fact, sometimes it may even appear to point in the opposite direction, away from expanded trade, as a way of finally reaching the desired destination.

Pat Choate and Juyne K. Linger, *Harvard Business Review*, January/February 1988.

The President would be required to initiate negotiations with those countries USTR identifies as showing a consistent pattern of market-distorting trade practices—including, but not limited to, Japan. The President would be required to report to Congress on agreements reached in eliminating the foreign practices and evidence of an increase in U.S. exports commensurate with the elimination of the barriers. In the event agreements are reached, commitments made, and then not lived up to, the mandatory retaliation provisions of Section 301 would then be applicable.

Actionable unfair trade practices would be expanded to include: practices which displace U.S. exports to third markets or cause diversion of a third country's exports to the U.S.; "targeting" industries for special development and advancement to the detriment of U.S. commerce; trading by a state-owned enterprise on other than commercial considerations; foreign government requirements that U.S. firms make some special concessions—such as licensing technology or building a foreign plant—in order to be permitted to export to that country.

Retaliation would end after 7 years, unless the industry seeking access to the foreign market requested its continuation. In that case, since the retaliatory import restrictions had burdened consumers but had not convinced the foreign country to eliminate its unfair trade practice, USTR could substitute a different retaliatory measure to increase pressure on the foreign country. . . .

U.S. Trade Problems

Finally, I would like to make the point that unfair foreign trade practices are only one reason for the poor U.S. trade performance. Others include large U.S. budget deficits, relatively poor productivity, the appreciation of the dollar from 1980 to 1985, slower growth in other developed countries, and reduced purchases by indebted LDC [less developed] countries.

But eliminating such practices are important for two reasons. First, they result in lost U.S. exports. . . . Second, unless and until the American public has confidence that its government is taking regular, swift and tough action to eliminate such practices, it will not be willing to address the other causes of our trade deficit.

"Far from opening markets, retaliation tends to provoke nationalism and xenophobia, generating even more pressure to keep out American goods."

The U.S. Should Not Retaliate Against Unfair Trade Partners

Jim Powell

Jim Powell is an author whose books include *The Gnomes of Tokyo: Why Foreign Investment Is Good for Us.* In the following viewpoint, he argues that retaliation against foreign countries does not open foreign markets for U.S. goods. He explains that eliminating U.S. trade barriers is the best way to encourage other countries to do the same.

As you read, consider the following questions:

1. How have retaliatory measures hurt U.S. companies, according to Powell?
2. What examples does the author provide of trade retaliations that have backfired?
3. Why have more countries reduced their trade barriers, according to Powell?

Jim Powell, "Forget the Crowbar." Reprinted, with permission, from the March 1990 issue of *Reason* magazine. Copyright 1990 by the Reason Foundation, 2716 Ocean Park Blvd., Suite 1062, Santa Monica, CA 90405.

Can we open foreign markets by closing our own? One of the hottest ideas in Washington is that we should retaliate against protectionist countries by raising our own import barriers against them. We will remove our restrictions only when they remove theirs, the theory goes, forcing these countries to negotiate with us to eliminate all trade barriers. "Retaliation" is the rallying cry of a new economic nationalism that has gained support from powerful Republicans and Democrats alike. But it doesn't work.

Trade Law Changes

So far, the most important result of all this talk of retaliation is the so-called Super 301 law. Passed as part of the 1988 trade package, this measure amends Section 301 of the trade code, expanding the power of the U.S. trade representative to crack down on countries with "unfair" trading practices by erecting barriers to those countries' goods. When Super 301 was passed, House Ways and Means Committee Chairman Dan Rostenkowski (D-Ill.) proclaimed, "This is a positive step toward dismantling foreign trade barriers that adversely affect American interests."

President George Bush declared he would "work vigorously to break down trade barriers abroad." He gave the new U.S. trade representative, Carla Hills, a crowbar at her swearing-in ceremony, suggesting that trade retaliation is a crowbar to force open foreign markets.

Underlying all this is what we might call the "crowbar theory" of trade sanctions. In his 1981 study, *Economic Sanctions*, Robin Renwick, of Harvard's Center for International Affairs, expressed it this way: "The theory of sanctions rests on the assumption that if subjected to economic penalties a nation will, as a matter of self-interest, change its conduct." But it's hard to find any significant cases where the theory has worked. The United States has closed its market many times, and almost always foreign markets have just closed even tighter.

A Dismal Record

During the 1980s, the portion of U.S. trade subject to import restrictions increased about 50 percent. We closed our market mainly with import quotas, "voluntary" agreements with other countries to reduce their exports, antidumping duties, and retaliatory tariffs. Yet other countries didn't respond by opening trade to outsiders. The Europeans, for example, merely counter-retaliated with punitive tariffs, "voluntary" restraint agreements with the United States, antidumping duties, and local-content laws.

And if you look at particular American retaliatory actions, the record is dismal. Since 1974, when Section 301 first became law, the United States has brought 78 cases against foreign governments. Threats of American retaliation have forced only 13 market openings—and those were generally trivial.

Retaliation Counterproductive

Trade retaliation is inherently counterproductive. By reducing the flow of dollars from the U.S., foreigners will have fewer dollars to spend in the U.S, which eventually will harm American export industries. American exports generally fall once imports are reduced. Consequently, employment in export-related industries, which account for as much as one-fifth of all employment in the U.S., will fall.

Thomas J. DiLorenzo, *The Freeman,* July 1988.

In 1975, for example, the American Farm Bureau complained that Canadian egg import quotas were harming American producers. After lengthy talks with the U.S. trade representative, the Canadians agreed to increase their quota limits. In the world of Section 301, that was designated a market opening. . . .

The most significant "victory" for the crowbar theory was the opening of the Japanese cigarette market in 1987. But although cigarette exports to Japan have increased substantially, they still account for less than 2 percent of total exports to Japan. And overall American exports to Japan jumped 40 percent over the same period—largely because lower exchange rates and higher quality made American products more competitive. Retaliatory threats had nothing to do with these big changes.

Harming U.S. Businesses

Over the years, many American companies have actually been harmed by Section 301 actions. In 1978, for example, American broadcasters filed a complaint because Canada had abolished tax deductions for advertising on stations in the United States. The United States retaliated by removing tax deductions for advertising on Canadian-owned stations. The consequence, of course, was that American advertisers had a harder time reaching the Canadian market. Twelve years later, these retaliatory measures are still in place—and Canada has not changed its original policy.

In 1982, after failing to resolve a dispute about European steel subsidies, Ronald Reagan ordered higher tariffs on imported European steel—making it more difficult for American automakers and appliance manufacturers to get competitively priced supplies. Georgetown University economist Gary Hufbauer argues that steel quotas cost Americans $1.5 billion to $3 billion in 1988. Similarly, the U.S.-engineered 1986 semiconductor agreement led to shortages of memory chips and a quadrupling of chip prices, harming American computer companies and consumers. . . .

Far from opening markets, retaliation tends to provoke nationalism and xenophobia, generating even more pressure to keep out American goods. This rising nationalism—notable today in South Korea and Japan—is undoubtedly driven at least as much by resistance to free trade as by resentment of U.S. trade barriers. But, either way, the crowbar will prove ineffective if not counterproductive.

South Korea began its first vigorous antismoking campaign, for instance, after the United States pressured it to eliminate barriers to American cigarettes. Anti-American Korean leaders promote greater self-sufficiency and oppose letting in more imports. Their rallying cry is *Minjok chajo*: "We can do it alone." Similar sentiments are on the upswing in Japan. Facing the threat of U.S. retaliation, those (such as South Korean and Japanese farmers) who oppose lowering trade barriers simply on self-interested grounds, can gain allies by appealing to patriotism.

This response is not a new phenomenon. The U.S. government has a long history of attempting to open other countries' markets by raising its own trade barriers. And it has a long history of failure. . . .

Markets Are Becoming Open

Over the last five decades country after country has opened its markets *without* pressure from the United States. Finding themselves with economic problems brought on by trade barriers and oversized government, these countries have been driven by their own self-interest to remove trade restrictions. Through it all, the United States' biggest role has been to serve as a model of a relatively open economy.

In Chile, for example, markets were unilaterally opened after an almost total economic collapse. The Marxist politician Salvador Allende had pursued economic policies that led to 600-percent annual inflation, chronic shortages, and stagnation. In 1973, his successor, General Augusto Pinochet, began removing trade barriers, investment restrictions, and business subsidies. Chile's GNP [gross national product] is now growing 10 percent annually, more than five times the Latin American average. It was self-interest, not economic sanctions, that forced these changes.

Nor did American retaliatory threats have anything to do with the deregulation of Japanese financial markets. During the mid-1970s, soaring budget deficits forced the Japanese government to issue far more bonds than the nation's heavily regulated financial markets could handle. To finance its deficits, the government had to chop away red tape binding financial institutions. As part of this program, it abolished most exchange controls, permitting capital to move freely in and out of the country for the first time since World War II.

For years, Mexico pushed economic nationalism as far as any country, with its economy a jungle of restrictions and subsidized, nationalized enterprises. But falling oil prices precipitated a crisis in 1982. Having exhausted its credit, the government began to create a somewhat more hospitable environment for foreign investors. Mexico signed a tariff-reduction deal with the United States, and *maquiladora*, factories owned by American companies, began to thrive near the U.S. border. Today, northern Mexico is growing 6 percent annually, almost as fast as Japan. . . .

Eliminate Trade Barriers

When one country unilaterally opens its market and prospers, other countries may begin exploring ways to open their markets—not because of retaliatory threats, but because they see that open markets are in their self-interest. No one wants to be left behind.

Of course, not every country will emulate free-market successes and unilaterally open its markets. But when one compares the results of unilaterally dropping trade barriers with the results of economic sanctions, it's no contest: Although there are no guarantees, the best way for a government to open up foreign markets is to eliminate its own trade barriers.

This is true even though access to foreign markets usually isn't the main reason people open their own market. Most countries remove their trade barriers so they can buy lower-cost, higher-quality goods. The subsequent opening of foreign markets is just a pleasant by-product.

If Americans really want to tap foreign markets, we should pressure our government to eliminate the trade barriers it has already erected. Consumers would gain access to new and less expensive products, businesses would pay less for raw materials and equipment, and the federal government could even cut its deficit a little bit by dismantling the bureaucracy that enforces all those trade restrictions.

The resulting increase in our own prosperity might make people in other countries demand that their governments get rid of trade restrictions. And even if other governments didn't change, we would still be better off.

a critical thinking activity

Evaluating Sources of Information

When historians study and interpret past events, they use two kinds of sources: primary and secondary. Primary sources are eyewitness accounts. For example, the congressional testimony of an American businessperson discussing Japan's restrictions on American imports is a primary source. An article in *The Wall Street Journal* quoting the testimony would be a secondary source. Primary and secondary sources may be decades or even hundreds of years old, and often historians find that the sources offer conflicting and contradictory information. To fully evaluate documents and assess their accuracy, historians analyze the credibility of the documents' authors and, in the case of secondary sources, analyze the credibility of the information the authors used.

Historians are not the only people who encounter conflicting information, however. Anyone who reads a daily newspaper, watches television, or just talks to different people will encounter many different views. Writers and speakers use sources of information to support their own statements. Thus, critical thinkers, just like historians, must question the writer's or speaker's sources of information as well as the writer or speaker.

While there are many criteria that can be applied to assess the accuracy of a primary or secondary source, for this activity you will be asked to apply three. For each source listed on the following page, ask yourself the following questions: First, did the person actually see or participate in the event he or she is reporting? This will help you determine the credibility of the information—an eyewitness to an event is an extremely valuable source. Second, does the person have a vested interest in the report? Assessing the person's social status, economic interests, professional affiliations, nationality, and religious or political beliefs will be helpful in considering this question. By evaluating this you will be able to determine how objective the person's report may be. Third, how qualified is the author to make the statements he or she is making? Consider the person's profession and how he or she might know about the event. Someone who has spent years being involved with or studying the issue may be able to offer more information than someone who simply is offering an uneducated opinion; for example, a politician or layperson.

Keeping the above criteria in mind, imagine you are writing a paper on U.S. trade policy. You decide to cite an equal number of primary and secondary sources. Listed below are several sources which may be useful for your research. *Place a P next to those descriptions you believe are primary sources. Place an S next to those descriptions you believe are secondary sources.* Next, based on the above criteria, *rank the primary sources, assigning the number (1) to that which appears the most valuable, (2) to the source likely to be the second-most valuable, and so on, until all the primary sources are ranked. Then rank the secondary sources, again using the above criteria.*

P or S		*Rank in Importance*
_____	1. Statistics compiled by the U.S. Department of Commerce in a yearly report on the trade deficit.	_____
_____	2. The text of the 1989 Super 301 law that strengthened the 1974 301 trade law.	_____
_____	3. An editorial in the Japanese daily newspaper *Asahi Shimbun* reassuring Americans that they are welcome trading partners for Japan.	_____
_____	4. Articles in *The New York Times* discussing the changing trade relationship of Asian countries.	_____
_____	5. A position paper written by the United Auto Workers union protesting the importation of Japanese cars to the United States.	_____
_____	6. A book by a leading economist examining U.S. involvement in trade wars from 1890 to the present.	_____
_____	7. A television report in Britain predicting the future trade relationship between the United States and the European Community (EC).	_____
_____	8. Viewpoint one in this chapter.	_____
_____	9. A review in a popular magazine of a book on ways to evade new trade restrictions.	_____
_____	10. An article in *Business Week* magazine examining the possibility of a Pan-American free-trading zone.	_____

Periodical Bibliography

The following articles have been selected to supplement the diverse views presented in this chapter.

Robert F. Black	"Ins and Outs on America's Trade List," *U.S. News & World Report*, August 21, 1989.
Joe Cobb	"Tradespeak," *Reason*, October 1988.
Susan Dentzer	"Trade's Most Wanted List," *U.S. News & World Report*, May 22, 1989.
Bill Emmott and Clyde V. Prestowitz Jr.	"A Charade That We've Played Before," *Los Angeles Times*, April 29, 1990.
James Fallows	"Getting Along with Japan," *The Atlantic Monthly*, December 1989.
Robert T. Green and Trina L. Larsen	"Only Retaliation Will Open Up Japan," *Harvard Business Review*, November/ December 1987.
John R. Hayes	"Who Sets the Standards?" *Forbes*, April 17, 1989.
Alex Huemer	"Dumping: An Evil or an Opportunity?" *The Freeman*, April 1989. Available from The Foundation for Economic Education, Irvington-on-Hudson, New York 10533.
Tetsuya Kataoka	"Stop Bashing Japan for U.S. Deficits," *USA Today*, January 1989.
Brink Lindsey	"Anti-Dumping's Dirty Secrets. . ." *The Wall Street Journal*, October 15, 1990.
Lawrence Minard	"Pressure Has Its Uses," *Forbes*, June 12, 1989.
The Nation	"The Yen Menace," March 12, 1990.
Robert N. Noyce	"A Unique Approach Against Trade Violators," *Vital Speeches of the Day*, August 15, 1989.
Kurt Stanberry	"Piracy of Intellectual Property," *Society*, September/October 1990.
Karel van Wolferen	"The Japan Problem Revisited," *Foreign Affairs*, Fall 1990.
C. William Verity	"Piercing the Ultimate Trade Barrier," *Fortune*, December 19, 1988.
Raymond Vernon	"Can the U.S. Negotiate for Trade Equality?" *Harvard Business Review*, May/ June 1989.

Should Trade
Be Restricted?

Chapter Preface

Trade can be restricted by national governments in several different ways. A government can hinder imports, for example, by imposing a tariff—a tax paid for every item imported. Another method of restricting trade is the quota, in which a country sets limits on the amounts of certain imported items. Examples of quotas include the "Voluntary Export Agreements" between the U.S. and Japan in which limits are set on the number of Japanese-manufactured cars that can be sold in the U.S. Exports can also be limited by governments. The U.S. government has laws forbidding the trade of military and technologically advanced items to such countries as the Soviet Union, for example.

Government leaders who pass legislation to restrict trade often argue that while free trade may be best for individual consumers (who enjoy wider choice and lower prices), it may be bad for nations as a whole. National security, the protection of U.S. jobs, and environmental concerns have all been cited as reasons free trade should be restricted. Whether or not trade restrictions actually succeed in their social objectives is a matter of debate, however. Economists Milton and Rose Friedman, for example, argue that restricting trade for almost any reason is a bad idea. They write, "the gains to some producers from tariffs and other restrictions are more than offset by the loss to other producers and especially to consumers in general."

The viewpoints in this chapter examine whether trade restrictions harm the U.S.

"The United States advanced to first place among the industrial powers behind protective tariff walls."

The U.S. Should Restrict Trade to Protect National Security

Anthony H. Harrigan and William Hawkins

Anthony H. Harrigan is president of the Business and Industrial Council, a business lobbying organization. William Hawkins is a consultant to the Council, and has taught economics at Radford University, Radford, Virginia, and at the University of North Carolina at Asheville. In the following viewpoint, Harrigan and Hawkins argue that, unlike the U.S., many countries restrict free trade to develop their own industries and attain other economic goals. The authors argue that the U.S. should do the same.

As you read, consider the following questions:

1. What utopian vision lies behind many people's support of free trade, according to Harrigan and Hawkins?
2. How do other countries take advantage of U.S. trade policy, according to the authors?
3. Why do Harrigan and Hawkins argue that there is no such thing as a global economy?

Excerpted, with permission, from *American Economic Pre-eminence: Goals for the 1990s* by Anthony H. Harrigan and William Hawkins. Washington, DC: United States Industrial Council Educational Foundation, 1989.

American policy is based on the concept of free trade. This theory argues against nations maintaining economic diversity and independence. Instead, it presents a global division of labor in which nations specialize and become complementary, or interdependent, rather than competitive in trade. Each country only produces what it does best—its comparative advantage. David Ricardo, an early 19th century economist, conceived his classic cloth-wine model to illustrate this. This model "proved" that agricultural Portugal should not try to compete with British manufacturers of cloth but be content to only produce wine. It could then trade wine for cloth. As has often been pointed out, this economics lesson had important strategic ramifications for the continuation of England's industrial dominance. It was an attempt to convince other nations not to challenge England's industrial leadership. But, other nations soon realized that it was impossible to be a Great Power without an industrial base. Thus England soon had plenty of competitors. Free trade provided London with no answer to these challengers and England declined after 1870. By the eve of World War I, Germany and the United States, both rejecting free trade, had surpassed England in manufacturing output. . . .

Utopian Dreams

The free trade myth has continued intellectual success in the face of real world defeats because it is based on a utopian vision of the world that many people find inviting. Ludwig von Mises, the famed libertarian economist, has given the utopian vision as follows:

> The goal of liberalism is the peaceful cooperation of all men. It aims at peace among nations too. When there is private ownership of the means of production everywhere and when laws, the tribunals and the administration treat foreigners and citizens on equal terms, it is of little importance where a country's frontiers are drawn. . . . War no longer pays; there is no motive for aggression. The population of every territory is free to determine to which state it wishes to belong, or whether it prefers to establish a state of its own. All nations can coexist peacefully, because no nation is concerned about the size of its state.

There is scant evidence that the world has moved towards the degree of peaceful coexistence that would allow governments to lose their concern over the "size" of their state. For what is at stake in "size" is more than just geography. It is resources: population, raw materials and industrial complexes. How economic resources are allocated between nations determines both the wealth of citizens and the power of government in the world arena. Von Mises felt that governments could safely ignore the location, ownership and control of resources and productive assets. But any government that adopts such an attitude in the current unstable environment is behaving irresponsibly.

The more practical, mercantilist vision is given by Friedrich List, an economic thinker who was deeply impressed by the spirit of enterprise he saw in America. Economic strength was the key to national wealth and power. Governments had a duty to adopt policies that would increase that strength. The dream of a peaceful world united by free trade should not be confused with the reality he argued. . . .

The American Tradition

"There are some who maintain that trade will regulate itself and is not to be benefitted by the encouragements or restraints of government," wrote Alexander Hamilton in 1782. But, he continued, "This is one of those wild speculative paradoxes, which have grown into credit among us, contrary to the uniform practice and sense of the most enlightened nations." As the nation's first Secretary of the Treasury, Hamilton's 1791 *Report on Manufactures* has become a classic statement of economic strategy. Hamilton was not alone in his rejection of free trade theory or in his belief that power and independence required a diversified industrial economy.

The Nation's Interest

The simple recognition that the goal of trade policy is to serve the nation's interest, and that the nation's interest requires an effective trade policy to protect it, we see, requires a fundamental change in American attitudes and stereotypes on foreign trade and trade policy. "Free trade" becomes an obviously self-destructive policy. The use of the slur-label, "protectionism," to blacken any and all forms of regulation of foreign trade becomes an obviously intolerable abuse of language.

John M. Culbertson, *The Trade Threat and U.S. Trade Policy*, 1989.

The United States advanced to first place among the industrial powers behind protective tariff walls. It was a central tenet of the Republican Party after the Civil War. A hundred years after Hamilton, Iowa Congressman John A. Kasson argued that protectionism "creates a sure foundation for the maintenance of national industry, without which no nation can be independent." The 20th century dawned with the United States the world's leader in industry. President Theodore Roosevelt exclaimed "Thank God I am not a free trader." He stated that American economic policy rested "on certain fixed and definite principles, the most important of these is an avowed determination to protect the interest of the American producer, be he businessman, wage-worker or farmer."

Not that anyone wanted to cut the United States off from the rest of the world. The country has always sought export markets for its agricultural goods and manufacturing surplus. There has been a willingness to negotiate reciprocal trade arrangements with foreign powers and American leaders supported an active diplomatic effort to promote trade such as the "Open Door" in China. But it was one thing to push open a door for American exports and another to open a door to foreign imports. Policy could be flexible, but the objective was firm: in a world of competing nation-states, trade policy was not a matter of economic abstraction. It was an arm of foreign policy which must serve the national interest. . . .

Economic Nationalism

Of course, there are some who do not think such concerns are important. Most are on the Left, people who we would normally expect to rejoice at the collapse of American power. But there are even some on the Right who should know better. For example, George Gilder has repeatedly denounced "nationalistic sentiments" in regard to international economic policy. He embraces the notion that "National economics are no longer nationally owned or controlled," dismissing concerns about such a development as "nationalistic fetishes." Gilder thus leaves out of his framework one of the most powerful motivators of human action.

A more realistic appraisal of the benefits of mercantilist policies come from Charles P. Doran, an international relations specialist at Johns Hopkins University. He has attributed the success of the "Japanese Model" to cultural discipline, a high savings rate, government-business cooperation and "the capacity of the society to close itself off to foreign goods, thus ensuring itself a balance of payments surplus." He then goes on to state:

Japan's giant trading companies concentrated the bulk of their operations at home; the jobs they created were Japanese jobs; the income they generated was taxed by the Japanese government. . . . Part of the miracle of post-war Japanese growth was attributable to the capacity of the Japanese trading company to transfer through trade profits and jobs from abroad to the home economy.

There are things that the United States needs from the international economy. Raw materials, in particular the exotic minerals essential for high technology production (those mined in South Africa), come readily to mind. But the United States also needs to gain access to, use, duplicate and improve upon scientific breakthroughs wherever they occur. A great deal of work is being done by foreign governments and industries and by multinational corporations. Under a "free trade" doctrine, we may only obtain the products generated by these new technologies rather than the technology itself and the advanced production methods involved. Such a system breeds dependence and vulnerability. Policymakers need to devise strategies that use the leverage available to us as the world's largest economy and most affluent market, in coordination with our sovereign authority as a nation-state, to insure that productive industry locates within the United States. These can't be just the "hollow corporations" that some have established here which serve only as assembly plants and marketing beachheads. Gaining knowledge and production capacity is more important for the United States than this year's model or generation of finished products whose value may be fleeting. . . .

A New Trade Policy Needed

The failure of the United States to address the foreign trade problem is rooted in a fundamental misunderstanding of the nature of trade in the world today. While other nations have waged trade offensives to penetrate the vast U.S. market and have targeted particular American industries for economic destruction, Americans have held to unrealistic and extremely naive ideas about international economic policy. The following key points are basic to a thoroughgoing reform of U.S. trade policy:

1. A trade deficit means that profits from production are earned by foreigners who are concerned, first and foremost, with the prosperity and security of their own countries.

2. A trade deficit inhibits growth in the deficit country; by definition, a trade deficit is a subtraction from GNP [gross national product].

3. The de-Americanization of the U.S. economy endangers the nation's ability and freedom to act in a crisis.

4. A trade deficit has resulted in foreign-owned plants in the U.S. that are only "hollow" corporations that engage in little more than assembly work. They are merely marketing beachheads used to circumvent expected legislation to curtail imports. Most foreign governments do not understand why the United States has not acted already to correct its trade deficit, but they eagerly exploit the delay.

5. A trade deficit leads to a shrinking industrial-technological core that serves as a base for future innovations, many of which are evolutionary or arise from interaction across disciplines. Losing a key industry now also means losing what it might become in the future.

6. The current trade deficit, 80 percent of which is due to loss of markets in manufacturing fields, means that workers are being pushed out of jobs with high productivity into service jobs

with low productivity. In the long-run, the standard of living depends on productivity.

7. A trade deficit that leads to devaluation cuts American purchasing power and leads to inflation. The terms of trade shift against the United States so that people have to work harder just to stay even.

8. The historical fact is that the United States became the largest, most productive economy in the world behind high "protective" tariff walls. By 1900, the U.S. economy surged ahead of England's economy, which declined steadily from the number one position by falling for the sophistry of "free trade."

9. General free trade is not possible because other countries do not believe in it or practice it; they never have and never will. When they talk of "free trade," they only mean keeping open the U.S. market for their products, just as the United States talked of an "Open Door" in China while practicing protectionism at home.

The Real Issue

The real question is what kind of environment we want to create for our economy. At issue is not pure free trade or total protectionism—we never have had and never will have either one; but rather what combination of free and managed trade we will have. It is not a matter of whether the U.S. government intervenes in the economy—it does and will intervene, massively; but whether it will do so in a way that helps or hurts. . . .

The most critical point is priority. As in Japan, maintaining the industrial, technological, and financial strength of the country must be at the top of the national agenda. The next president must see issues of trade and industrial leadership as worthy of the same attention as arms negotiation, because if he cannot maintain America's economic might, he will eventually have no arms over which to negotiate.

Clyde V. Prestowitz Jr., *Trading Places*, 1988.

---

10. Free trade allows American companies to be undersold by countries with low pay scales, oppressive domestic policies and few, if any, health, safety or environmental regulations. Competition under these conditions rewards those with the most antisocial behavior.

11. Increased exports will be an insufficient remedy for the trade deficit because either overseas markets are closed by foreign economic policies in rival industrial states and countries, or foreign populations are unable to buy American goods due to poverty or debt in the Third World. Just as the deficit was

caused by a jump in imports, it must be solved by a reduction in imports.

12. Even if trade can be brought into balance, it might not be sufficient to provide the industrial base the country needs. The United States has apparent "comparative advantage" in agriculture and services, but expanding exports in these fields will do nothing to support heavy industry and high technology.

13. International trade, just as other forms of competition, produces winners and losers. The game is won by whoever scores the most points, not whoever plays by the "cleanest" set of rules.

14. Denying that a trade war is in progress will not prevent the United States from losing it. The war started some two decades ago, but it took a long time to erode America's initial superiority. Now the danger is upon us and little time remains to mobilize our resources to fight back. . . .

America's Rivals

National legislators and policymakers must bear in mind that many of America's trade rivals have very different economic systems and philosophies of political economy. They have aggressive, export-oriented national industrial policies. They finance steel mills, auto plants, shipyards and other industrial operations, all of which are often owned by the government itself. Foreign laws and customs permit longer time horizons and less vulnerability to the business cycle than is true for American firms. Foreign governments work more closely with their private firms and allow them to combine, exchange labor, undertake joint projects, coordinate strategies and make other arrangements that are not currently possible under the restrictive antitrust laws of the United States. Foreign companies are often subsidized so that they can maintain operations and employment with low prices and only marginal profits from sales in order to gain or expand market share in America.

These foreign trade strategies are not "evil," but simply practical and successful. It is not "bashing" another country to recognize that it is following its own interests. This is how the world works. The United States needs to learn from the experiences of others and from the lessons of history. Only then can it determine its own interests and devise strategies to advance them. . . .

Any economic program for America has to be based on a clearsighted, comprehensive understanding of Japan's economic objectives, just as any American military defense program has to be based on the objective of the Soviet Union. Central to such an understanding is the fact that the economic struggle of our time is between nations, not simply between companies.

"The role of government in a borderless world is to. . .protect the interests of its people, not of its companies or its industries."

The U.S. Need Not Restrict Trade to Protect National Security

Kenichi Ohmae

Kenichi Ohmae is the managing director of McKinsey & Company, Inc., an international management consulting firm. He has written many books on international trade and economic issues, including *Triad Power* and *The Borderless World*. In the following viewpoint, he argues that trade has made nation-states and their governments less relevant to the lives of most people. Efforts by national governments to restrict or redirect trade, he argues, are counterproductive and unnecessary.

As you read, consider the following questions:

1. What is the fundamental truth of the world economy, according to Ohmae?
2. How have multinational corporations changed, according to the author?

Kenichi Ohmae, "Toward a Global Regionalism," *The Wall Street Journal,* April 27, 1990. Reprinted with the author's permission.

The pleas for "coordination" of economic policies being made by finance ministers of the world's leading countries are not convincing. What these helmsmen don't seem to understand is that their economies are already coordinated. The role of national governments is much less important than they think; governments are little more than spoilers who disrupt markets with their interference and announcements.

The economic coordination isn't perfect. Some resources (money) are mobile, others (jobs) are not. Some industries are global (autos), others (many services) are not. Moreover, some regions of individual countries are more coordinated than others because of local trade and investment patterns.

Despite these imperfections, the most fundamental truth of today's economic world is this: Man's ability to create, compete and consume will not be denied by those politicians and bureaucrats who try to restrict the flows of capital, technology and information. This is a lesson not only for Eastern European communists, but Japanese and American nationalists.

The two traditional "products" of governments—military protection and access to natural resources—are losing their value. Commodities can be arbitraged across producing countries, and if you have the wealth to buy these commodities you certainly have access to them. Just 10 years ago, during the second energy crisis, we were worried about the supply of primary commodities and resources. We don't worry so much today. The price of energy might rise, but innovative products or services can produce much higher per capita GNP [gross national product] than natural resources. Switzerland, for example, doesn't even have a flat stretch of land, yet it has a $25,000 per capita GNP, the world's highest.

Access to Information

Thus, there is diminishing need for military power to protect a country's "scarce" resources. Moreover, no amount of military power can make a people more productive. An educated populace with free access to information is the truest source of wealth and national security. That's the reality that brought down the Berlin Wall and is the fundamental reason the world needs less military muscle.

Besides military forces, another benefit governments offer their people is ideology. With their taxes, people pay for the "truth." But Cable News Network and the tales of the good life it spreads throughout the world have made standards of living, not political dogma, the criteria by which governments are judged. Communism, Japanism, Monroe-ism are merely packaging for this "core product."

Government "advertising"—which basically asks people to pay

124

for dogma—no longer sells. People want the best goods and services, whatever their origin. Along with the right to vote, they want the right to buy.

Consumers and Nationalism

Economic nationalism flourishes during election campaigns and infects what legislatures do and what particular interest groups ask for. But when individuals vote with their pocketbooks—when they walk into a store or showroom anywhere in Europe, the United States, or Japan—they leave behind the rhetoric and mudslinging.

Do you write with a Waterman or a Mt. Blanc pen or travel with a Vuitton suitcase out of nationalist sentiments? Probably not. You buy these things because they represent the kind of value that you're looking for.

At the cash register, you don't care about country of origin or country of residence. You don't think about employment figures or trade deficits. You don't worry about where the product was made. It does not matter to you that a "British" sneaker by Reebok (now an American-owned company) was made in Korea, a German sneaker by Adidas in Taiwan, or a French ski by Rossignol in Spain. What you care about most is the product's quality, price, design, value, and appeal to you as a consumer.

Kenichi Ohmae, *The Borderless World,* 1990.

So governments must deliver standards of living in this new market for political control. Some politicians think they can do that on a national basis. They are wrong. National standards of living have always hidden disparities in well-being—disparities between families and between regions. The dirty little truth is that politicians rob other regions to buy votes in their own. But global competition is making these larcenies more obvious.

If, for example, a government protects its steel industry with tariffs, other steel-intensive industries in that country, or their customers, suffer because of the higher prices they must pay. Now that markets are global, cross-regional transfers result not only in a loss of profits and higher prices, but in lost jobs as national companies lose to foreign competition.

Multinationals in the late '60s and early '70s were structured more or less according to a hierarchical, colonial model. Most production was done "at home." Today's global companies are decentralized and willing to manufacture, design, or assign managerial authority wherever they can best serve the customer. The objective of Honda, IBM and other global firms is to serve customers, not governments, worldwide.

Thus we now see as much intranational as international competition. For North Carolina to prosper, it has to attract European and Japanese investment. In fact, one-third of investment in that state since 1988 has come from Japan. North Carolina is not competing with Japan or Europe; it is competing with Boston and Silicon Valley for foreign high-tech investments. Boston is its biggest "enemy" in this regard. What should Washington do in this contest except stay out and make sure there is a "level playing field" between these two competitors—for example, equal access to educational grants?

Japan's economy is just as regional as that of the U.S. When people talk about Japan's prosperity, they are basically talking about the prosperity of three cities, Tokyo, Osaka and Nagoya. The rest of the country is holding on by getting money from the central government at the expense of urban taxpayers.

Restoration Needed

Like the Meiji Restoration in the second half of the 19th century, a Heisei Restoration is needed to transform Japan's government to one more suitable for a developed country in a global economy. Japan needs a new constitution that would divide the country into nine or 10 regions, each with some degree of autonomy. These regions would be able to negotiate with foreign nations on matters such as air rights and immigration.

The governor of the northern island of Hokkaido, for instance, would declare independence from Tokyo. He would abolish its 3:30 a.m. sunrise based on Japan standard time and open stock trading two hours earlier than Tokyo. Sapporo would then attract all the financial institutions now in Tokyo, Sydney and Wellington. And, because Sapporo would be able to negotiate air rights with foreign governments, it would become a hub for transpacific flights. It would also have direct flights to Seoul, Taipei, Hong Kong and other major cities in the Pacific. Hokkaido, with its beautiful lakes and mountains, would become the Switzerland of Asia.

Centrally governed countries such as Japan, the Soviet Union and China will have to go through turmoil that in the long run will be good for them. The solution is to reconstruct on a regional basis. In order to modernize, China must create 20 "Singapores." To a lesser extent, but still in the same fundamental way, America must continue to allow each region to integrate itself into the world economy elsewhere.

Most politicians are still living in the 19th century. In Japan, for example, most politicians come from small towns and try to promote a concept of narrow regionalism. They ask one region to make sacrifices in the name of "national" interest. They say they can protect the rice farmers from foreign pressure and build bridges and gymnasiums with the central government's money. They use voters' nationalistic feelings to funnel money into special interest groups or their own constituencies. Nowhere is this hypocrisy more clear than in Japan-U.S. trade talks, which take on artificial nationalistic overtones when in truth they are battles among special interests. Whose interests are being represented by the negotiators? America's? Japan's?

Global Regionalism

Only a global regionalism that ignores national boundaries makes sense. Local communities will develop natural partners, sometimes close geographically, sometimes remote. Through these pairings, alert regions with global views and aspirations will develop and prosper, the same way that alert companies with a global perspective are already prospering. For example, Southern California can flourish through its ties with Australia, Japan, South Korea and Taiwan—not so much through its ties with Washington, D.C., New York or Chicago. Similarly, Toronto and Vancouver can flourish because of their ties with Hong Kong and Wales and, more recently, Alsace-Lorraine can flourish through investments from Tokyo, etc.

If I had my way, I'd pay a third of my taxes to an international fund dedicated to solving world problems, such as the environment and famine. Another third would go to my community, where my family lives and my children are educated. The final third would go to my country, which each year does less and less for me in terms of security or well-being and instead subsidizes special interests.

The role of government in a borderless world is to represent and protect the interests of its people, not of its companies or its industries. It should let in the light and then allow its people to make their own choices. Anything less is to put the class and career interests of government bureaucrats ahead of the people they are sworn to serve.

"The U.S. export-control system subordinates the country's economic competitiveness to military concerns at a time when economic concerns are growing in importance."

Trade Restrictions with the Soviet Union Should Be Relaxed

Kevin F. F. Quigley and William J. Long

Ever since the Export Control Act of 1949, the United States has restricted trade with the Soviet Union and other communist countries in order to maintain a U.S. advantage in military technology. In the following viewpoint, Kevin F. F. Quigley and William J. Long argue that such restrictive trade policies harm the U.S. economy and are no longer necessary because of changes in the Soviet bloc. Quigley is director of public policy at the Pew Charitable Trusts, and was formerly a Council on Foreign Relations international affairs fellow. Long is an assistant professor of international relations at American University in Washington, D.C., and an international trade attorney.

As you read, consider the following questions:

1. What basic principles should be used in reforming U.S. export control policy, in the authors' opinion?
2. According to Quigley and Long, why is controlling the spread of technology more difficult for the U.S. than ever before?
3. How much money have export controls cost the U.S., according to Quigley and Long?

Kevin F. F. Quigley and William J. Long, "Beyond Export Controls: Moving Beyond Economic Containment," *World Policy Journal* 8:1 (Winter, 1989-90), pp. 165-188. Reprinted with permission.

Former Soviet leader Nikita Khrushchev reportedly jested that the United States should restrict the export of buttons because they are used to hold up Soviet soldiers' pants. The U.S. system of export controls, put in place at the onset of the Cold War to prevent the transfer of sensitive technologies to the Soviet bloc, is not nearly as all-encompassing as Khrushchev's facetious remark implied. Nevertheless, its extensive scope and rigidity make it seriously out of step with today's international realities.

An Outdated Policy

At a time when the dramatic transformations taking place in the East bloc are bringing an end to the Cold War, a control regime that affects nearly one-third of all U.S. exports seems highly anachronistic. Not only is such a system out of touch politically with the new era in East-West relations that is emerging, but as a practical matter it is economically untenable in today's competitive global marketplace. On the one hand, technological diffusion and the growth of international trade and communications have rendered U.S. export controls more difficult to enforce and thus subject to circumvention by other countries. On the other hand, the U.S. export-control regime, by virtue of being considerably broader and more complex than the regimes of our major trading partners (and competitors), imposes serious costs on U.S. businesses that have hurt their ability to compete in the world economy.

In short, the U.S. export-control system subordinates the country's economic competitiveness to military concerns at a time when economic concerns are growing in importance. Moreover, the system does not even succeed in safeguarding U.S. national security, because its extensive scope stifles the civilian technological advancement that is increasingly essential to maintaining a strong military.

Background

Sometimes called the economic arm of containment, the present system of U.S. export controls dates to the Export Control Act of 1949. That act authorized the president to embargo most exports to the Soviet Union and other communist countries in order to further U.S. national security interests. (The act also envisaged the use of controls for the furtherance of U.S. foreign policy goals not directly related to national security; an example of such controls was the grain embargo against the Soviet Union in response to the Soviet invasion of Afghanistan in 1979.) The original grant of authority encompassed goods of both direct and indirect military utility, and gave the president the power to determine which articles would require export licenses and which countries would be denied licensable goods or technologies. Beginning in the late 1950s and culminating in the revised Export Control Act of 1969, the United States relaxed this comprehensive embargo policy in favor of selective export controls on only those items that would make a significant contribution to the military strength of potential adversaries. The avowed purpose of such a strategic embargo was to safeguard the West's technological lead over the East in defense-related technologies without inhibiting U.S. export growth.

WARNING!!!
DO NOT
SHIP ABROAD
BECAUSE OF
NATIONAL SECURITY
REASONS

Reprinted from *USA Today* magazine, July copyright 1988 by the Society for the Advancement of Education.

In addition to devising a system of unilateral controls, the United States has sought to promote multilateral cooperation in implementing export controls. To this end, the United States organized the Coordinating Committee on Multilateral Export Controls (COCOM) in 1949. This informal organization, which includes Japan, Australia, and all the NATO [North Atlantic Treaty Organization] states except Iceland, is charged with enlisting the voluntary participation of member states in limiting the export of militarily significant goods and technology to the East bloc. COCOM's mandate, however, has always been narrower than that of the U.S. export-control regime: COCOM restricts only exports that have potential military utility, such as dual-use technology that is adaptable for civilian or military use, and, in contrast to the United States, does not impose foreign-policy export controls.

In one sense, it is possible to claim that export controls—at least those of the national security variety—have worked, in that they have allowed the West to stay significantly ahead of East-bloc countries in the development of essential military-related technologies. The United States and other COCOM member countries, for example, have maintained a lead of five to 10 years in computer technology. This success, however, has not been without heavy economic and political costs for the United States.

Effects on Trade

The economic costs of export controls are seldom fully appreciated, in part because it is widely assumed that the restrictions apply only to the relatively insignificant amount of U.S. trade with the East bloc. Yet the most profound consequence of the U.S. export-control regime is in restricting so-called West-West trade—that is, U.S. transactions with allies and neutrals. Because of the potential for diversion to East-bloc countries all commercial exports, including those to noncommunist countries, must be licensed. There are two kinds of licenses: general licenses that permit export without explicit permission, and validated licenses that require formal application and governmental approval. In 1987, the Department of Commerce, which has primary jurisdiction over export licensing, processed 104,320 validated licenses involving more than $80 billion worth of goods. Nearly 90 percent of these licenses involved West-West transactions. The impact of this system on inhibiting trade and undermining the U.S. export position should not be underestimated.

The damage done by export controls to alliance harmony is likewise seldom fully appreciated. With the far-reaching reforms initiated by Soviet President Mikhail Gorbachev, a serious rift has developed between the United States and its COCOM allies over the scope of COCOM restrictions. Even in the pre-Gorbachev days, COCOM allies were becoming increasingly restive with U.S. attempts to dictate export-control policy. Tensions occasionally flared up into acrimonious disputes, as occurred in the early 1980s after the declaration of martial law in Poland, when the United States tried to force its allies to comply with a ban on exporting equipment for a massive Soviet oil and gas pipeline construction project. . . .

Clearly, the export-control regime is in urgent need of a fundamental reform to align it with political and economic realities. The system is overly broad in scope, excessively burdensome on West-West trade, and increasingly deleterious to both alliance cohesion and East-West relations. Moreover, it relies far too much on unilateral measures, which are increasingly ineffective in an interdependent world, and on extraterritorial application of U.S. law, which is viewed by our allies as a direct affront to their national sovereignty and a violation of international law. As a 1987 National Academy of Sciences report concluded, the existing export-control regime serves neither the national security nor the economic interests of the United States. . . .

In crafting a viable new export-control policy, U.S. policymakers should follow several basic principles. First, the system must be modified so that it acknowledges and supports the market-oriented reforms taking place in the East bloc. Second, the United States must eschew unilateralism and use a more cooperative leadership style within COCOM. Third, and most important, the United States must recognize that the commercial marketplace, with its free flow of goods and information, is the engine of technological advancement and economic growth. This means that Western security interests, COCOM harmony, and U.S. competitiveness would all be better served by a less extensive regime that regulated only the most critical military-related items. . . .

An Overburdened System

An array of international economic and political developments have made an ambitious export-control regime both unenforceable and unaffordable.

The exponential rise in the volume and importance of international trade is perhaps the most obvious development affecting the functioning of the export-control regime. While all the COCOM countries have seen their levels of foreign trade increase sharply, this change has had particularly great ramifications for the United States. Traditionally, foreign trade has made up a much smaller part of the gross national product of the United States than of other Western nations. Since 1950, trade's share of total U.S. economic activity has more than doubled, from less than 10 percent to 20 percent today. It was far easier for the United States to advocate stringent export controls when its own economic activity was relatively unaffected and when the overall volume of exports was small.

The accelerating rate of technological diffusion has also worked to undermine the effectiveness of the export-control regime. In the early days of COCOM, the United States was the world's preeminent technological leader and primary source of such advanced products as aircraft, radar, sonar, radio, and television. Of the approximately 23,000 patents issued by the U.S. patent office in 1948 to today's major trading countries—the United States, Japan, Germany, Great Britain, and France—the United States received almost 20 times as many as all the other countries combined. Of the approximately 70,000 patents issued in 1988, however, the U.S. share was only one-and-a-half times larger than that of all its major trading partners combined. The Japanese received nearly half of all patents issued to foreigners.

Moreover, even technology invented in the United States frequently has its first commercial application overseas, as was the case with video cassette recorders and compact disks. With its monopoly on the development of advanced technology ended, the United States can no longer dictate export-control policy to its allies. . . .

In sum, U.S. export controls can be no more effective than the cooperation the United States is able to gain from other producers and exporters of advanced technologies. Ignoring this reality and refusing to compromise with other countries on export-control issues would risk destroying the basic multilateral framework that has served U.S. interests well in the past, and that will be necessary to meet new export-control and security problems in the future. . . .

Economic Costs

The elaborate U.S. system of export controls has become untenable not simply because of the enforcement problems created by the rapid movement of goods, capital, and information around the globe, but also because of the system's rapidly mounting costs to the U.S. economy.

Overly extensive export controls hinder the commercial openness that is increasingly essential to technological progress, and impair U.S. competitiveness at a time when U.S. industrial dominance is increasingly threatened by the rise of Europe, Japan, and the newly industrializing countries. The persistently large U.S. trade deficit, which ballooned to $170 billion in 1987, is only the most obvious evidence of the U.S. inability to compete in an increasingly demanding world marketplace. Of course, U.S. competitiveness suffers from a variety of complex, interrelated factors, not the least of which is a fiscal policy that increases the cost of capital and discourages longer-term investment. But an overly burdensome export control system compounds the problems facing U.S. business. . . .

The effects of the outdated system of export controls have been most devastating in the U.S. high-technology sector. Although export controls are not the primary cause of the current trade deficit in high technology, they have exacerbated this sector's competitiveness problems. Ironically, controls on high technology have not only hurt U.S. economic interests, but have also been detrimental to the military security they are supposedly safeguarding. Today, defense procurement is no longer the catalyst of technological advancement; instead, advances in civilian technologies often drive the development of the military sector. Thus, a competitive high-tech industry is increasingly essential to maintaining a military edge. As the National Research Council's study of the global computer industry concluded: "Unlike past decades, COCOM military establishments now have more to gain than to give the commercial computing technology base. Consequently, U.S. policymakers must be concerned with the impact of control options on the domestic computer sector as well as their impact on the COCOM lead overall."

Different Approaches

Where the United States has viewed trade policy as a tool of containment, West Germany has sought to use trade and other kinds of economic cooperation to stabilize East-West relations. Like the United States, West Germany supports denying the transfer of militarily critical goods and technology to the East. But the Germans favor a more narrowly drawn list of restricted products and are opposed to controlling goods that are of no potential military value or that are available from uncontrolled sources.

As the contrasting U.S. and West German approaches illustrate, controversy has frequently arisen in COCOM as a result of fundamentally differing perceptions of the Soviet threat and the role of trade and export controls in the East-West relationship. For West Germany and a number of the COCOM members, assisting Eastern Europe and the Soviet Union with reform has always seemed a surer path to security than the more vigilant U.S. approach. In private conversations, many European officials express the view that the security gains of consolidating reform in the Soviet Union and Eastern Europe outweigh any risks associated with relaxed technology transfer restrictions.

Kevin F. F. Quigley and William J. Long, *World Policy Journal,* Winter 1989/1990.

Estimates suggest that the current system of export licensing imposes direct costs to the U.S. economy of $7 to $10 billion per year (total direct and indirect costs are roughly twice that) and results in the annual loss of 188,000 jobs. Moreover, by restricting the participation of U.S. companies in joint ventures and industrial alliances, the system circumscribes their prospects for success in the global marketplace, reducing their profit margins as well as restricting their access to technological exchange. This in turn limits the ability of U.S. firms to maintain the levels of investment in research and development critical to keeping pace with the dynamic process of technological innovation.

In a world where the old distinctions between economic and security interests are breaking down, and where the rules of the international marketplace are being remade by transnational joint ventures and corporate alliances, the costs of the export-control regime go well beyond the lost trade between the United States and East-bloc countries. If current global economic trends are reinforced in the years ahead, as can be expected, the economic costs to the United States of the export-control system will grow more severe. If the United States continues to adhere to a broader and more rigid export-control regime than its trading partners, it could find U.S. companies increasingly discriminated against and left out of the emerging pan-European economy, with their capacity for technological innovation and commercial success impaired as a result.

Moving Beyond Economic Containment

The dismantling of the Berlin Wall symbolizes the end of the artificial division of Europe and the beginning of a new era of expanding East-West relationships. As we move beyond containment, we must design an export-control regime flexible enough to encourage greater economic interaction while safeguarding U.S. and global security well into the twenty-first century. We need a simpler, more flexible system that is less prone to bureaucratic inertia and capable of responding to a range of future international political and economic developments.

In some ways, even with the remarkable changes in Eastern Europe and the Soviet Union, COCOM's mandate has not changed fundamentally. COCOM members still believe in the need to restrict Soviet access to the West's most sensitive technology. However, the existing system of export controls fails to adequately reflect either the diminished level of threat from the East bloc or the emergence of new security threats. It also fails to reflect the blurring of the distinction between economic and security interests in today's international environment. Historically, the basic export control dilemma was to design a system that attempted to balance the often antithetical interests of economics and security. Today, this dichotomy seems patently false. The profound effect of global forces on the U.S. economy has forced Americans to acknowledge that economic competitiveness is an essential component of national security, and that export expansion is not a threat to security but an enhancement.

"This is not the time for the U.S. to abandon export controls."

Trade Restrictions with the Soviet Union Should Not Be Relaxed

Baker Spring

The waning of the Cold War has led to debate over whether U.S. laws restricting exports to the Soviet Union should be changed. In the following viewpoint, Baker Spring argues that the Soviet Union remains a military threat to the U.S., and that export controls should be retained to help the U.S. keep its lead in military technology. He writes that such policies do not greatly damage U.S. trade. Spring is a policy analyst for The Heritage Foundation, a conservative think tank in Washington, D.C.

As you read, consider the following questions:

1. What are the four myths concerning export restrictions, according to Spring?
2. Why does Spring question the wisdom of selling high technology to East European countries?
3. What changes in the Soviet Union are necessary for export restrictions to be lifted, according to the author?

Baker Spring, "Controls Still Needed on High Technology Exports to the USSR," The Heritage Foundation *Backgrounder*, August 2, 1990. Reprinted with permission.

The United States needs advanced military technology to maintain a winning edge against potential enemy forces. This need will continue despite the decline of the Soviet threat in Europe. For one thing, the Soviet Union remains a formidable military power around the globe. For another, the U.S. will need advanced military weapon systems to combat terrorism, the spread of ballistic missiles in the Third World, international drug trafficking, and regional challenges to U.S. interests. America thus must continue fielding better weapon systems and equipment than its adversaries.

To protect its military technology edge in the past four decades, America carefully has restricted the sale or other transfer of technology to its potential adversaries. These restrictions understandably are being reviewed in the wake of the real decline of the Soviet military threat in Europe. . . .

COCOM

The Coordinating Committee for Multilateral Export Controls, or COCOM, was established in 1949 to prevent the export of strategically significant technologies and commodities to the East. Such technologies have been computers, machine tools, and electronic equipment, which can be used to manufacture such advanced weapons as self-guided rockets and elaborate military command and control systems, and to make submarines more difficult to track. Seventeen countries participate in CO-COM: the U.S., Australia, Belgium, Britain, Canada, Denmark, France, West Germany, Greece, Italy, Japan, Luxembourg, the Netherlands, Norway, Portugal, Spain, and Turkey. These countries have agreed to prohibit the export of those technologies designated by the unanimous agreement of COCOM members. . . .

The fall of the Berlin Wall and the collapse of the Warsaw Pact have convinced some COCOM governments and some members of the U.S. Congress that the Soviet military has weakened significantly. They thus argue for relaxing controls over the export of militarily significant technologies not only to the emerging democracies of Eastern Europe, but to the Soviet Union as well. Said Representative Don Edwards, the Democrat of California, on the House floor last June 6, 1990, ". . . the events in Europe and the Soviet Union over the past year have brought dramatic changes not only in terms of national security and military strategies, but also in terms of international trade."

The campaign to relax export controls is led by American and foreign businesses that seek markets in Eastern Europe and the Soviet Union. Among U.S. companies pressing for lighter controls are International Business Machines Corporation, Digital Equipment, Inc., and American Telephone and Telegraph Company. The U.S. Chamber of Commerce supports the House of

Representatives bill to loosen export controls. In the House, the most outspoken advocates of eased controls are Connecticut Democrat Representative Sam Gejdenson and Wisconsin Republican Toby Roth. The foreign government pushing hardest for eased export controls is West Germany. In fact, proposals were made in 1989 in the West German Bundestag, its parliament, to abolish COCOM altogether. . . .

Chuck Asay, by permission of the *Colorado Springs Gazette-Telegraph.*

The case for fewer restrictions on the export of advanced technology to the Soviet Union and its allies is based on four myths. They are:

Myth #1: Giving the countries of Eastern Europe high technologies is the key to modernizing their economies.

Representative Sam Gejdenson of Connecticut and others argue that Czechoslovakia, Hungary, Poland and other emerging democracies in Eastern Europe will not be able to modernize their economies without high technology equipment. They cite the need for modern telecommunications for the banking system, computers for business management, and automated production equipment for food processing. A May 10, 1990, report by the House Foreign Affairs Committee states: "As long as one cannot pick up a phone and get a dial tone in Warsaw, and as long as Hungary's banking system and hotel reservation system lack up-to-date computers, the economic development of Poland and Hungary, and other countries in Eastern Europe will be retarded, thereby making it more difficult to maintain their economic and political independence from the Soviet Union."

High Technology Is Unnecessary

It is true that Eastern Europe will need some advanced technologies, particularly in telecommunications, but reliable and affordable technologies will be more important than sophistication. What Hungarian and Polish industries need are machine tools to produce reliable consumer products, not expensive and highly sophisticated technologies to produce high quality propellers for submarines. The key to Eastern Europe's economic future is economic reform, not advanced technology. Economic policies that encourage productivity and efficiency will do more to promote economic growth than high technology which the relatively backward economies of Eastern Europe may not in some instances be able to absorb. To rely on high technology to transform East European economies is to repeat the mistake made in the past quarter-century's failures to transform the African economies.

Myth #2: Export controls on high technologies prevent U.S. companies from exporting to Eastern Europe and the Soviet Union.

Some U.S. business leaders believe that the U.S. export control policy on high technology is the principal barrier to U.S. exports to Eastern Europe and the Soviet Union. But only 6 percent of the dollar value of U.S. exports to the U.S.S.R. and its allies have been subject to export bans since 1987. Only high technology manufactured products such as advanced computers or microelectronic equipment are prohibited. All other goods can be exported, although some are subject to a license requirement. Some 85 percent of exports to the Soviet Union are agricultural products and not subject to controls at all. And, of the $3.6 billion worth of U.S. products licensed before export to the U.S.S.R. from 1987 to 1989, about $2.6 billion was approved for export. Nothing in the current export control law prevents U.S. businesses from exporting fertilizers, food, oil production equipment and a vast variety of other products to most countries in the world. U.S. export controls are not a serious economic barrier to trade with the East.

Myth #3: U.S. export restrictions on technologies are out of date.

Businessmen from the U.S. and other COCOM nations frequently say that many technologies controlled by the West are already available elsewhere on the world market. Echoing this sentiment, the House Committee on Foreign Affairs report stated: "The Commodity Control List [the list of sensitive commodities prohibited from export to the East and managed by the Department of Commerce] is cumbersome and out of date.

Items are on the List absent justification and just remain there."

In some instances this is true. The earlier list includes steel alloys and floating dry docks. These provide the Soviets with no military advantage. Yet the standard for restricting technology transfers should not be based on what is generally available in the world market, but on what the Soviet military currently lacks. The aim of U.S. and COCOM export control policies is to restrict the ability of the Soviet Union to produce advanced weaponry. Moscow is still lagging behind world standards in most militarily significant technologies, including computers, fiber optics, and microelectronic circuits. Giving the Soviets such advanced technology, which they do not yet have and which could improve the performance of their military equipment and weaponry if they obtained it, is against the security interests of the West. In some instances this could include technologies that the West views as unsophisticated, such as some kinds of microelectronic and telecommunications equipment. Products using this kind of technology include certain types of computers and telephone modems for computers.

Myth #4: The Soviets already have obtained the technology they want from spying on the West.

Though Moscow does steal Western technology, Soviet spying and illegal purchases clearly do not make U.S. export control policies meaningless. The Pentagon calculates that of the 32 categories of deployed weapon systems, the U.S. has more sophisticated weapon systems in fifteen, including strategic bombers, ballistic missile submarines, and sea-based aircraft. Were the Soviet spy program able to obtain advanced technologies from the West at will, Soviet weapons would be on a par with U.S. weapons. The Soviet spy program, despite its vigor, cannot by itself close the gap between the Soviet Union and the U.S. in advanced military technologies. Moscow must rely on technology imports to do that.

A Prudent Policy of Export Restrictions

Most COCOM members have more lenient standards on restricting high technology exports to the East than the U.S. and they are seeking even lower standards. While they argue that high technology exports to the new democratic governments of Eastern Europe will help these countries modernize their economies, the main motive for COCOM members to push for lower restrictions is to give their domestic industries expanded export markets. It is up to Washington, as it has been for nearly a half-century, to make it clear to the other COCOM nations that collective security must not be sacrificed for the sake of potential export markets for specific industries. The Administration can do this by:

• *Maintaining U.S. leadership in COCOM.* The U.S. should remain COCOM leader. There have been occasions. . . when the U.S. has been the sole opponent of proposals to ease export restrictions. . . . Because COCOM makes decisions only by unanimous consent, a firm U.S. position can prevent or slow an opening of the floodgates on technology exports to the Soviet Union. The U.S. should block the decontrol of particular commodities after the new core list is established. If the U.S. refuses to okay decontrolling a particular commodity, it will not be taken off the list. Other COCOM members may be tempted to propose easing export restrictions on specific items. . . . The U.S. should resist this as it could become an indirect way to eliminate all export restrictions as the more lax members of COCOM continually whittle away at the list of restricted commodities. . . .

Foolish Policy

There is great danger in any U.S. policy that weakens opposition to strategic trade with the Soviets or permits the transfer of technology needed by Moscow. It is extremely foolish to provide the USSR with massive credits that would allow Moscow to build up its power at our expense. The new detentists, both in government and the private sector, fail to see—or greed blinds them to seeing—that aid to the Soviet Union is completely contrary to the national interests of the United States. A "new and improved" Soviet economy would only provide the Kremlin with the means to build more threatening weapons systems and to engage in a more intense political-military struggle around the world. U.S. trade with the Soviet Union should be limited to agricultural commodities and consumer goods which are desired by the Russian people rather than the factories and high-tech equipment desired by the Soviet leaders.

Anthony H. Harrigan and William R. Hawkins, *American Economic Pre-eminence,* 1989.

• *Distinguishing between exports to the Soviet Union and the new democracies in Eastern Europe.* The emerging democracies of Eastern Europe, specifically Czechoslovakia, Hungary, and Poland, should be exempted from strict COCOM restrictions if they continue to divorce themselves from their military and intelligence relationships with the Soviet Union. As democratic nations, these countries pose no significant military threat to the U.S. and its allies. The new, lower standards for exporting high technology commodities to the emerging democracies of Eastern Europe, however, should take effect gradually. These countries have been members of the Warsaw Pact for over 40 years. Military and intelligence ties to the Soviet Union will not dissolve overnight. As these ties are loosened, COCOM restrictions can be eased. At the same time, COCOM must impose on the new East European governments strict rules against transferring Western technology to the Soviet Union. COCOM will have to develop new ways to enforce the rules, perhaps requiring the exporter to identify the customer and to reveal the stated purpose for which the product is intended. Periodic inspections to ensure compliance with regulations will be required.

• *Ensuring strict controls on exports to the Soviet Union.* The Soviet Union (or even an independent Russia) will remain a significant military threat to the U.S. and its allies long into the future. The Soviet strategic modernization program continues, and as its conventional forces shrink, Soviet generals will seek through advanced technologies to achieve what American military experts call "force multipliers," which enhance the capability of the combat force using them. The U.S. should insist that COCOM link further relaxation of export restrictions to the U.S.S.R. to a demonstrable decline in Soviet military capabilities. The West should demand that Moscow deploy a military force no larger than needed for defense of Soviet territory. For U.S. export policy toward the Soviet Union to be relaxed almost completely, the Soviet Union would have to become a multi-party democracy with a market-based economy; this is the best way to ensure friendly intent toward the West. Barring these actions the Soviet Union should not be eligible for high technology exports from the West. . . .

Military Advantage

This is not the time for the U.S. to abandon export controls and give up what has been the trump card of Western security—its clear advantage in military technology. What the ongoing changes in Eastern Europe and the Soviet Union require is a careful review of export control policies and the easing of restrictions based on a clear-eyed assessment of the risks to Western security. This will require that the Bush Administration establish a policy that properly balances the competing interests of East European economic modernization, expanded foreign markets for U.S. producers, and American and allied security. Given the fact that the Soviet Union retains an extremely potent military force, Western superiority in military technology is still essential to maintaining a military balance and world peace. Until the Soviet Union dismantles its huge conventional and strategic forces, the U.S. has no choice but to restrict the flow of advanced technologies to the U.S.S.R.

"The United States. . . . needs to buy American for national defense and prevent foreign acquisition of sensitive American technologies."

America's Defense Industries Must Be Protected

Anthony H. Harrigan

Anthony H. Harrigan is president of the Business and Industrial Council, a business lobbying organization. He has written numerous books on trade, including *Putting America First: A Conservative Trade Alternative*. In the following viewpoint, Harrigan argues that the U.S. is in danger of losing its industrial base as more and more industries are eliminated or weakened by foreign competition. He argues that this development leaves the U.S. too dependent on foreign suppliers for essential industrial goods, and that in the case of war or trade breakdown such dependency could cripple the U.S. Harrigan calls for policies that would ensure the protection of U.S. industries deemed vital to America's defense.

As you read, consider the following questions:

1. How has the U.S. industrial base changed since World War II, according to Harrigan?
2. Which industries are important to U.S. national security and should be preserved, in the author's opinion?
3. What kind of military threats should the U.S. be prepared for, according to Harrigan?

Anthony H. Harrigan, testimony before the U.S. House of Representatives Subcommittee on Economic Stabilization, of the Committee on Banking, Finance, and Urban Affairs, May 17, 1989.

The U.S. is becoming increasingly dependent on foreign sources for its defense equipment. This is the result of the erosion of our industrial base. It is a fact of our national life. The erosion is taking place because of the underselling of U.S. production by foreign production and the shift of production to other countries in industry after industry. The U.S. has suffered severe setbacks in industries such as steel, machine tools, electronics, optical equipment, aluminum, shipbuilding, mining and computers. America's capacity for carrying out military commitments worldwide in the years ahead, in producing essential, sophisticated armaments, in executing a swift build-up in future crisis situations, or rapid mobilization and equipping of our forces in time of large-scale conventional war is endangered.

A New Development

This is something new for the United States. In the post-World War II era, America's industrial resources and capabilities were unrivaled. It's also something new for military professionals to consider in their estimates the ability of the United States to respond to threats in remote regions.

Spokesmen for strategic industries attest to deindustrialization. John F. Mitchell, president of Motorola Inc., one of the nation's leading high tech companies, has said: "We are simply losing our industrial base." *Business Week* has noted that American steel producers "have shuttered 25 million short tons of capacity since 1977—16 percent of the nation's total."

The ominous consequences of deindustrialization are not lost on many observers. Alfred E. Eckes, a member of the U.S. International Trade Commission, has said: "No great power in human history has watched its industrial base decline and remained a great power for long."

The New York Times has noted that the Defense Department is increasingly concerned that a rapid deterioration of the American microelectronics industry will leave the United States dependent on other nations for computer chips.

Loss of Defense Capability

The loss of defense capacity is to be found in a number of fields. As long ago as 1985, the Joint Logistics Commanders Bearing Study found that the U.S. bearing industry has lost almost 40 percent of the market, and that the erosion is continuing. The study noted that manufacturers have begun to turn to foreign sources for bearings used in military engines.

Kevin P. Phillips, the public affairs commentator, writing in his book "Staying on Top," opened his study of deindustrialization with the assertion that "Relative to our present economic circumstances, the United States is trying to defend too much of the world—to uphold the Pax Americana rooted in the very different economic circumstances of the late 1940s and the 1950s." All this has impacted on the strategic-military interests of the United States. W. R. Timken, Jr., Chairman of Timken Co., has noted that the United States is "the only country keeping [the Soviets] from their goal of world hegemony." Mr. Timken asked where the nation would be if it "didn't have steel, aluminum, chemicals, machinery and transportation industries or the necessary parts industries." Arguing against the theories of a post-industrial society for the United States, he said "Perhaps it is treasonous to advocate their elimination, that is, the elimination of the basic industries necessary to national defense."

Strategic Trade Policy

Strategic trade policy ensures that the United States does not become overly dependent on foreign suppliers—as might occur were the international division of labor to operate freely—and that it does not lose its technology base. One may disagree over the proper balance between economic efficiency and requirements of trade restrictions in the interest of national security, but national security does have a legitimate claim on the formulation of trade policy.

Mackubin T. Owens, *Orbis*, Fall 1989.

Dr. Paul Seabury of the University of California at Berkeley has written in an Institute for Contemporary Studies publication that "the United States simply cannot afford to allow its industrial base to wither away." With its enormous strategic burdens and responsibilities on all the world's oceans, the United States has a national requirement for an industrial base that makes possible the building of ships, aircraft, tanks and weapons in large numbers and the equipping of defense forces with the most sophisticated electronic devices and capabilities. Moreover, with relatively small standing forces, it has to be prepared in terms of equipment manufacture to outfit vastly larger numbers of personnel if the need arises. Almost a decade ago, Gen. Alton Slay alerted the country when he stated in *The Ailing Defense Industrial Base: Unready for Crisis* that "It is a gross contradiction to think that we can maintain our position as a first-rate military power with a second-rate industrial base. It has never been done in the history of the modern world."

Gen. Slay was then president of the American Defense Preparedness Association. He spoke of "a genuine concern with and interest in the capabilities of our industrial base to respond to the hardware requirements of our forces." He said that the

United States didn't have a "defense industry base that produces military hardware in an efficient and timely manner" and didn't have "a surge capability for use in an emergency short of mobilization."

In his article for the Institute for Contemporary Studies, Dr. Seabury suggested that the condition of America's industrial base should ring alarm bells in the nation.

Severe Problems

The United States already has severe problems with the manufacture of military hardware. Shipyards capable of building sophisticated warships are few and strained to the limit. The U.S. armed forces have chronic shortages of ammunition, spare parts, and missiles—what Adm. Thomas H. Moorer (USN-Ret.) has referred to as "consumables." These are indicators of a declining defense sector in the United States. And a decline means that the United States is less and less prepared to undertake swift mobilization in a crisis or to institute crash programs in defense necessitated by dramatic military advances on the part of powers that threaten America's security.

The defense debate in the United States focuses largely on the near-term, on the next group of ships, aircraft or tanks to be authorized. Defense thinking and planning almost never gets beyond the yearly defense budget struggle to consideration of the industrial base needs for the development and maintenance of forces over the long haul. While the U.S. was deficient in preparedness in the 1930s, including a lack of plans for rapid war production, its basic industrial production system was strong and capable of adaptation within months after the surprise attack on Pearl Harbor.

Today, the United States has strong defense forces but a deteriorating industrial posture. The United States already is dependent on imports for a wide variety of strategic materials. According to *Industry Week*, "foreign sources provide more than 90 percent of the country's supply of manganese, chromium, cobalt, and platinum, as well as more than 50 percent of its bauxite, zinc, tin, tungsten, and cadmium." In the main, these strategic minerals come from politically unstable areas.

In terms of defense production, machine tools are critical items. However, U.S. companies have lost 60 percent of the domestic market for computerized machine tools. The National Machine Tool Builders Association, expressing concern about imports of machine tools, states that "The national security of the U.S. is being impaired by current levels of imports of machine tools because such imports threaten to debilitate the domestic machine tool industry." It would be foolish indeed to dismiss this as one industry's special pleading. The industry makes a solid case that it is critical to America's "defense and deterrence posture." Machine tools are needed to produce every ship, plane, tank, missile, transport vehicle and other armament employed by the U.S. armed forces.

A Strategic Policy Needed

This situation has caused the U.S. Business and Industrial Council to advocate a "strategic economic policy" for the United States. Such a policy would aim at a restoration of industrial and technological capacity sufficient to support the defense structure required for the security of the United States.

A strategic economic policy for the United States would be based on a belief that military threats to the United States take a variety of forms and that a conventional, protracted war on the ground or at sea must be considered one of the possible forms. The United States can't rule out this type of confrontation, given the commitment of its principal adversary to conventional forces and weapons as well as to intercontinental ballistic missile warfare. If the conventional threat is real, then the United States must possess the industrial resources essential for such a conflict and for the rapid mobilization required to deal with it.

The U.S. needs adequate capabilities in production of basic metals, basic machinery such as motor vehicles, advanced machinery such as aircraft, and, of increasing importance, advanced electronics.

The United States needs adequate defense production facilities. It needs to safeguard small and medium-size companies that are producing leading-edge defense equipment. It needs to buy American for national defense and prevent foreign acquisition of sensitive American technologies. America can't afford to rely on foreign producers.

"Defense protectionism, like other forms of protectionism, is unnecessary, ineffective, and even dangerous."

Protecting America's Defense Industries Is Bad Policy

William J. Long

William J. Long is an international trade attorney and assistant professor of international relations at American University in Washington, D.C. In the following viewpoint, he attacks the argument that the U.S. needs to protect certain industries from foreign competition for national security reasons. Long argues that U.S. dependence on foreign suppliers for industrial goods is not necessarily bad. He asserts that sheltering U.S. industries from foreign competition ultimately weakens them. Thus protectionism, Long concludes, can cause more harm than good to America's defense capabilities.

As you read, consider the following questions:

1. How has free trade benefited the U.S., according to Long?
2. Why is dependence on foreign industrial suppliers not necessarily a threat to U.S. security, according to the author?
3. In Long's opinion, what three questions should be asked of any proposed strategic trade policies?

William J. Long, "Expand the Military-Industrial Complex? No—It's Unnecessary and Inefficient." Reprinted with permission from the Fall 1989 issue of *Orbis: A Journal of World Affairs* published by the Foreign Policy Research Institute.

Although the United States has traditionally pursued a policy of relatively free trade and investment, many are now calling for a more managed approach to defense-related industries. In large measure, these calls have been provoked by America's unprecedented trade deficits, by foreign challenges to its technological lead, and by the sudden reversal in its status from the world's leading creditor to the leading debtor. Should these voices be heeded? Should an effort be made to preserve or encourage domestic "strategic" industries, that is, industries that contribute to technological advancement, national income, or defense programs? The issue breaks down into three component questions. Do imperfections in the market (such as industry concentration or export targeting by foreign governments) demand remedial U.S. action that departs from free trade norms? If so, are government agencies capable of discovering the remedies that will nurture the appropriate industries? And can the political process produce appropriate and effective policies?

The Department of Defense (DOD), among others, already has answered all three of these questions in the affirmative, and its decisions could profoundly affect the course of U.S. trade and investment policy. In so deciding, however, the DOD has ignored basic objections to so major a shift in America's economic stance. And a close look at those objections suggests that defense protectionism, like other forms of protectionism, is unnecessary, ineffective, and even dangerous.

Free Trade Versus Strategic Trade

American free-trade liberalism holds that the distribution of resources should be left to market mechanisms and that the provision of collective goods (such as stable exchange rates) should be the province of international organizations. Although the United States has never completely realized this ideal, its postwar trade and investment policy has usually favored free trade. The reason for this policy was stated by President Reagan in September 1983, and it is a reason that would have been given by any of his predecessors: "The United States believes that international direct investment flows should be determined by private market forces. . . . We believe there are only winners, no losers, and all participants gain from it." Thus, with regard to capital barriers, the United States has maintained an open-door policy that has few exceptions. With regard to trade barriers, it has led an international movement away from high tariffs and toward a more open international trading system. To be precise, it has stood for the principle of negotiating diffuse, reciprocal trade liberalization through multilateral institutions such as the General Agreement on Tariffs and Trade. . . .

This system of relatively open trade and investment has unquestionably served U.S. and Western interests well. The increase in global trade and capital flow since the days of the Smoot-Hawley Tariff Act (1930) has been dramatic and unprecedented. Between 1933 and 1980, for example, real, price-adjusted U.S. exports more than doubled as a share of U.S. goods production. With expanded trade and investment has come an era of global and national prosperity.

© Matt Wuerker. Reprinted with permission.

Nevertheless, the argument that free trade and investment policies best serve the nation is presumptive only. It can and should be overridden by an argument for government intervention where compelling evidence in a particular case supports the need for national security. Indeed, U.S. trade and investment policy has long recognized such conflicts. Perhaps the best known departure from free-trade liberalism is embodied in the Export Administration Act, under which the Commerce Department, in consultation with other agencies, grants or denies export licenses for reasons of national security or foreign policy. The Department of Defense is entitled to review these license applications for the export or re-export of specified commodities and technical data to communist countries, or to certain noncommunist countries thought to pose a significant risk of diversion.

Nor are export controls the only justifiable limits that national security can impose on free trade. Even in the nuclear age, it makes sense for the United States to safeguard select production capacities from economic, political, or military disruption.

But in terms of large-scale economic policy, the Defense Department traditionally has held that open trade and investment policies were vital to maintaining the U.S. technological advantage over the Soviet Union, and in this way made an essential contribution to U.S. defense. The Defense Department also opposed import restrictions because it wished to maintain the option of procuring goods and components on a worldwide market and because it viewed its ability to deal with economic competitors as more important than securing domestic suppliers. The department's support for the co-development of the FSX aircraft with Japan indicates that this view still predominates, on occasion. These premises are now changing rapidly, however, and the changes mark a turning point in the executive branch's approach to trade and investment.

The New Defense Protectionism

Increasingly, the argument is heard in defense circles that a sound strategic trade and investment policy entails governmental protection of, or encouragement for, certain industries. In the narrow version of this argument, the industries are said to be vital to U.S. defense programs. In the broad version, they are merely linked to the economic health upon which U.S. military power is based. During the 1980s, such notions of a strategic trade and investment policy spread quickly from the academic to the policy-making realm and took institutional root at the Department of Defense. This change was prompted in part by the precipitous decline in the fortunes of the U.S. high-technology sector, once a showcase of the U.S. economy and prime source of America's defense superiority. From 1980 to 1985, America's high-technology trade balance declined drastically, from a surplus of $27 billion to less than $4 billion. In 1986, the United States incurred its first high-technology trade deficit. As a result, a fissure developed in the executive branch's traditionally solid support for liberal free trade and investment policies. Elements in DOD began to argue that "strategic industries" —semiconductors, numerically controlled machine tools, high-speed computers, telecommunications equipment, and a variety of other sophisticated technology products—should be protected from foreign competition and acquisition because of their role in the industrial requirements of the U.S. military. . . .

In mid-1988, the department released *Bolstering Defense Industrial Competitiveness*, an important examination of the U.S. defense industrial base that outlined a general strategy for preserving and strengthening domestic industries of strategic importance. Focusing on America's increasing dependence on foreign hardware and technology and on the erosion of U.S. competitiveness in defense-related industries, the report concluded that "United States institutions have not responded adequately or quickly enough to basic shifts in economic or manufacturing power among nations." It recommended a more active role for the Defense Department in U.S. foreign and domestic economic policy, the establishment of internal DOD mechanisms for addressing defense manufacturing issues, and the formation of a Defense Manufacturing Strategy Committee at the National Academy of Sciences to undertake a comprehensive analysis of the interplay between foreign trade and domestic defense procurement policies. . . .

The Defense Department's new-found interest in the economy is of truly staggering scope. It has begun to advocate active government participation in the market through trade and investment policies that protect and promote those industries it believes are strategic. Clearly, the time has come to raise hard questions about DOD's understanding of its role in a free economy.

National Security Concerns

To be sure, the presumption in favor of free trade can be overridden when that policy potentially endangers vital national security concerns. But such a move presumes that the proposed intervention is necessary, that it will be effective, and that it can be accomplished in a way that yields more benefit than harm. Does DOD's campaign for a strategic trade and investment policy meet these three criteria?

Like most major industrial countries, the United States already protects essential military, food, energy, communications, transport, and core production needs through a host of selective measures. The U.S. government promulgates over 600 pages of regulations governing strategic exports. It prohibits or limits foreign acquisitions in the atomic energy, airline, and communication industries. It stockpiles and subsidizes food and energy, and protects such manufactures as steel, automobiles, textiles, semiconductors, and machine tools. It finances research and development in national defense, aerospace, health, and medicine. The cost of protecting and promoting these many "strategic" sectors already amounts to an enormous burden. DOD efforts to identify new strategic industries will further add to these costs without significantly improving national security.

The argument for an expanded DOD role in managing the U.S. economy ignores certain basic realities. First, contrary to the assumption underlying the new DOD economic interventionism, U.S. national security does not require total reliance on domestic supplies. In an era of growing economic and technological interdependence and transnational corporations, the industrial base of American security must to some degree depend on the resources of U.S. allies and on companies not completely under

U.S. national control. Indeed, sensible procurement of manufacturing equipment, weapons, and technology should exploit the innovation and competitive discipline that foreign suppliers can provide.

Undoubtedly, domestic or accessible foreign supplies could meet U.S. security needs for nearly all products under a wide variety of wartime scenarios. Invariably, in the past, U.S. industries petitioning for import protection on national security grounds have failed to prove that competing foreign suppliers would be unavailable sources in wartime. One reason is that the proliferation of technological competence throughout the West means alternative suppliers can be found in Western Europe, Japan, and elsewhere.

Reduced Economic Resources

Second, a reduction in conventional forces—and hence the economic resources needed to sustain them—is at the top of both the U.S. and Soviet arms control agendas. Success in controlling arms will allow the DOD to shift funds from present expenditures to building reserve capacity and mobilization potential. Too, should there be similar progress in lessening the probability of a major and protracted conventional war, the U.S. force structure will shift accordingly, and the structure of the U.S. defense industry with it. Almost certainly, this will mean a move away from large-scale production capacity.

Third, many problems thought to require government's intervention could be better resolved by getting the government out of the marketplace. As one study of a defense industrial policy put it:

> The government should stop taking actions that work against. . . market trends. Overly stringent antitrust policies work against the cooperative development and subsequent diffusion of new technologies. Overly zealous export restrictions prevent U.S. firms from reaping the profits from proprietary-product development.

Similarly, a government effort to put its fiscal affairs in order and to increase the rate of domestic savings might go far toward improving America's industrial base. . . .

Is Defense Protectionism Effective?

Strategic trade and investment policy is fraught with uncertainty. The United States has no tradition of successful government involvement in economic decision making, and no evidence suggests that the U.S. government as a whole, let alone the Department of Defense, knows how to improve national welfare and security by developing sectors of the economy that will produce higher rates of return on investment or extraordinary technological benefits.

For example, government intervention in the semiconductor market yielded less than optimal results. This is not for lack of trying. In addition to supporting voluntary export restraints, DOD involvement in the semiconductor industry has included the funding, research, and development of semiconductor manufacturing techniques through Sematech; opposing in late 1986 Fujitsu Corporation's acquisition of Fairchild Semiconductor (a U.S. firm owned by a French parent company); and, recently, committing itself to operate its own semiconductor manufacturing plant under a contract with National Semiconductor.

Protectionism Inefficient

By harming certain key domestic industries, trade can allegedly impair a nation's defense. But trade protection is a very inefficient means of preserving the production capacity of an industry deemed essential to national defense. A far cheaper way is to pay for the capacity and such stockpiles of products are as necessary to defend the nation directly out of the federal budget.

Robert Z. Lawrence and Robert E. Liton, *Harvard Business Review*, May/June 1987.

The Pentagon has little to show for these efforts. The voluntary restraint agreement with Japan raised the costs and reduced the competitiveness of U.S. semiconductor-using industries; drove Japan toward the high end of the semiconductor market, where it will compete more directly with U.S. manufacturers; encouraged Japan to build sophisticated micro-processors not covered by the agreement; and created a market niche for Korea's nascent semiconductor industry. It is too early to assess the outcome of the Sematech project, but it does mark a major departure from traditional American reliance on the market to allocate capital for commercial undertakings, and may set an ominous precedent. . . .

For those concerned with the future course of U.S. trade and investment policy, Department of Defense activism in the economic arena should be worrisome. The Defense Department's institutional weight and influence may overwhelm other institutions in the highly decentralized and delicately balanced economic policy-making process and foreclose effective debate. Moreover, the manifold benefits of economic freedom, and the potential for harm in economic interventionism, make government policies to shelter defense industries prima facie unwise. A defense industrial policy should therefore not be launched until thorough study has proven that national security requirements make it unavoidable.

"The United States is asking nations around the world to surrender the authority to protect their environment. . .in pursuit of the notion of 'free trade.' "

Environmental Concerns Should Restrict Trade

Robert Schaeffer

Robert Schaeffer is senior editor of *Greenpeace* magazine, a bimonthly journal published by Greenpeace, an environmental activist organization. In the following viewpoint, he argues that international trade is dominated by rich countries and corporations that have limited concern for the environment. Examples of the environmental harms of free trade, according to Schaeffer, include the logging of rain forests for wood exports and the selling of U.S.-banned pesticides to other countries. Schaeffer writes that environmental protection should receive higher priority than at present, and that trade between nations should be restricted when necessary to preserve the global environment.

As you read, consider the following questions:

1. Why are many environmentalists opposed to the General Agreement on Tariffs and Trade (GATT), according to Schaeffer?
2. What examples does the author provide of environmental laws being overturned for the sake of free trade?
3. According to Schaeffer, what simple question should be asked about proposals to expand free trade?

Robert Schaeffer, "Trading Away the Planet," *Greenpeace Magazine*, September/October 1990. Reprinted with permission.

Meeting in secret, U.S. government negotiators are revising the rules of international trade. If they persuade the 98 members of the General Agreement on Tariffs and Trade (GATT) to adopt their radical proposals, environmental protection could suffer for years to come.

Trade Rules

Since 1948, international trade has been governed in part by the GATT agreement. GATT is a rule book that establishes how companies in different countries should buy and sell their products. About once every five years, the world's trade ministers meet, usually at the urging of the United States, to renegotiate the rules of the agreement. For the most part, these reforms have been restricted to encouraging nations to stop placing taxes on foreign goods.

In 1986 the world's trade ministers met at a posh seaside resort to begin the "Uruguay Round" of negotiations. This time, the United States is pushing for a bigger prize. They want the rule book to be rewritten and expanded to permit international corporations to set up shop in any corner of the world with as little government interference as possible. This means free access to natural resources with the minimum of social and environmental "strings" attached—few regulations, emissions standards or other hedges against pollution, habitat loss or exploitation of labor. Any nation that decides to impose limits on the rights of foreign companies, for environmental or social reasons, can be retaliated against for creating a "restraint on trade."

The Bush administration will present the new GATT as a more perfect realization of "free trade." Through arrangements like the recent trade agreement between Canada and the United States and the "borderless Europe" of 1992, national governments are organizing the global economy around this definition of free trade. It is a concept that meets with either blank stares or unquestioning approval from most people in the developed world. Because the news media has focussed narrowly or not at all on the implications of rewriting the rules of international business, few Americans are well-informed enough to comment.

But many scholars, environmentalists, labor and human rights activists and Third World leaders are strongly opposed to the notion of free trade as defined by corporate interests and their allies in the U.S. government. If the United States gets its way in the Uruguay Round, they contend, much of the authority to protect the environment, food, labor and small businesses will be taken from communities, states and nations and put in the hands of government-appointed trade ministers, multinational corporations and obscure international agencies.

In 1981, in response to a growing garbage crisis, Denmark

passed a law requiring that beer and soft drinks be sold only in returnable bottles. In 1987, the European Commission took Denmark to the European Court of Justice, arguing that the law was an unfair restraint on free trade because it imposed, in the words of the *Economist*, a "disproportionate level of environmental protection." In 1990 the court backed Denmark, but only on returnable bottles. A plan to demand refillable bottles from industry was struck down as a restraint on trade.

Canada's western forests are also victims of free trade. After being pushed by the Bush administration, British Columbia ended a government-funded tree-planting program. Planting trees, the United States argued, was an "unfair subsidy" to Canada's timber industry.

Trade and the Environment

If a government wants to stop the export of the country's very precious natural resources—tropical wood, for example—it might be accused of being against the principles of free trade. If a government would like to ban the import of toxic waste or of food considered dangerous because of excessive pesticides, it might be similarly accused.

Martin Khor, quoted in *Los Angeles Times*, July 29, 1990.

This is how free trade can destroy the environment. The examples from Canada and Denmark are just the beginning of what may well become a full-scale trade war on the planet's natural resources if U.S. GATT proposals are accepted. "GATT represents an unprecedented abolition of national sovereignty on the part of nations around the world," says David Morris of the Institute for Local Self-Reliance. "Under the new GATT rules," says Martin Kohr, an analyst with the Malaysia-based Third World Network, "the country that exploits most, whether it be the environment or the worker, wins." These proposed reforms will affect all aspects of national policy. Some examples:

Health Standards. In recent years, California voters approved the anti-toxic Proposition 65 initiative, state legislators have passed air-quality and waste-disposal regulations that are more stringent than federal law, and European governments have adopted measures that prohibit the import of beef contaminated with artificial hormones.

Harmonizing Standards

U.S. negotiators are proposing to "harmonize" standards governing food safety to eliminate what they call "nontariff" barriers to trade such as food-labeling or recycling requirements.

Instead of allowing local, state or national governments to set standards, U.S. negotiators would make international standard-setting bodies, such as the U.N.'s [United Nations] Codex Alimentarius Commission, responsible for creating uniform global food standards.

Because this tiny agency based in Rome sets extremely low standards for some commodities, the proposal to make Codex responsible for food safety would degrade protection for consumers and the environment. Current Codex standards, for example, would allow the import of bananas containing up to 50 times the amount of DDT permitted by the U.S. Food and Drug Administration. It would allow a 10-fold increase of DDT residues in imported carrots and potatoes, a 20-fold increase in strawberries and grapes, and a 33-fold increase in pineapple, broccoli and lettuce. Under GATT rules, if California, for example, attempted to set higher standards or restrict the import of food contaminated with pesticides now banned in the United States, foreign governments could sue the United States for establishing nontariff barriers to trade. When trade barriers come down in Europe in 1992, West Germany faces the prospect of being forced to import captan, the toxic fungicide banned by Bonn but used freely in Denmark and Great Britain.

Under the new GATT rules, U.S. efforts to label tuna as dolphin-safe, Denmark's ban on the use of polyvinylchloride food containers, British rules on labeling irradiated food, and the West German law requiring beverage containers to be recyclable could all be attacked as nontariff trade barriers by governments at the behest of corporations that consider themselves disadvantaged.

Natural Resources. U.S. negotiators are eager to prevent countries from restricting food exports for any reason, even when they are facing food shortages at home. In addition, they want to eliminate export restrictions on natural resources, such as the raw log export bans adopted by Asian and Pacific nations to slow the destruction of rainforests. GATT rules could make it extremely difficult for countries anywhere to develop their raw materials and natural resources on a sustainable basis. Proposed GATT rules could also prevent countries from restricting the import of goods, such as hazardous wastes, simply because they apply higher environmental standards than other countries.

Agriculture

Subsidies. U.S. negotiators want to eliminate agricultural subsidies. U.S. family farmers annually receive about $40 billion in aid from the federal government, most of it to support commodity prices, but some of it to promote soil and water conservation. This includes land set-aside programs designed to allow the soil to recover its natural fertility. All of this would go out the window if price supports were withdrawn and support for conservation-related farm activities were treated as "trade-distorting subsidies."

By changing GATT to prohibit government-funded agricultural programs, more land would be put to the plow. Commodity prices would fall, family farmers would be ruined, and land would be consolidated in the hands of corporate farmers. Under these conditions, groundwater contamination and soil loss would become a serious problem. The conscientious family farmer may replenish or keep soil loss at a minimum, but the corporate farmer can lose up to 35-40 tons annually.

Free Trade vs. the Environment

At least one decision of the European Commission shows the problems inherent in favoring free trade over the environment. The Court of Justice of the European Community ruled in a case involving Denmark's returnable bottle law that although no actual restraint of trade had actually arisen, the reuse regulations could be more expensive for importers than domestic producers. The Court concluded, "There has to be a balancing of interests between the free movement of goods and environmental protection, even if in achieving the balance the high standard of the protection sought has to be reduced." In other words, free trade permits Denmark to have a returnable bottle bill, but not a refillable bottle bill.

David Morris, *Trading Our Future: Talking Back to GATT*, 1990.

Technology. U.S. and European negotiators want patents, trademarks and other "intellectual property rights" to be recognized internationally. While the reforms are advertised as an effort to stop bootlegging of U.S. and European products such as watches, luggage and audio recordings, the implications are considerably more far-reaching. Drugs that are produced cheaply for distribution to the poor in India would suddenly become too expensive to offer. Even worse, as corporate-controlled biotechnology advances, a poor Mexican farmer might find himself unable to afford seeds for drought-resistant tomatoes because the patent on the seeds is held by a U.S.-based chemical corporation. This despite the fact that the genetic material that established the plant's resistance to drought could well have originated in Mexico.

The United States is asking nations around the world to surrender the authority to protect their environment, their workers and their small businesses in pursuit of the notion of "free trade." The unquestioned assumption of this demand is that the unfettered access of major corporations to every corner of the world will produce a host of mutual benefits.

Contemporary free traders argue that GATT is responsible for the 10-fold increase in the volume of world trade since 1950. This may or may not be true (some economists argue that the increase in international trade is more the effect than the cause of the general increase in global wealth). But it is also beside the point. Trade has expanded, but it has not made poor nations rich.

According to Giovanni Arrighi, an Italian economist who measured the Gross National Product per capita of countries around the world from 1938 to 1979, the global distribution of wealth has been rigidly stable, despite the expansion of trade. Arrighi's research found that the small number of rich countries stayed rich, the large number of impoverished countries remained poor by comparison, and a small group of intermediate-strata nations stayed where they were.

To put it simply, Guatemala was poor, and despite free trade it still is. When tariffs were averaging 40 percent in the 1940s, the United States was extremely rich. Today they average four percent, but the gulf between the world's poor countries and the United States remains as wide as it was in 1940. The only upwardly mobile countries during this period were Japan, South Korea and Taiwan. But their success, Arrighi says, had more to do with internal economic policies and a special relationship with the United States than with the effects of free trade.

Who Will Benefit?

For the sake of simplicity, any analysis of any major international development should ask the question, "Who will benefit?" In the case of the proposals to reform GATT, it is clear that the main beneficiaries will be a collection of international corporations that have no national loyalties. At risk are the global environment and the rights of people in California, Denmark or Mexico to set policies protecting their health and their natural wealth.

Consumer advocate Ralph Nader accuses GATT "of imposing a mega-corporate view of the world. It is designed to circumvent democratic institutions and override local and state government efforts to protect consumers and the environment." As the 20th century closes, the power that corporations wield over the workings of the planet is growing. At the same time, the power of people to assert their right to decide how to husband their natural resources and control their economic future is also on the rise.

The fight over GATT is really a fight over who will write the rules of international commerce—the corporations on behalf of their profits, or the people on behalf of the environment and the needs of the individual and the community. Speaking on behalf of a coalition of environmental groups, Lynn Greenwalt of the National Wildlife Federation said, "We have come together to note, and perhaps to prevent, the passing of an era—an era when local communities had a say in how their natural resources were used, and when state and federal governments could take steps to stop the destruction of our environment. These basic rights may be sacrificed by U.S. negotiators in the name of free trade."

> *"Free trade is compatible with, even essential to, both economic and environmental benefits."*

Restricting Trade Will Not Protect the Environment

Fred L. Smith Jr. and Daniel F. McInnis

Fred L. Smith Jr. is president of the Competitive Enterprise Institute (CEI), a Washington, D.C. public interest group which advocates market-oriented approaches to public policy issues. Daniel F. McInnis is an environmental policy analyst for CEI. In the following viewpoint they argue that efforts to protect the environment by restricting trade are unnecessary and counterproductive. Expanding free trade to all nations, they conclude, could have beneficial effects for the environment by encouraging people to use natural resources wisely and efficiently.

As you read, consider the following questions:

1. What are the flaws of current U.S. environmental policy, according to Smith and McInnis?
2. According to the authors, why should environmental and trade policies not be linked?
3. Why has a trade ban in ivory been harmful to the African elephant, according to Smith and McInnis?

Fred L. Smith Jr. and Daniel F. McInnis, "The New International Order," a 1990 position paper published by the Competitive Enterprise Institute, Washington, D.C. Reprinted with permission.

While the old Internationalists who have long sought to create a one-world government may be in retreat, a new coalition has been building on a greener foundation. The budget of the United Nations Environmental Program (UNEP), headed by Egyptian Mostafa Tolba, has ballooned to $1.3 billion dollars in 1990. The Montreal Protocol, an international agreement to phase-out the use of CFCs [chlorofluorocarbons], was ratified by over 58 countries. Even conservative stalwart Margaret Thatcher joined the environmental Chicken Littles by declaring support for a substantial decrease in carbon dioxide emissions as a response to the still unproven theory of global climate change. Thoughtful critics of socialist internationalism should take seriously green internationalism as a threat to individual liberty and national sovereignty. . . .

Environmentalists have learned to use the international political order to magnify their influence on national policies. Greenpeace, the radical environmental protest group, has been able to open offices in such disparate places as Argentina, Costa Rica, Germany, New Zealand, the Soviet Union, the United Kingdom, and even Antarctica. The World Resources Institute, headed by Gustave Speth, works closely with UNEP. The World Bank's Herman Daly is one of the leading proponents of the "sustainable development" movement, which argues that unfettered capitalism will destroy the world.

The Dangers of Centralization

In this battle, international law and trade policy have been the Greens' most effective tools. The Greens argue that ecological problems are best addressed by uniform multilateral action. Not surprisingly, they have moved to centralize environmental protection, influencing nations to bind themselves together in a series of treaties, conventions, protocols, resolutions, recommendations, and declarations.

Before we "globalize" environmental policy, however, we should examine the arguments for—and our experience with—centralized environmental planning. The United States created a centralized Environmental Protection Agency (EPA) in 1970. The EPA mandated over 750 billion dollars in spending during its first ten years (in 1986 dollars). Accordingly, the size and scope of government power increased enormously. Violation of the Clean Water Act of 1972 can result in arrest. One Pennsylvania property owner was jailed for nothing more than filling in a ditch on his land. The 1990 revisions of the Clean Air Act, first passed in 1970, will impose additional costs of perhaps 50 billion dollars a year. EPA programs worked to turn local problems into large-scale pork barrel programs, e.g. Superfund, which has wasted billions of dollars and failed to clean up the original waste dumps.

Clearly there are major risks—both economic and environmental—in these centralizing strategies. The vision of a large, coercive government is antithetical to free markets and the competitive spirit that drives people to be efficient. Moreover, global environmental advocates not only oppose ordinary competition but also market-oriented environmental policies. Decentralized environmental protection would endanger the global environment, they argue. For example, the Natural Resources Defense Council has for years tried to block the export of pesticides to foreign countries, since the use of these chemicals would not be as highly regulated as in the United States. Ironically, businesses have often supported these calls for further international regulation. They point out that much of the U.S.'s environmental regulations threaten the ability of American firms to compete in a world economy. Senator Frank Lautenberg (D-NJ) proposed legislation that would extend the unfair trading practice laws to address both these "problems." A nation that failed to duplicate our environmental laws might well find itself subject to trade sanctions.

Linking the Environment and Trade

We should be skeptical of linking environmental and trade policies. The problems of determining whether a specific trade policy will advance the economic interests of the United States is complex; to broaden this question to address environmental issues—particularly whether the environmental policies of a specific trading partner are "adequate"—would take us far beyond the possible.

These caveats do not mean that environmental policy on an international level is impossible. They suggest only that a centralized environmental bureaucracy will reduce the ability of diverse interests to advance their own environmental objectives. Competition, whether in trade or environmental protection, is a strong and positive force that we should be wary of suppressing. In short, an open world economy and a policy of free trade is compatible with, even essential to, both economic and environmental benefits.

Let us now consider some of the factors arguing against linking trade to environmental policies:

U.S. Environmental Policies Don't Export Well: American environmental policy costs hundreds of billions of dollars, mobilizes armies of technicians, relies upon a civil service largely immune to bribes and an independent environmental movement to monitor and police the process. The U.S. has been able to take this approach because we are rich, have an excellent professional and academic establishment, an honest civil service, and a large

164

and aggressive public interest sector. None of these prerequisites are present in the Third World. If Third World countries had money and technicians, they would hardly be Third World. Incorruptible civil servants with decent pay and training are rare in the developing world. Independent groups that stand up and resist Third World governments often find themselves lying down again very swiftly. Yet, the presumption of global environmental policy—specifically those policies that relate to trade—is that other countries should adopt our policies. That is both unwise and unworkable.

Anti-Market Policies

Environmental Policy Is Anti-Market: A second factor that should make us cautious in linking environmental and trade policies is the strong anti-market bias of current environmental policy. Conventional wisdom views pollution and other environmental problems as the inevitable consequence of "market failure." Since pollution is "external" to the market place, the market "fails" to consider its impacts. When the market "fails," political intervention is essential. The "market failure" model thus leads to regulating all economic activities that have environmental consequences. But all economic activities have environmental consequences; thus, the current approach seeks to regulate the whole economy.

Economic central planning has proven itself a failure throughout the world. Why should we expect ecological central planning to fare any better? After all, Vistula, Poland's largest river, is so corrosive that it is hardly fit for industrial use. Chernobyl, the world's worst nuclear disaster, is the product of Soviet central planning. Cracow, Poland suffers from some of the world's worst air pollution. Its ancient statuary is losing its features, the once milky-white marble is discolored and the gothic architecture is crumbling. Before treading down the path of economic central planning, we should reconsider the "market failure" model. The fact that markets are not perfect does not mean that political approaches necessarily are. In the real world, efforts to extend property rights to resources now at risk and to develop legal mechanisms to protect vulnerable environmental resources may work far better than political controls.

Special Interests

Environmental Trade Policy Is Likely To Be Captured By Special Interests: Government policies often represent the views of special interests rather than the public interest. Few individuals have the time or inclination to master complex policy questions and to monitor the process by which policy is made and enforced. Only groups having a strong economic or ideological stake are likely to participate. The economic groups that attend public hearings are often established firms whose commitment to competition is limited. Most ideological environmental groups are even less likely to favor diversity. Because of the almost universal acceptance of the "market failure" model in the environmental community, they are more likely to oppose market approaches and favor trade restrictions.

Failure of Trade Bans

Trade bans on wildlife products have failed to protect species for which there is a commercial demand. Many species of Latin American parrots, for instance, are "protected" by a CITES [Convention on International Trade in Endangered Species] Appendix I listing. Prices skyrocketed after the trade ban and the legal trade was taken over by poachers who make no effort to maintain birds on a sustainable basis. After all, the nest left today will in all likelihood be taken by someone else tomorrow. Native hunters go so far as to chop down nesting trees to get the parrots. The captured parrots are drugged, put in door panels and even hubcaps, and smuggled into the United States, where the few that actually survive are sold on the black market for more than $20,000. The return for trading in protected birds is often greater than what can be made from producing illegal drugs. Rather than reducing the slide in native parrot populations, prohibition has accelerated it.

Randy T. Simmons and Urs P. Kreuter, *Policy Review*, Fall 1989.

The inability of the political process to determine the public interest is already serious. Opening the door to environmental pleadings will only make it worse. Just as textile interests have come to champion human rights in oppressed Third World countries in hopes of limiting their textile exports, protectionist arguments are now being advanced on environmental grounds. Orange juice tariffs are already defended as necessary to protect tropical rainforests in Brazil. One Brazilian orange planter pointed out that while his exports have come under attack, his groves are about as close to the rainforest as the orange groves of Florida are to the forests of upstate New York.

Setting Environmental Priorities Is Difficult: Since much environmental policy is directed by the pressure of interest groups, environmental priorities often reflect politics and passion rather than science. Consider the environmental scares of the last few years: Alar, Chilean grapes, hormone residues in imported meat, asbestos. The EPA itself, in an internal study, *Unfinished Business*, found its spending priorities were inversely related to the scientific assessments of public health risks. The sensational rather than the serious dominate policy.

This policy dynamic will have serious consequences in the Third World. People routinely die of water contaminated by human waste in the Third World, but American environmentalists focus on industrial wastes as the major water pollution problem. Likewise, the elimination of trace levels of pesticides or herbicides can scarcely rival the improvements needed in basic diets and water quality to advance the welfare of Third World countries.

Saving the Elephant

Consider the way in which trade policies have become intertwined with efforts to save the African elephant. One of the most discussed international environmental treaties is the Convention on International Trade in Endangered Species (CITES). In 1989, the CITES directorate voted to move the African elephant to Appendix I status, effectively banning all trade in elephant products. The reasoning behind this action was familiar: elephant ivory prices had increased and these higher prices made poaching increasingly profitable. Thus African elephants were more likely to fall before poachers' guns. Since markets and trade created this threat, the obvious solution was to restrict the ivory trade.

Championed by leading environmental organizations such as the World Wildlife Fund, the ivory trade ban was very popular. Interests in Africa were also very active. Kenya, in a highly promoted event, burned over twelve tons of elephant tusks. The ban was opposed by a handful of countries in Africa that had pioneered a novel "conservation-through-use" strategy that had begun to integrate the elephant into the local economy. Zimbabwe was a leader in this effort. While elephant herds had been plummeting in Kenya from 65,000 to 19,000 over the last decade, Zimbabwean herds had grown from 30,000 to near 43,000. There was clearly more to this story than appeared in the press. (Botswana, Malawi, Namibia, and South Africa—all recorded population increases of around five percent.)

What was the difference? These latter countries allow and encourage property rights in elephants, giving African natives an incentive to protect their now valuable elephants. In Africa, elephants compete with natives for scarce resources. If there are no gains to offset these losses, then elephants become a massive pest. "If the ivory ban works" wrote Tom Bethel in *The American Spectator*, "the elephant will nonetheless remain a large, hungry, and destructive animal—a giant rat."

The CITES decision ignored the very different elephant management strategy pioneered by countries like Zimbabwe and blindly accepted the need to ban elephant ivory. But this is not surprising. Because trade policies reflect American perceptions rather than Zimbabwean realities, there was little understanding or sympathy for nations that have found creative ways to integrate economic and environmental values.

Trade and Elephants

Elephants are endangered in certain parts of Africa, not all Africa. Thus, the solution to saving the African elephant lies not in banning ivory trade, but in applying the successful elephant conservation policies of South African nations to East African nations that have mismanaged their resources. Where poaching and facilitation of poaching by corrupt officials occurs, the responsibility lies with the country's government. An international ban on trade in ivory will not solve internal problems and is an abrogation of responsibility to eliminate the true causes of elephant decline.

Randy T. Simmons and Urs P. Kreuter, *Policy Review*, Fall 1989.

Nations face vastly different environmental tasks—each country has its own geographic, economic, and political challenges. A diversity of local conditions encourages a wide range of experimentation. A non-use policy which may work well in the United States, may well fail in both Zimbabwe and Kenya. The fact that Zimbabwe's elephant population is increasing, while Kenya's is declining suggests that trade may be more pro-environment than environmentalists would like to admit.

CITES is no exemplar for rational environmental policy. Unfortunately, CITES is only one of the latest examples of the anti-trade bias of environmental policy. That bias has blocked the evolution of turtle ranches in the Cayman Islands. Strong efforts were made over a decade ago to find ways to commercially farm sea turtles—a species in danger throughout the world. That effort was blocked by the anti-trade bias of the Department of the Interior and a number of environmental groups. . . . Likewise, efforts to stop trade in tropical lumber are growing as are efforts to condition all agricultural trade on adherence to environmental standards. This latter trend is extremely serious when one contrasts the low to non-existent risks of trace contaminants in food with the very serious risks of starvation throughout the world.

Balancing Interests

The U.S. government has long sought to balance the conflicting interests of Americans concerned over trade policy. That task has been daunting. Today, policy makers are considering steps that might vastly complicate those deliberations and most often fail to advance environmental goals. This would merely add environmental policy to the list of "unfair" trading practices used to rationalize protectionist policies. . . .

What should policy makers do? First, they should reconsider the view that markets are to blame for environmental problems. Empirical evidence suggests otherwise—throughout the world, the correlation between environmental quality and markets is evident. Markets encourage everyone to consider carefully their use of materials and energy. Those incentives reduce the stress posed by economic activities to the environment. Moreover, market economies are based on secure property and contract rights. These institutional arrangements decentralize authority for preserving natural resources and encourage wise use. In contrast, resources owned in common and politically managed are rarely used wisely. Property rights give an owner both the incentive to manage the resource wisely and the means to protect that resource from harm. Often good economic policy is good environmental policy. Policy makers should consider policies likely to encourage the evolution of market economies for the sake of the environment.

Policy makers also should be skeptical of the motives of those who seek to restrict trade for an "environmental" cause. Green protectionists should be scrutinized as thoroughly as all other protectionists.

The Need for Skepticism

Skepticism should equally apply to special interests within the government. The information supplied by the Environmental Protection Agency or the Department of the Interior has often been criticized as biased in favor of these agencies. In any case, these agencies have their own agendas and trade expansion is not a high priority.

Finally, we should be receptive to creative ways whereby the poorer countries might best advance their environmental and economic welfare. Had Britain been dominated by environmentalists in our colonial times, they might have reacted with horror to the rapidity with which we cleared away the forests that blanketed North America. Yet, those early centuries of deforestation came to an end and now forests east of the Mississippi are expanding again. Are we to deny to Brazil and Indonesia this same right to transform natural resources into wealth? Supporting a new international order to enforce environmental perfection will result in the same disasters as the old international order's efforts to enforce economic perfection.

169

Ranking Concerns in Trade Policy

Berry's World

© 1985 by NEA, Inc.
7-c

"You like protectionism as a 'working man.' How about as a consumer?"

Reprinted by permission of NEA, Inc.

Determining what would be the best trade policy for the U.S. is complicated by many factors. The above cartoon illustrates one paradox. The man being questioned may support protectionism because he believes it helps prevent Americans (including himself) from losing jobs to foreigners. On the other hand, as a consumer he may support free trade because foreign goods can be purchased more cheaply. Thus, the trade concerns of consumers and producers may conflict, even when the consumer and the producer are the same person.

This activity will give you an opportunity to explore and discuss the values you and your classmates consider important in making U.S. trade policy.

Step 1: The class should break into groups of four to six students. Group members should rank the concerns listed below. Decide what you believe to be the most important concerns, and be ready to defend your answers. Use number 1 to designate the most important concern, number 2 for the second most important concern, and so on.

Step 2: Each group should return to the concerns and evaluate whether or not they call for a policy of restricting trade. Place an *R* beside each concern that seems to call for trade restrictions. Place an *F* beside each concern that seems to call for free trade.

Rank		*R or F*
_____	exposing U.S. businesses to foreign competition to force them to compete with foreign goods	_____
_____	giving U.S. consumers the widest selection and best prices on goods	_____
_____	protecting U.S. businesses from foreign competition	_____
_____	making sure the U.S. keeps a steel industry in case of war	_____
_____	protecting the environment	_____
_____	keeping technological secrets out of the hands of military rivals	_____
_____	keeping technological secrets out of the hands of economic rivals	_____
_____	protecting U.S. jobs	_____

Step 3: Compare your answers from steps one and two. Is your group generally in favor of free trade, or in favor of trade restrictions? Why? Compare your answers and explain your reasoning with other groups in a class discussion.

Periodical Bibliography

The following articles have been selected to supplement the diverse views presented in this chapter.

Harry Anderson	"Mainframes for Moscow," *Newsweek*, May 14, 1990.
J. Michael Cleverley	"The Problem of Technology Transfer Controls," *Global Affairs*, Summer 1989.
John P. Cregan	"Building an American Consensus—A National Interest Trade Policy," *Vital Speeches of the Day*, March 7, 1990.
Clyde H. Farnsworth	"Why a U.S. Trade Pact Is Crucial to Gorbachev's Economic Hopes," *The New York Times*, May 27, 1990.
Martin Feldstein	"Trade Economic Aid for Soviet Arms Cuts," *The Wall Street Journal*, June 28, 1990.
Dan Glickman and James A. McClure	"Should the United States Lift Trade Restrictions with the Soviets?" *American Legion Magazine*, May 1990.
Seymour E. Goodman, Marjory S. Blumenthal, and Gary L. Geipel	"Export Controls Reconsidered," *Issues in Science and Technology*, Winter 1989/1990.
Ethan B. Kapstein	"Losing Control—National Security and the Global Economy," *The National Interest*, Winter 1989/1990.
Deborah M. Levy	"Export Controls: Benefit or Bust for U.S. Business?" *USA Today*, July 1988.
Multinational Monitor	"Trading Away Rights," May 1990. Available from Essential Information, Inc., PO Box 19405, Washington, DC 20036.
Kenichi Ohmae	"Managing in a Borderless World," *Harvard Business Review*, May/June 1989.
Steven Shrybman	"International Trade and the Environment," *The Ecologist*, January/February 1990. Available from MIT Press Journals, 55 Hayward St., Cambridge, MA 02142.
Richard L. Stroup and Jane S. Shaw	"The Free Market and the Environment," *The Public Interest*, Fall 1989.
Jacob Weisberg	"Playing Favorites," *The New Republic*, June 18, 1990.
E. Allan Wendt	"U.S. Export Control Policy: Its Present and Future Course," *Department of State Bulletin*, October 1988.

How Critical Is the U.S. Trade Deficit?

Chapter Preface

Every month the U.S. Department of Commerce reports U.S. trade figures, estimating the value of goods and services sold to foreign countries as well as the value of goods and services imported from abroad. If the U.S. sells more than it buys, the difference becomes a trade surplus. If the reverse happens, the result is a trade deficit.

For most of the twentieth century the U.S. has had a trade surplus. For example, as recently as 1981 the U.S. sold $12 billion more goods than it imported. During the 1980s, however, the U.S. began building up trade deficits. The trade deficit peaked in 1987 at over $152 billion and in subsequent years remained over $100 billion annually. Many observers believe the high trade deficit is evidence that U.S. industry is not competitive. They argue that the U.S. cannot indefinitely continue to buy more than it sells. As author and textiles manufacturer George Vargish writes, "The U.S. is producing less and less of the goods it consumes. Each year we become more dependent upon foreign manufacturers than we were the year before. Where will it all end?"

But other analysts argue that the trade deficit does not signify U.S. economic problems. They contend that all commerce—imports and exports—provides jobs and helps the U.S. economy. Some economists go so far as to conclude that the trade deficit symbolizes U.S. economic strength. Economist Paul Craig Roberts writes that "A trade deficit can be a sign of investor's confidence and serve as a leading success indicator."

The following chapter examines the question of what impact the U.S. trade deficit has on the economy and what role the deficit should play in debate about free trade.

"Evidence indicates that the succession of deep U.S. trade deficits has had a significant net adverse impact on the U.S. economy."

The Trade Deficit Harms the U.S. Economy

Committee for Economic Development

The Committee for Economic Development (CED) is a research and educational organization composed of over two hundred business executives and educators. It publishes periodic reports on U.S. and international economic issues. In the following viewpoint, CED argues that large and persistent trade deficits are detrimental to the U.S. economy. Trade deficits, they argue, cause unemployment, hamper U.S. industry and leave the U.S. in debt to other nations.

As you read, consider the following questions:

1. What industries have been especially affected by the U.S. trade deficit, according to CED?
2. What significant change in U.S. economic status occurred in 1985, according to the authors?
3. Why is CED concerned about the U.S. national debt?

Committee for Economic Development, *Toll of the Twin Deficits.* New York: Committee for Economic Development, 1987. Excerpted with permission.

The U.S. economy has run up huge deficits in its international trade and current-account balances in the 1980s. The 1986 trade deficit reached a record $170 billion (cost, insurance, and freight, or c.i.f., basis), surpassing the previous high of $148 billion in 1985. Such trade imbalances are not characteristic of the U.S. economy. In fact, throughout most of the post-World War II period, this country realized current-account and trade surpluses. U.S. merchandise trade performance deteriorated somewhat in the 1970s, but trade deficits did not become the rule until the 1980s. The current-account balance remained positive until 1982, because of favorable balances in the service and investment income accounts.

The huge deficits in recent years are unsustainable and pose a major threat to the nation's long-term economic growth. The trade deficit now appears to be turning down, but only very gradually. . . .

Current-Account Deficit

A broader measure of a country's performance in international transactions is its current-account balance.

The current account includes not only merchandise trade, but also trade in services, income from international investments, and unilateral transfers. Thus, the current-account balance covers all international transactions except capital flows. Unlike the trade account, the U.S. current account did not start to show a consistent deficit until 1982. In prior years, the worsening trade deficits had been partly offset by surpluses in the services account, particularly net receipts of investment income on U.S. investments abroad. Since 1982, however, the shrinking surpluses in the much smaller services account (particularly in net receipts of investment income abroad, which peaked at $34 billion in 1981) failed to offset the widening U.S. trade deficits, and the total current account also fell into deep deficit.

There is no inherent reason for either a country's trade balance or its current account to be balanced every year. But the deep and prolonged deterioration in both the U.S. trade and current-account balances since 1981 clearly reflects seriously declining competitiveness relative to our trading partners. Today's huge trade deficits and the prospects of continued large deficits in the future have generated grave concerns about the stability of the dollar, the international competitiveness of the U.S. economy, and the ability of the United States to continue its leadership of the free world.

Damage from U.S. Trade Deficits

International trade has strong influences on U.S. economic growth, the level of employment, and the incomes of workers. Recent studies of the impact of U.S. trade deficits lead us to believe that the deepening deficits since 1981 have, on balance, had a significant negative impact on U.S. economic growth and employment. . . .

Although the precise effects are very difficult to estimate, the deterioration in the U.S. trade balance appears to have contributed to the below-average domestic growth rates. From mid-1984 through the end of 1986, the average GNP [gross national product] growth was only about 2 percent a year, well below the estimated potential rate of 3 to 3.5 percent per year.

© Hofoss/Rothco. Reprinted with permission.

A report by the National Association of Manufacturers (NAM) estimates that the annual GNP growth rate would have been about 1.2 percentage points higher during this period if the deficit in net exports of goods and services in our GNP accounts had not worsened. Such foregone GNP growth implies a corresponding lag in the incomes of individuals and businesses.

Unemployment Level

A Department of Commerce economist [David C. Lund] estimates that the U.S. unemployment level would have been 1.1 percentage points lower if the trade deficit had not deteriorated in the 1980-1984 period. He further estimates that the trade-related job loss in the manufacturing sector totaled about 1.2 million to 1.9 million per year in 1984 and 1985, respectively.

Of necessity, such quantitative estimates of the impact of trade deficits are based on numerous assumptions and uncertain data bases. In particular, they implicitly assume that the potential dampening effects on overall demand from budget-deficit reductions that are of key importance in narrowing the trade deficit will be offset by monetary policy actions aimed at achieving a healthy overall growth rate. Such estimates also do not take into account the hard-to-measure secondary effects of trade deficits, such as the possible reemployment of laid-off workers in different sectors of the economy. These feedback effects tend to reduce the degree of negative effects on overall U.S. economic growth and employment. Taking all this into account, however, we believe the evidence indicates that the succession of deep U.S. trade deficits has had a significant net adverse impact on the U.S. economy, especially its manufacturing sector.

Dislocation in Trade-Sensitive Industries

The worsening trade deficits, which represent a net result of the increase in U.S. imports and weak U.S. export growth, have seriously affected those industries that are particularly sensitive to foreign trade. As international competition intensifies, many U.S. manufacturing industries are being confronted with painful problems of sales losses, dislocation, and adjustment. Some of these industries are experiencing shrinking domestic demand for their traditional products as well as growing foreign competition. In many export-dependent industries, U.S. producers are losing world market share. The report of the President's Commission on Industrial Competitiveness warned that even in high-technology industries, which are often regarded as a barometer of international competitiveness, the United States has lost world market share in seven out of ten sectors. The disproportionately large loss of market share in these high-growth and high-technology industries is bound to have enormous implications for future U.S. competitiveness.

International trade accelerates structural changes among industries. Over the long run, foreign trade benefits most industries because it promotes the efficient use of resources. In the short run, however, gains and losses resulting from trade and structural changes are not evenly distributed. Some industries, suffering from import competition and structural changes, create unemployment and hardship for those who lose jobs, even as others create new employment opportunities.

The effects of foreign competition have been most notable in such U.S. industries as steel, automobiles, consumer electronics, textiles, apparel, and shoes. Many firms in these industries were heavily affected. Faced with shrinking sales, declining profits, or drastic changes in market conditions, some companies had to close plants and lay off workers, creating untold hardships for those displaced workers and their communities. . . .

Losing the Trade War

In seven short years, from 1980 to 1987, America went from a relatively comfortable trade position to a humiliating $160 billion deficit. If this had been a seven-year trade war, the United States would have lost battles against every country, leaving our once mighty economy in a perilous condition.

America's defeats on the economic battlefields of Europe were significant, but our heaviest losses shifted from the Atlantic to the Pacific theater, where Asian imports battered our Western frontier. To the north, the United States was in retreat from Canada's preemptive attacks on our domestic economy. The news was not much better on the southern border, where conventional U.S. economic strikes were no longer hitting their targets in debt-ridden Latin American countries.

Even more worrisome was the absence of any overall U.S. strategy to deal with the crisis. Throughout most of the early 1980s, the United States did not realize it was in a trade war, let alone that it was losing badly and retreating in virtually every major sector of the economy.

Don Bonker, *America's Trade Crisis,* 1988.

Although foreign competition has affected many other industries, the steel and auto industries have drawn much public attention in recent years because they are large and geographically concentrated. Consequently, any plant closings and worker layoffs have a particularly large economic impact on the geo graphic areas where the plants are located. Furthermore, these industries have a large multiplier effect (interindustry linkage effect) on other sectors of the economy. More recently, however, the high-tech industries (computers, semiconductors, telecommunications, analytic instruments) have been added to the list of the important U.S. industries that are experiencing strong import competition and a decline in the foreign trade balance. A congressional report on the U.S. trade in high-technology products expressed serious concern about the erosion of U.S. competitiveness in these high-growth industries.

Businesses and workers who have been hard hit by foreign trade competition often feel that the solution to their problem lies in import restrictions and other protectionist trade barriers. But systematic actions to restrict trade do not solve the trade deficit problem; they can only shift the burden of adjustment to other industries. . . .

A more subtle and longer-run adverse influence is the buildup of net U.S. debt to foreigners as private and public entities borrow abroad to pay for their spending. The United States had been a net international creditor since 1914, but the cumulative effects of the rising trade deficits in the 1980s turned this country into a net international debtor by 1985.

World's Largest Debtor

The rising U.S. trade deficits have been financed by net capital inflows, which represent the difference between what the U.S. invests overseas and what foreigners invest here. A preliminary estimate put U.S. net foreign indebtedness through the end of 1986 at about $264 billion, and it is rising at a rate of about $140 billion a year. The fact that the United States has borrowed so much money from foreigners to finance its trade deficit has been a key element in changing it from a net creditor to the world's largest debtor in just three years. The size of this foreign debt is now becoming a burden large enough to affect the country's future prosperity.

Net capital inflows, which finance the trade and current-account deficits, fill a gap between U.S. saving and investment levels. This capital inflow allows the United States to finance its consumption and investment at a time when it is suffering from record budget deficits.

In other words, the inflow allows the United States to live beyond its means.

A more helpful way to analyze this turnaround in the U.S. international investment position is to think of the country as a private household living on credit. The United States borrows from foreigners to finance its current account deficit in the same way a private household buys goods and services using credit cards or consumer loans. . . .

No nation can continue indefinitely to incur very large trade deficits and borrow heavily from abroad to in effect finance its consumption. As in any individual household, eventually it will reach a credit limit. When that credit limit is reached, foreign investors will no longer be willing to accumulate dollar denominated assets. . . .

Potential Dangers

If foreign investors stop all further lending to the United States, this country will be forced to cut back drastically on its imports and its standard of living. In this situation the dollar will have to depreciate far enough to eliminate the current account deficit. At the same time, if the budget deficit is still large, domestic interest rates will have to rise because competition for funds will increase and pressures on domestic saving will be intensified. In the worst case, the United States, as a reserve currency country, could reduce its real debt burden through inflation and the consequent depreciation of the dollar. But such a policy would be extremely risky because it would bring on all the familiar sorrowful consequences of domestic inflation and could eventually set off panic selling of U.S. financial assets. This, in turn, could bring the viability of the entire financial system into question.

Another uncertainty created by the increasing total of U.S. debt held abroad is the need for increased allocation of investment to export industries. Historically, export surpluses have been a chief means of servicing foreign debt, and large international borrowers generally have had to run trade surpluses for this purpose. Because the balance on the U.S. investment income account will soon change to a deficit, the need to achieve a trade surplus by that time becomes doubly important. Otherwise, the total U.S. current-account deficit could worsen at a rapid rate.

Potential Decline in Living Standard

As long as the United States remains a large international borrower for purposes of consumption rather than productive investment, it will eventually have to allocate more resources to the sectors producing exportable goods and away from those sectors catering to domestic demand. This shift will mean a decline in the potential living standard of future U.S. generations, a legacy that no previous generation has passed on to its children since the Civil War. The disappointment and potential disruption that could ensue would be a major challenge to our society.

"The trade deficit is good *for the American economy."*

The Trade Deficit Helps the U.S. Economy

John Rutledge and Deborah Allen

John Rutledge is chairman and Deborah Allen president of the Claremont Economics Institute, a California consulting firm. In the following viewpoint, they argue that the trade deficit benefits the U.S. by providing foreign capital that can be invested in the U.S. economy. They argue against measures to restrict foreign trade and investment.

As you read, consider the following questions:

1. What problem faces the U.S. economy, according to Rutledge and Allen?
2. In what three ways do the authors disagree with the standard view on the cause of U.S. trade deficits?
3. Why do Rutledge and Allen predict that the U.S. will have trade surpluses in the near future?

John Rutledge and Deborah Allen, "We Should Love the Trade Deficit," *Fortune,* February 29, 1988. Copyright © 1988 Time Inc. All rights reserved. Reprinted with permission.

The trade deficit, according to many politicians and economists, is the Darth Vader of the American economy. It exports high-paying manufacturing jobs to low-wage countries, makes us the biggest debtor nation in the world, and threatens to impoverish our children. Having totaled an estimated $173 billion in 1987, critics say, the deficit must be cut at any cost, by raising taxes to discourage Americans from buying foreign goods and by punishing those foreign countries, like Japan and Taiwan, that don't buy enough U.S. products.

We take another view: that the trade deficit is *good* for the American economy. Our highly publicized international indebtedness—the U.S. became a net debtor in 1985 after being a creditor for the better part of this century—represents nothing more than future export sales for American companies. That's because U.S. debts can be repaid only by exporting American-made goods.

America's Money Problem

The U.S. does not have a deficit problem; it has a capital problem. Abnormally low savings rates, tight money, and the loss of a number of tax exemptions in the 1980s have created a great shortage of funds and of capital goods in the American economy. This is much like the capital shortages experienced by Japan and Germany at the close of World War II. The trade deficit is the result of our need for capital flows to redress the nation's shortage.

Basic accounting demands that if you run a deficit, then you must have capital inflows to finance it. But it is also true the other way around: The deficit provides foreigners with the dollars they are now using to make new investments here. As such, the deficit is part of a reverse Marshall Plan, in which the capital-rich countries of the world, like Japan and Taiwan, are investing in the reindustrialization of America. It is the window through which we are importing the machines and other capital goods we need to retool our industrial companies.

During the early part of the decade the strong dollar made capital goods cheaper to import than to produce at home. The failure of U.S. capital goods producers to invest in plant and equipment also meant that these imports were of better quality than the goods we manufactured domestically. Without the trade deficit we could not earn our way back to competing in the world marketplace.

If they are allowed to work their magic without political meddling, the rejuvenating capital flows from abroad are exactly what's needed to push the U.S. trade position from deficit back into surplus. . . . Foreign buyers will be ready then, in effect, to exchange the U.S. stocks, bonds, and office buildings they now own for U.S. exports. But protectionist-minded politicians, particularly in an election year, will likely try to cut the deficit and so dam up those capital flows. It is not the trade deficit but misguided attempts to make it go away that represent the real risk to the world economy—the possibility of a complete trade meltdown and worldwide recession.

Why the Standard View Is Wrong

According to standard arguments, the trade deficit was caused by a consumer spending binge on Hondas, Toyotas, and now Hyundais made with cheap foreign labor. The result was less work and lower incomes for American workers, whose high-paying manufacturing jobs were being exported to Japan, Taiwan, and Korea.

Deficits and Economic Growth

Persistent large trade deficits are supposed to be proof of the loss of American competitiveness. Yet during. . .a period of record trade deficits, average U.S. real economic growth at 4% has been about the same as in Japan (4.2%) and two-thirds more rapid than in Germany (2.4%). U.S. growth in 1982-89 was 44% faster than it was in the 1970s when the trade balance was generally positive. Why? Because these deficits are symptoms of a rejuvenated, not a declining, economy.

Mack Ott, *The Wall Street Journal,* January 19, 1990.

The standard view is wrong on three counts: First, the U.S. economy in the 1980s was the most incredible job-creating machine the world has ever seen. Although America was losing manufacturing jobs until the dollar declined, it has added over 13 million net new jobs since 1980—more than all of Europe has created since 1960. Employment rates are at an all-time high, and unemployment is down to 5.7% of the labor force. New employees aren't all filling low-paying McJobs, either. Any way you measure real output and total income, they have increased significantly in the 1980s.

Second, foreign labor is no longer cheap. On a productivity-adjusted basis, at today's deflated dollar exchange rates, U.S. labor costs are now among the lowest of the major industrial countries. That's a reason why so many foreign and domestic producers are moving plants to the U.S. For the past two years, U.S. manufacturing productivity has apparently grown faster and unit labor costs have fallen further than in Japan. Since 1982 productivity growth in U.S. manufacturing has been running at a phenomenal 4.7% per year, double the 2.4% growth we enjoyed between 1960 and 1982.

Manufacturing labor costs per unit of product have *fallen* by 1.5% per year since 1982, compared with an increase of 4.3% per year from 1960 to 1982. In 1987 the decline in U.S. unit labor costs accelerated to 2.5%. This means that U.S. producers can lower their prices and raise their profits at the same time. And it means American manufacturers are getting more competitive again.

Other Factors

Third, Hondas and other consumer goods are not the only factors in the trade deficit. According to a Morgan Stanley report, *America's Persistent Trade Gap*, by Stephen Roach, capital goods were the single largest contributor to the worsening of the merchandise trade deficit during the 1980s. Measured in 1982 dollars, these imports accounted for $51 billion, or 31%, of the $167 billion swing from a $3 billion surplus in the third quarter of 1980 to a $164 billion deficit in the third quarter of 1987.

The next largest contributor was not cars but industrial supplies and materials, which account for 25%, or $42 billion, of the swing in the trade deficit. Altogether, capital goods and industrial supplies and materials accounted for $93 billion, or 56%, of the swing in the trade deficit, vs. $73 billion, or 44%, of the swing accounted for by autos and other consumer goods. So the ships that arrive in Long Beach haven't been bringing us only Hondas; they have also been unloading the machines and other supplies to help build the Honda factory in Ohio or the Toyota plant in Kentucky.

Since fewer jobs mean fewer votes, however, our fearless leaders are hellbent (for election) to get rid of the trade deficit at any cost. Many of the presidential candidates have announced their intentions to balance trade and reduce imports. Both houses of Congress have passed bills that included measures to restrict trade. The Commerce Department is looking into whether the Japanese are dumping because they are not raising prices fast enough to reflect the full drop in the dollar. The White House and the Treasury Department, while talking free trade out of one side of their mouths, have been dollar-bashing out of the other in an attempt to stanch imports.

These policies have been a total flop. Exports are rising in actual dollars, but the value of imports has risen too, and the trade deficit, like Old Man River, just keeps rolling along. In fact, it seems that the more the Treasury tries to beat the dollar down, the bigger the trade deficit gets.

But this shouldn't worry us, since the capital goods we import are essentially stockpiles of future output waiting to be released by American workers. Adding to our stock of capital goods increases our capacity to produce in the future. This ultimately means lower prices for consumers. For example, we will have the capacity to produce about two million Japanese cars each year right here in the U.S. In an already soft auto market, these extra cars mean better prices for the consumer. Workers who are hired for these new factories will be more productive and better paid. These new jobs will replace the work that will be lost at outdated factories.

Economy Will Adjust

While importing capital goods helps create a trade deficit, employing those capital goods to produce high-quality, low-cost products to take the place of imports and be used for export helps make it go away. For example, every Camry that rolls off the assembly line at Toyota's Georgetown, Kentucky, plant will be sold to one of two kinds of customers. Someone will buy the car who was already going to buy a Toyota, in which case Toyota will have to ship one auto fewer from Japan to the U.S. and the trade deficit will decline. Or, a driver who was going to buy a different car will buy a Camry, which will increase Toyota's U.S. market share and help force U.S. rivals to cut prices or increase quality, becoming more competitive in world markets. The effect is already occurring: The deficit is declining and Toyota's market share is growing.

Not a Sign of Weakness

Having a trade deficit is not a sign of low productivity or economic weakness. Poor, weak countries—like Brazil—can have trade surpluses. Rich, strong countries like us can have trade deficits.

Herbert Stein, *The Wall Street Journal*, May 16, 1989.

Honda likes its U.S. operation so well that it will build a second plant in Ohio to take advantage of our high productivity and low costs. Some of the output from these factories is scheduled for export to Japan and to other countries. Even though the profits may go back to Japan, these exports will have long-term benefits for the U.S.

In the 1990s, when our new low-cost capacity is producing goods to export or to replace imports, the U.S. trade accounts will switch from deficit to surplus in a big hurry. As we argued above, it is not possible to import capital without running a matching trade deficit. In the same way, foreign owners of U.S. assets—the assets they acquired because of our multibillion-dollar net foreign debt position—can cash in and bring their money home only by buying American-made goods. We should view our foreign debts the same way a store looks at customers who hold gift certificates: as future export sales in the cash drawer.

The Flow of Capital

As long as Japan and our trading partners have a large stockpile of funds and the U.S. has an effective capital shortage, private capital is going to flow from those countries where it earns a low return to the high-return U.S. We will continue to have a trade deficit until this capital imbalance is repaired. Attacking foreign investors with protectionist legislation both delays the capital flow we need and makes it, and our stock and bond markets, more volatile. We should be welcoming the capital goods that are reindustrializing American industry and making us competitive again.

"The nation's terrible trade deficit has had devastating effects on employment and production in this country."

The Trade Deficit Creates Massive Unemployment

AFL-CIO Department of Economic Research

What impact the trade deficit has on employment is highly controversial. The following viewpoint is excerpted from a report by the American Federation of Labor-Congress of Industrial Organizations (AFL-CIO). The authors of the report argue that the U.S. trade deficit has resulted in massive unemployment as U.S. factories close down and more work is done overseas. The AFL-CIO is comprised of ninety labor unions with fourteen million members and is the largest organization of its kind in the U.S.

As you read, consider the following questions:

1. What sources do the authors use to support their argument that jobs have been lost because of the trade deficit?
2. In what economic sectors have job losses been most severe, according to the AFL-CIO?
3. How have multinational corporations contributed to the trade deficit, according to the authors?

Excerpted, with permission, from *America's Trade Crisis* by the AFL-CIO Department of Economic Research, Washington, D.C., 1987.

The enormous U.S. trade deficit has caused massive economic upheaval and much individual suffering and now is pushing the U.S. economy to the brink of a recession.

The trade imbalance cost the United States 2.5 million jobs in 1986 alone. Saving those 2.5 million jobs would have reduced the unemployment rate from 7.0 percent to 5.0 percent.

Numerous well-paying and high-quality job opportunities in the middle tier of the nation's income structure are being forfeited. America is losing its middle class—and with that, losing the buying power that made the U.S. market the envy of the world.

The trade gap has already undermined income and equity in the United States, and has contributed to making the U.S. the largest debtor in the world. This represents a heavy burden for members of future generations, who not only are likely to have fewer good job opportunities and slower income growth, but who will also have to repay the burdensome debt to other nations which the United States is now accumulating.

The Trade Gap Has Cut Employment and Incomes

The impact on employment has been severe. The year 1986 was only one of ten post-World War II years with an unemployment rate above 7 percent, yet six of those years were 1981 through 1986 as America's international trade position nosedived. Closer analysis of trade's employment effects reveal that as much as two percent of 1986's 7 percent unemployment rate resulted from the trade imbalance.

While total employment has grown since 1980, that growth has taken place solely in the service sector. Employment in manufacturing has actually declined by some two million jobs. Further, the rate of employment growth since 1980 is 29 percent below average growth rates of the 1970s.

The upheaval within the manufacturing sector has been harsh and tempestuous during the 1980s, and imports arc the source of most of the employment losses. Since peaking in 1979, the jobs in numerous manufacturing industries have plummeted dramatically. Among durable goods manufacturers, lumber, furniture, stone, primary and fabricated metals, machinery, motor vehicles and other transportation equipment have all suffered considerable job losses. In nondurables, employment is down from 1979 levels in food, tobacco, textile, apparel, paper, chemicals, petroleum, and leather. These devastating losses have shattered the livelihoods of millions of families.

In a study of displaced workers released in October 1986, the Bureau of Labor Statistics reported that between 1981 and 1986, 13.1 million lost their jobs to plant closure, slack work or layoffs—years when the nation's trade deficit was growing dramatically. More than five million of these displaced workers had been at their jobs for at least three years. Of these, the survey found that 18 percent remained unemployed and an additional 15 percent had left the workforce entirely. For those fortunate enough to find other jobs, 10 percent were working part-time, and of those securing full-time work, 40 percent were forced to accept lower pay.

Employment Changes in Manufacturing Between 1979 and 1987

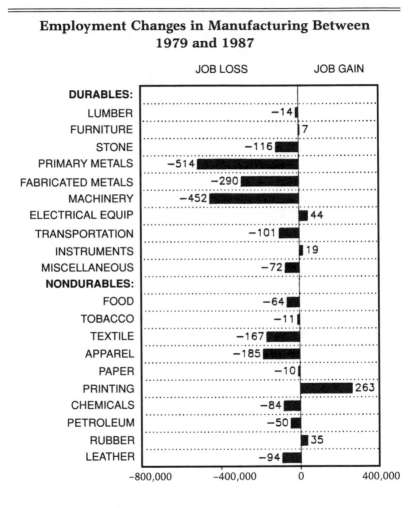

SOURCE: U.S. Bureau of Labor Statistics

Under that impact, average weekly earnings for U.S. non-supervisory employees are currently $305, declining about 7 percent from 1979 to 1986 in constant dollars. The reduction of employment in manufacturing and the growth of jobs in services contributed to this decline in pay. Average weekly earnings for manufacturing workers reached $395 in 1986. Workers averaged $176 in retail trade and $265 in the service industry, two sectors where the employment growth has been largest. In all, 60 percent of the new jobs created since 1979 paid less than $7,000 a year.

The distribution of income among families has also undergone a dramatic shift. For the period from 1980 to 1985, the top 20 percent of all families increased its share of family income to 43.5 percent, the highest concentration in the history of the series which began in 1947. By contrast, the bottom 20 percent of families received only 4.6 percent, the smallest share since 1954.

Hidden Lost Jobs

The jobs lost to the trade deficit have been even greater than seems evident from the above look at the employment trends during the 1980s.

The officially reported net job changes in various industries do not capture all of the jobs lost because of the trade gap. This doesn't mean that the official numbers are wrong; such numbers are properly designed to measure actual employment in each industry. But actual employment levels reflect the influence not of trade alone, but of all the factors that combine to determine employment.

Reported employment doesn't show the job opportunities that would have been available if the nation's trade balance were better. For example, given the growth in the nation's economy and the demand for various goods and services, if trade had been balanced and demands were satisfied to a greater extent by domestic production, many domestic industries that lost jobs would have had job increases, and industries that posted net employment additions would have enjoyed even greater increases.

Further, an evaluation cannot focus just on the direct effects of exports and imports on jobs in each industry, but must also account for the many indirect effects that reverberate throughout the economy.

Trade, Output, and Employment

Several organizations, both public and private, have studied these relationships and traced the myriad interconnections among industries involving trade, output, and employment. Such investigations uniformly demonstrate that the nation's terrible trade deficit has had devastating effects on employment and production in this country, and that manufacturing industries and the regions dependent on manufacturing have suffered the most.

One detailed evaluation of trade's employment impacts, based on the experience in 1984, was published by the U.S. Department of Commerce in January 1986. The United States suffered a $123 billion deficit in its merchandise trade in 1984. Using two different assumptions concerning the composition and size of the trade deficit, the Commerce Department estimated that employment was between 1.3 percent and 2.7 percent lower than it would have been if trade were balanced. This represents between 1.1 and 2.4 million jobs in 1984.

Lost Jobs

The current level of imports is costing us conservatively 460,000 auto jobs, 370,000 apparel jobs, 280,000 in high-tech components, 130,000 in consumer electronics, 67,000 in machine tools, and 66,000 in steel. And these numbers don't include the ripple effect through the economy.

The government's own rule of thumb is that for every billion-dollar increase in our trade deficit, 25,000 American jobs are lost.

Lee A. Iacocca, *Journal of Business Strategy*, Spring 1987.

A third analysis showing an estimated loss of 1.8 million jobs in 1984, assessed trade within the context of the overall economic environment. This approach assumed that the United States would undertake a set of policies designed to bring about a trade balance. These policies included negotiations with other nations that resulted in their reducing trade barriers and unfair trade practices that harm the United States, along with agreements that key trading partners would implement government spending, tax, and monetary measures to boost their economies and thereby help reduce the U.S. trade deficit. The additional element in this phase of the Commerce Department's analysis was the allowance for the feedback from such factors as interest rates and inflation when the pace of the economy quickened because of the trade deficit's decline. Simultaneously, employment and output were traced through the nation's industrial structure, as in the Department's two other analyses.

Updating these job loss estimates to 1986 for the 40 percent deterioration in the nation's trade balance over the last two years indicates that *the United States lost 2.5 million jobs* because of the trade deficit in 1986.

While the influence of the import surge has spread throughout the nation's economy, the harmful effects have disproportionately fallen on particular industries, occupations, and areas. Of the nation's many different products and services, manufacturing has been most heavily affected.

The Commerce Department's estimates, revised to 1986, indicate that job opportunities in U.S. manufacturing dropped most heavily in the following industries: textiles, 631,000; electrical and electronic equipment, 475,000; the three metal industries combined (primary iron and steel, primary nonferrous, and fabricated metal products), 342,000; leather and leather products, 208,000; and motor vehicles, 171,000. . . .

Multinationals

The unrestrained, self-directed actions of U.S.-based multinational corporations have adversely affected America's competitive position in world trade.

Corporations shift the production of goods out of the United States to take advantage of policies of other nations affecting wages and working conditions, labor standards, taxes, and changes in currency values. And they actively seek to shape the national policies that affect them. They can shift U.S. technology and production know how, quickly erasing the technological advantage of the United States in producing goods.

A large share of exports and imports are under the control of multinational corporations. Multinational corporations, in 1983, received 46 percent of all U.S. imports with one-third of their imports shipped by their own affiliates in foreign countries.

The large number of workers employed in foreign countries by American companies shows the size of the foreign production capability of American firms. American multinational companies' employees in other nations now account for 6.6 million or 26 percent of the total; and in manufacturing, foreign employment accounts for 4.8 million or 31 percent of the employment of U.S. multinational manufacturing corporations.

By shifting production abroad, American multinationals can prosper regardless of the health of the U.S. economy. The U.S. share of world trade in manufacturing, for example, fell by 35 percent between the late 1950s and early 1980s. Yet, American multinationals, by shifting their production and exporting from other countries, showed no loss in their share of the world export market. In 1983, almost half of the exports of American multinational corporations came from their production facilities outside of the U.S.

For example, American Telephone and Telegraph recently stopped producing ordinary telephones at its equipment plant in Shreveport, Louisiana, throwing more than 1,000 people out of their jobs. At the same time, AT&T opened a similar production facility in Singapore to export to the U.S. The movement of this production will hasten the end of telephone handset production in the U.S.

The destruction of jobs and production will continue according to the plans of multinational corporations. For example, automakers are planning to buy massive numbers of foreign made cars. Ford has opened a $500 million plant in Mexico which will produce vehicles for the American market. General Motors has a joint venture with Daewoo in Korea to produce cars for the U.S. And Chrysler plans to join with a Taiwanese car company to build a subcompact car that would be exported to the U.S.

The Commerce Department estimates that the practice of American companies selling foreign made cars will raise imports to 40 percent of sales and cost 90,000 more jobs.

In many cases, American multinationals have cut back or ceased production of product lines, preferring to buy foreign made goods and sell the products under the American company's name. Several American companies are buying video cameras, recorders, and other consumer electronic equipment from Japanese companies and putting the American brand name on them. A large computer firm sells two mainframes which it buys from Japan and gets the central processing circuitry ("the brain") for its biggest mainframe from a Japanese manufacturer.

The Destruction of Purchasing Power

The multinationals are buying labor cheap overseas and re-selling products here in the U.S., the country with the greatest consumer market in the world. In the process, however, they are destroying the economic balance which helped to create and sustain the U.S. market. That balance was facilitated by a U.S. system which allowed workers to gain higher wages through collective bargaining as advanced technology was developed and yielded higher productivity. As workers received part of that productivity in higher wages, markets expanded and encouraged further investment and employment. Increased economies of scale then contributed to further productivity gains and permitted wage gains.

Many of the countries in which U.S. multinational corporations are locating new plants have hourly compensation costs for production workers in manufacturing—including wages and salaries, supplements, and employer payments for social security, and other employee benefit plans—which are significantly below those in the United States. Generally, the new plants include the latest production technology and equal or exceed in efficiency the older plants in the United States that have been shut down. The economic balance that sustained a growing market in the U.S. does not prevail in the global economy the way it is reshaped by the multinationals. The U.S. economy and its workers are being affected adversely.

Before too long, because of the lower levels of wages and economic imbalances, the multinationals will have to sell in a world market less affluent than when workers producing the products received a better share of the sales value of the product. Their sales volume, benefits of economies of scale, and profits will be reduced. However, given the drive of U.S. corporate management to show profits in the short run, it is unlikely that changes would occur unless there are changes in laws and policies that affect multinationals.

U.S. trade and tax policies should at least offset the subsidies and labor policies that cause jobs to be moved out of the country.

"There is empirical evidence that imports do not destroy jobs. "

The Trade Deficit Does Not Create Massive Unemployment

Lloyd R. Cohen

Lloyd R. Cohen is an associate professor of law at California Western School of Law in San Diego, and was formerly special counsel to the United States International Trade Commission. In the following viewpoint, he attacks the argument that the U.S. trade deficit creates unemployment. He argues that such a view belies a false understanding of how the job market works. While foreign trade may cause short-term job displacement, Cohen argues, in the long run trade helps the U.S. economy and creates jobs.

As you read, consider the following questions:

1. What premise about trade underlies Cohen's arguments?
2. How are jobs misunderstood by many people, according to the author?
3. Why does Cohen have limited sympathy for steelworkers and others laid off from high-paying jobs?

Lloyd R. Cohen, "'Chicken Little' and the Myth of International Trade." This article appeared in the October 1988 issue and is reprinted with permission from *The World & I,* a publication of The Washington Times Corporation, © 1988.

My analysis. . . is bottomed on a simple premise: The purpose of economic activity is to provide goods and services; the best economies provide those things in as much abundance as cheaply as possible.

Trade Is Good

Let me begin with the widely held and damaging picture of trade as either a zero-sum or negative-sum game. A broadly shared illusion is that the nation would be better off if it did not trade at all. The truth is that foreign trade, like domestic trade, serves to increase the wealth and well-being of countries participating in it. The opposite may sometimes appear to be the case because there will indeed be individuals who will be hurt by increases in trade, and you may be sure that they will make themselves heard. The damage done to these individuals will be more concentrated and visible, and therefore more newsworthy, than the gain to the larger, more diverse and dispersed set of individuals who benefit from the influx of low-priced imports and the resulting growth in exports. Television news lacks the expertise, the format, and the inclination to present a balanced view of trade issues. Thus the public's misunderstanding is reinforced by the six o'clock news. . . .

Although the United States as a whole is better off because inexpensive foreign steel is being imported, there are pockets of workers, investors, or suppliers in the domestic steel industry competing with imported steel who are worse off as a result of trade. Their loss, although it has its origin in imports, is fundamentally no different from any suffered as a result of technological change or the increased bounty of God. Any time products are available more cheaply from an alternative source, those who originally were providing them are likely to suffer.

Absurd Examples

I am reminded of a petition written in jest by the nineteenth-century French economist Frederic Bastiat asking for import relief on behalf of the candlemakers of France. His petition reads: "We are suffering from the intolerable competition of a foreign rival, placed, it would seem, in a condition so far superior to ours for the production of light that he absolutely inundates our national market with it at a price fabulously reduced. The moment he shows himself our trade leaves us—all consumers apply to him; and a branch of native industry, having countless ramifications, is all at once rendered completely stagnant." This fiendish competitor was none other than the sun. The petition requested that all buildings be required to shut their windows.

We need not resort to fiction to illustrate the point. From 1811 to 1816 in England, groups of workers known as Luddites rioted and destroyed property in an effort to prevent the use of more productive labor-saving machinery. Another illustration, closer to home, comes from western Pennsylvania. Prior to this century, the gauge of railroads was not the uniform 4 feet 8 1/2 inches that it is now. The attempt to create such uniformity led to bloody riots in Erie, Pennsylvania, in 1853. Erie was a junction where three different widths of railroad gauge met. Hundreds of residents were profitably employed loading and unloading the trains, jacking up the cars, and replacing the wheels. Naturally they were quite exercised over the prospect of losing so many well-paying jobs when the railroads sought to make the gauge uniform. At one point, a mob of women took sledgehammers and tore up the tracks. Fortunately neither the Luddites nor the women of Erie succeeded in stemming the tide of progress.

Jobs and Deficits

From 1982 to 1986, while the trade deficit soared, the United States created jobs three times as fast as Japan and 20 times as fast as West Germany; America's GNP [gross national product] grew 43 percent faster than that of Japan or West Germany in that time, though both nations have huge trade surpluses with the United States.

The fact is that surpluses or deficits in the balance of trade—in and of themselves—are neither good nor bad. They are not correlated with growth, decline, competitiveness, or noncompetitiveness. What matters is *why* they occur.

Phil Gramm, *The World & I,* May 1987.

Although these examples appear absurd, they are fundamentally no different in their effect or reasoning from any plea for import relief. Whether a valuable product arrives in our market as a result of technological change, manna from heaven, or—more prosaically—from the hard work and productivity of Korean steelworkers, you may be assured that some domestic competitor will suffer as a result and will attempt to protect his welfare, even if this imposes a much higher cost on the rest of the nation. Most economic change entails gains to some and losses to others. If improvement in the material condition of all people were a political prerequisite of all economic change, our economy would still be mired in the misery of feudalism.

Trade and Jobs

This brings us to another myth about international trade. The most frequently voiced objection to imports is that they destroy jobs. This misunderstanding results from focusing on the trees, branches, and twigs rather than on the forest. First, it fails to reflect the fact that, in general, nations *must* export in order to import. For example, when the Koreans sell us steel, they wind up with U.S. dollars. Those dollars can only be used directly, or indirectly, to purchase products or services in this country. Though U.S. dollars may take a while to get back to us, foreign countries will ultimately use our currency to purchase from us. In the long run, we can expect that there will be jobs created in exporting industries to replace those lost in our import-competing industries.

It is true that if the Koreans do not spend their dollars, or alternatively decide to lend those dollars back to us, a trade deficit will result and our export industries will not prosper. We are suffering from such a trade deficit. In 1984 it reached $123 billion and continued to rise until a drop in December 1987 and January 1988. Some pundits have asserted that for every billion dollars of trade deficit, twenty-five thousand jobs are lost. There is a grain of truth in this. In the short run, before an economy can make any adjustments, workers in import-affected industries will be displaced by those imports. However, I believe that the tendency to focus on this short-run relationship between imports and jobs reflects a pervasive misunderstanding about jobs.

How the Market Functions

Too many people view the labor market as consisting of a necessarily limited number of jobs. Under this view, if a job is eliminated by imports, there is no replacement. But as long as our wants are not limited, neither are the jobs to be done. The very reason that jobs are lost in import-affected industries is that labor is more highly valued elsewhere. The reason that automatic elevators have largely eliminated the occupation of elevator operator is that in a capital-rich, technologically advanced economy such as ours, even unskilled labor is too valuable to waste on operating elevators. The market sends the signals and performs the task of shifting people out of an occupation by raising the wage rates to such a level that it is sensible to install automatic elevators as a cheaper substitute. In precisely the same spirit, the international trade market sends a signal to our unskilled labor-intensive industries, such as textiles, that labor is too valuable a resource to be wasted on such an activity, that their products can be provided to consumers more cheaply by imports. The workers can almost always be assimilated into some other productive activity at essentially the same wage. Naturally this is not a costless or painless process, but it can be and is done.

I hear you asking: "What about the steelworkers? What about highly paid workers who lose their jobs as a result of imports, and who have no comparable employment available to them?"

In the jargon of economics, these steelworkers are earning "economic rents." Economic rents are payments above what workers could earn in their next best opportunity.

Other Causes

It should be noted that the effect of trade on long-term employment is generally small when compared to other determinants of employment, even though in a protectionist environment all job losses are attributed to trade. For example, recent estimates indicate that in the steel industry, 209,000 jobs were eliminated between 1976 and 1983 because of a long-term decline in the demand for steel while only 37,000 jobs were lost (reallocated) because of import competition. The recessionary difficulties of the late 1970s and early 1980s accounted for the loss of another 27,000 jobs.

J.R. Kearl, *The Freeman*, October 1986.

How is it that steelworkers earn twenty-two dollars an hour, a wage twice as high as what they could receive anywhere else? What are the implications of this? Through their union, steelworkers have managed to exclude from their labor market millions of workers who would willingly do the same work at considerably less than the union wage. My sympathy for the plight of steelworkers who lose their jobs as a result of cheap foreign steel is counterbalanced by my conviction that fairness is not served by forcing consumers to pay to protect the economic rents that steelworkers receive by preventing other workers from competing with them.

A Long-Term View

Jobs are not a benefit that we should seek to preserve, but a cost that we should seek to eliminate. The more jobs that we can eliminate either through technology or imports, the more labor we can free for other productive activities. This is sometimes not immediately apparent when we focus on the short-run effect on a small industry. But fortunately it becomes obvious when we examine changes in a large industry over a long time. The farming industry is a very good illustration. For most of human history, the vast majority of mankind was employed in agriculture. Even shortly before the turn of the century, half of the population of this country lived on farms. Now it has fallen to less than 5 percent. What would life be like if an additional 45 percent of the labor force had to return to the farm in order to produce enough food to feed the nation? Obviously we would be much poorer. The changes in technology, increases in capital, and improved organization that *destroyed* jobs in this industry thereby freed that labor for the productive nonfarm employment that gives this nation a prosperous way of life. We should seek to consume as much as we would like with as little work as possible, not to work more for less.

Another illustration is provided by the telephone industry. Historically, most telephone operators have been women. If we were still switching telephone calls today as we were in 1920, most of the working women in America would be telephone operators—otherwise, our phone system would not be capable of handling the current level of phone calls. Technological change has destroyed the jobs of all those women. Lo and behold: They are not in unemployment lines or on welfare. They are employed. I cannot emphasize too strongly that goods and services are of value. Jobs are merely a cost of achieving that end.

Imports Do Not Destroy Jobs

Although I hate to even acknowledge the argument that trade destroys jobs, it keeps cropping up and needs to be countered by every available weapon. In summary: First, focusing on jobs is, in effect, trying to maximize inputs, which should not be our concern. Second, the dollars we send abroad come back one way or another to fuel investment, consumption, or government spending. Finally, there is empirical evidence that imports do not destroy jobs.

While our trade deficit rose to one hundred billion dollars in 1984 from a surplus of nine billion dollars in 1980, employment also rose by seven million and labor-force participation by half of a percent. At the same time, the Europeans virtually eliminated their trade deficit and, nonetheless, experienced no increase in employment. The explanation of this seeming paradox is that the level of employment is not determined by the presence or absence of a trade deficit, but rather by the number of people who want to work at a wage that does not exceed the value of their productivity. . . .

A Changing World

Some readers, I am sure, are tempted to respond by asserting that all that I have written may have once been true, but that the world has changed and the old verities no longer hold. My response is that the world has changed and the old verities are more important than ever! How has the world changed? Over the last several hundred years, there has been a relative decline in the costs of transportation and communication over distance. In other words, the cost of moving a ton of wheat one hundred miles has fallen farther and faster than the cost of the wheat. And the cost of finding out the price of wheat and establishing credit in a market one hundred miles distant has fallen still faster, particularly in the last forty years. As a result, foreign trade and international capital movements, which are ultimately driven by comparative advantage and constrained by transportation and transaction costs, have become a more prominent part of all economies.

Substantial Gains in Wealth

As the transportation and transaction costs have fallen, more trade opportunities have opened up. The gains from trade have always been of material importance to the welfare of the citizens of all countries, but now that the costs constraining trade have fallen, the gains in wealth have become more substantial. At the same time, of course, domestic firms are subject to even more competition. To those firms who lose as a result, this increased trade is a disaster. For the nation as a whole, however, it is a wondrous benefit. Yes, the game has changed. It is better. There is more to be gained from trade and more to be lost from artificial restraints.

Recognizing Statements That Are Provable

We are constantly confronted with statements and generalizations about social and moral problems. In order to think clearly about these problems, it is useful if one can make a basic distinction between provable statements for which evidence can be found and unprovable statements which cannot be verified because evidence is not available, or the issue is so controversial that it cannot be definitely proved.

Readers should be aware that magazines, newspapers, and other sources often contain statements of a controversial nature. The following activity is designed to improve your skill at distinguishing between statements that are provable and those that are not.

The following statements are taken from the viewpoints in this chapter. Consider each statement carefully. *Mark P for any statement you believe is provable. Mark U for any statement you feel is unprovable because of the lack of evidence. Mark C for any statement you think is too controversial to be proved to everyone's satisfaction.*

If you are doing this activity as a member of a class or group, compare your answers with those of other class or group members. Be able to defend your answers. You may discover that others come to different conclusions than you. Listening to the reasons others present for their answers may give you valuable insights into recognizing statements that are provable.

> P = *provable*
> U = *unprovable*
> C = *too controversial*

203

1. The trade deficit totaled $173 billion in 1987.

2. During the 1980s, the United States created jobs three times as fast as Japan and twenty times as fast as West Germany.

3. America's huge deficits pose a major threat to the nation's long-term economic growth.

4. U.S. labor costs are now among the lowest of the major industrial countries.

5. It is not the trade deficit but misguided attempts to make it go away that represent the real risk to the world economy.

6. U.S. employment rates are at an all-time high.

7. The United States has lost 2.5 million jobs because of the trade deficit.

8. While total employment has grown since 1980, that growth has taken place solely in the service sector.

9. By shifting production abroad, American corporations can prosper regardless of the health of the U.S. economy.

10. U.S. trade and tax policies need to offset the subsidies and labor policies that cause jobs to be moved out of the country.

11. Multinational corporations, by buying cheap labor overseas and reselling products here in the U.S., destroy the economic balance that helps to sustain the U.S. market.

12. Sixty percent of the new jobs created since 1989 pay less than seven thousand dollars a year.

13. Foreign trade serves to increase the wealth and well-being of countries participating in it.

14. The United States has borrowed so much money from foreigners to finance its trade deficit, it has become the world's largest debtor.

15. American steelworkers earn twenty-two dollars an hour, a wage twice as high as what they could receive anywhere else.

16. America's trade deficits are symptoms of a rejuvenating, not a declining, economy.

17. America is losing its middle class.

18. Sales and profits will decrease in the long run because multinational corporations will have to sell to a world market whose workers are less well off.

Periodical Bibliography

The following articles have been selected to supplement the diverse views presented in this chapter.

C. Fred Bergsten	"Attacking the Deficits Now Will Bring Years of Prosperity," *Fortune*, January 2, 1989.
Willard C. Butcher	"Action Time for the Trade Deficit," *Vital Speeches of the Day*, February 15, 1990.
Edmund Faltermayer	"Is 'Made in the U.S.A.' Fading Away?" *Fortune*, September 24, 1990.
Roger Nils Folson and Rodolfo Alejo Gonzalez	"U.S. Trade Deficits Aren't a Problem," *The Freeman*, August 1990. Available from The Foundation for Economic Education, Irvington-on-Hudson, New York 10533.
George Gilder	"Trade Gap Is Inevitable—and Good," *The Wall Street Journal*, January 15, 1988.
William R. Hawkins	"Whose Wealth of Whose Nation?" *Chronicles*, January 1990.
Richard T. McCormack	"Competitiveness in the Global Marketplace," *Department of State Bulletin*, July 1989.
Richard B. McKenzie	"American Competitiveness—Do We Really Need to Worry?" *The Public Interest*, Winter 1988.
Paul Magnusson et al.	"Will We Ever Close the Trade Gap?" *Business Week*, February 27, 1989.
Mack Ott	"Trade Deficit Myths," *The Wall Street Journal*, January 19, 1990.
C.K. Prahalad	"The Changing Nature of Worldwide Competition," *Vital Speeches of the Day*, April 1, 1990.
Robert B. Reich	"Who Is Us?" *Harvard Business Review*, January/February 1990.
Paul Craig Roberts	"Time to Trade in Our Old Notions About Deficits," *Business Week*, November 13, 1989.
Abu K. Selimuddin	"The Selling of America," *USA Today*, March 1989.
Herbert Stein	"Don't Worry About the Trade Deficit," *The Wall Street Journal*, May 16, 1989.
Langdon Winner	"Let Them Eat Competitiveness," *Technology Review*, August/September 1988.

What Is the Future of the World Trading System?

Chapter Preface

A major issue confronting the world trading system is the uncertain fate of the General Agreement on Tariffs and Trade (GATT). Established in 1947 with twenty-three signatory countries, the agreement sought to establish rules of trade to which all member countries would agree. Such a multilateral agreement was thought necessary to prevent a repeat of the trade wars of the 1930s, in which countries enacted protectionist trade barriers to cope with economic depression and retaliate against other countries' trade barriers. The resulting collapse of trade made the worldwide depression worse and was one of the contributing causes to World War II.

GATT successfully prevented a repeat of the 1930s disaster and increased its membership to 107 countries. Through several rounds of negotiations, GATT made significant progress in reducing tariffs and other barriers to free trade. But as international trade grew in both size and complexity, negotiations to liberalize trade became more difficult.

These difficulties cause some people to argue that GATT is obsolete. "Multilateral free trade is a thing of the past," writes business columnist Douglass F. Lamont. Lamont and others argue that, rather than relying on GATT, the U.S. should instead negotiate trade agreements with other countries on an individual or bilateral basis.

The 1989 U.S.-Canada Free Trade Agreement and the economic unification of the European Community in 1992 are bellwethers of a development some observers believe will supersede GATT: the rise of rival trading blocs consisting of nations with free trade agreements among them, but restricting trade with outsiders. Most forecasters, including economist Jeffrey E. Garten, foresee three blocs: a unified European bloc, an American bloc composed of nations in North and possibly South and Central America, and an Asian bloc led by Japan.

Disagreements exist, however, on whether such a scenario is likely, and whether it would repeat the harmful trade wars of the 1930s. The viewpoints in the following chapter examine several predictions for world trade, and how the U.S. might be affected.

"We are operating with an obsolete American trade policy."

The U.S. Should Abandon the General Agreement on Tariffs and Trade

Pat Choate and Juyne Linger

U.S. trade policy since World War II has been based on the General Agreement on Tariffs and Trade (GATT), which is designed to liberalize trade among all of its member countries. In the following viewpoint, Pat Choate and Juyne Linger argue that GATT has become obsolete. The member countries operate under a variety of economic systems, they argue, and a single trade agreement involving all countries is no longer possible. Choate and Linger conclude that the U.S. should negotiate separate trade agreements with each country rather than continue with GATT. Choate is a former director of Policy Analysis for TRW, a U.S. aerospace and defense company. Juyne Linger is an economics consultant and author. Together they have written many articles and the book *The High-Flex Society: Shaping America's Economic Future.*

As you read, consider the following questions:

1. What two outdated premises do Choate and Linger believe underlie U.S. trade policy?
2. How do the authors classify the world's differing economic systems?
3. What advantages do Choate and Linger see in bilateral trade arrangements?

Pat Choate and Juyne Linger, written testimony submitted to the U.S. Senate Subcommittee on International Trade, of the Committee on Finance, March 13, 1989.

The United States is floundering in the global marketplace, incurring devastating losses in market position, profits, equity, and jobs. The real problem is less with America's products than it is with America's trade policy. We face the prospect of continuing economic loss until American business and political leaders recognize the fundamental differences between U.S. and foreign economic systems. Today the key trade issue is not free trade versus protectionism but diminishing trade versus expanding trade.

We are operating with an obsolete American trade policy, an artifact of the mid-1940s when the United States and Britain dominated the global economy, tariffs were the principal obstacle to trade, and U.S. supremacy was uncontested in virtually all industries. In the intervening decades, economic circumstances have shifted radically. United States trade policy has not.

Today America's trade policy seems frozen by intellectual and political inflexibility, paralyzed by the relentless conflict between proponents of "free" and "fair" trade. The free traders argue that American markets should be open, and the movement of goods and services across national borders unrestrained. The fair traders assert that access to American markets should be restricted until U.S. businesses are granted equal access to foreign markets. They contend that free trade is impossible as long as other nations erect barriers to U.S. exports.

Outdated Premises

Of course, both are correct: fair trade requires equal access and equal access leads to free trade. The problem is that both sides base their positions on the same two long-held and now outdated premises:

1. Global commerce is conducted under the terms of the General Agreement on Tariffs and Trade (GATT) and dominated by the United States and similar economic systems abroad.

2. Multilateral negotiations are the most effective way to resolve pressing trade issues.

Both assumptions are wrong. The 40-year-old GATT now covers less than 7% of global commerce and financial flows. More important, world trade is no longer dominated by the free-trade economies. . . .

The loss of dominance by the free-trade economies must bring a dramatic shift in the overall goal of U.S. trade policy. The United States has long operated on the premise that a multilateral world requires multilateral negotiations. But reliance on multilateral negotiations has become a risky proposition at best. The bulk of U.S. trade negotiating efforts over the past four decades has taken place in multilateral talks under the auspices of the GATT. Indeed, U.S. policymakers have mistaken the

GATT negotiation process for an end in itself. Making the GATT work has become an American trade objective. But as the number of GATT signatories has more than quadrupled from 23 countries in 1948 to 94 today, the task of forging a multilateral trade policy consensus has become virtually impossible.

The new players—all with their own trade objectives and most with economic systems unlike Uncle Sam's—are often reluctant to engage in substantive multilateral trade negotiations. When nations finally do confer, moreover, new rules come slowly: the Tokyo Round of trade talks began in 1973 and did not end until 1979.

Evading GATT

More and more, trade flows are governed by arrangements made outside the GATT framework. The GATT now covers, at most, 50 percent of world trade, as countries have sought special arrangements for the industries they consider most important. The United States appears to be a particularly prominent violator of the GATT, but this may be because measures are debated openly in the United States and are exercised in a far less subtle fashion. (It is an interesting question whether this can be attributed to American naïveté in international negotiations or to the residual attitude of a hegemonist.) Europeans seem more accomplished at giving the appearance of technical compliance with the GATT, while subverting it in substance.

Timothy Wendt, *Proceedings of the Academy of Political Science*, vol. 37, no. 4, 1990.

While multilateral talks drag on, the United States misses opportunities for international economic cooperation and trade expansion. The new reality is that a multilateral world requires more options, both inside and outside the GATT, than multilateral negotiations provide. . . .

Five Economic Systems

Five types of economic systems confront the United States. Four of them are not founded on our free-trade economic model: centrally planned (like the Soviet Union); mixed (France); developing (Mexico); and plan-driven (Japan). Only the Anglo-American system is rooted in a free- and fair-trade approach.

Within this framework, there are, of course, variations. The mixed economy of France differs in many ways from the mixed economy of Sweden; Japan's version of a plan-driven system differs from South Korea's plan-driven economy; and even between America and Canada there are clear distinctions. Yet each model possesses characteristics that are important to the design of future U.S. trade policies. It is possible, for example, to sketch the differences among the five systems by comparing them along four dimensions: the role of government in the economy; the ownership of industry; the relationship between process and results in the system; and how trade is conducted.

In the rule-driven, market-oriented Anglo-American economic model, for instance, government sets the economic backdrop but takes few direct positions on which industries should exist, grow, or decline. In contrast, plan-driven economies, like Japan's, and mixed economies, like Sweden's, skillfully blend the strength of government with the flexibility of the marketplace. Once decisions are made, government backs them with resources and, at strategic moments, with trade protection.

In free-market and plan-driven economies, private ownership of business and industry is the rule. The mixed economies, like France's, are based on a combination of state and private ownership, market and nonmarket decisions. Major industries are either owned by the state or tightly regulated. The major enterprises in the centrally planned economies, of course, are state owned.

Rules vs. Results

The Anglo-American economies are process oriented; once rules are established, market processes dominate.The plan-driven economies are results oriented; business and government shape a national "vision" that often includes targeting certain industries like semiconductors or computers. To guide the economy toward desired results, governments of plan-driven economies will provide special financing, encourage joint research, and offer adjustment assistance like worker retraining. The mixed economies rely on a combination of market processes and government planning. The command economies are dominated by state planning.

The process-oriented Anglo-American economics are heavily influenced by economists and lawyers who make, interpret, and enforce the rules under which market processes operate. Because the plan-driven economies are results oriented, they have far less need for lawyers and economists to make and enforce rules. As recently as the mid-1970s, Japan's huge Ministry of International Trade and Industry had only two Ph.D. economists. Instead, politicians and business leaders direct the results-oriented economies. In trade talks, therefore, U.S. and Japanese trade negotiators often have different orientations: the Americans focus on rules that will facilitate market processes while the Japanese focus on measures that can advance their national economic vision. . . .

In fashioning their economic systems, the developing nations have borrowed from each of the other four systems, patching together combinations of public and private sector initiatives. In virtually all these countries, however, government predominates in designing and implementing a national trade strategy.

American policymakers, devoted to free trade and open markets, have ignored the often vast differences between U.S. and foreign economic systems. Rather, they still operate on the free-trade premise that policies that are neutral to the fate of American industries will produce the same market-oriented benefits globally as they do domestically. Consequently, American trade policies are doing enormous harm to U.S. industry.

Even where there is ample evidence of harm—as in the case of consumer electronics—industries have been unable to get relief from predatory foreign practices like dumping, theft of American intellectual property, foreign regulation that forces U.S. companies to move plants and jobs offshore as a condition of market entry, and nontariff barriers that restrict exports of America's most competitive goods and services. Free-trade advocates have exacerbated the problem of gaining legitimate relief by discrediting reciprocal market access as a negotiating strategy. And they mistakenly brand tough negotiating tactics as protectionism.

Multilateral negotiations via the GATT have been unable to bridge the differences among the world's five economic systems. If we continue to depend on these agreements, the United States must resign itself to failure. . . .

Two Courses

Despite America's spirited urging of other nations to adopt the U.S. economic model—reliance on market forces, free trade, and deregulation—this system has enjoyed little appeal abroad. It suits us, but it would never fit many other nations—and they know it. Consequently, U.S. trade policy is at a crossroads: we can either continue to urge other nations to adopt our free-trade economic model or we can change U.S. trade policy to deal with other nations as they are, rather than as we wish they would be.

Clearly, only the second course makes sense. It is pure folly for us to presume that we can somehow convince other nations to abandon economic systems that serve their interests and adopt a system that serves ours. Nor can we blindly continue to look the other way. America can no longer afford its missionary work on behalf of global free trade. When the United States had huge trade surpluses and was the world's largest creditor, we could afford to give other nations special trade concessions as a means of inducing them to become free traders. But now that the United States has chalked up an unprecedented $400 billion in indebtedness and faces unprecedented trade deficits far into the future, a "beggar thyself" policy to help our neighbors is impractical. We need a new U.S. trade strategy. . . .

There is a recent benchmark for such a strategy: the newly negotiated U.S.-Canadian bilateral trade pact. This agreement—a strong sign that the otherwise arthritic U.S. trade strategy may have some flexibility—has produced a sweeping change in the trade arrangements between the world's two largest trading partners. It created a framework and time schedule for eliminating tariff and nontariff trade barriers between them. Moreover, the U.S.-Canada talks were completed in less than 16 months, breakneck speed for trade negotiations. And they were comprehensive, covering imports, exports, and investment.

No Enforcement

The GATT dispute-settlement mechanisms are ambiguous, slow, and unenforceable. For example, the United States pleaded unsuccessfully for 12 years for the European Community (EC) to reduce its import barriers to American citrus. In 1982, the United States took the issue to the GATT; in 1985, a GATT panel found in favor of the United States; the EC ignored these findings, precipitating a minor trade war. This example is so common that most nations are unwilling to involve the GATT in trade disputes.

Pat Choate and Juyne Linger, *Harvard Business Review*, January/February 1988.

At the same time that the two nations established a larger framework for their bilateral trade, they addressed and partially resolved several thorny micro issues, such as the 1965 Automotive Products Trade Agreement and Canadian restrictions on U.S. investment. Finally, and perhaps most important, the agreement established a powerful and quick dispute-settlement mechanism, based on arbitration panels composed of experts. . . .

Bilateral Agreements

Bilateral arrangements have their limitations, of course. They would expand trade, for example, but only between the participating countries. Moreover, a system of global trade based exclusively on bilateral or "plurilateral" (involving several nations with mutual interests) relations could easily create so much fragmentation and discrimination that net global trade would be reduced.

When carefully drawn, however, bilateral or plurilateral arrangements can also facilitate the expansion of trade. Such arrangements are quite common; most other nations conclude them as a matter of course. As the U.S.-Canadian agreement illustrates, these agreements have great potential for expanding U.S. trade.

A tailored-trade approach would elevate bilateral and plurilateral negotiations from a secondary to a primary role. This would enable American representatives to match the negotiations to the economic system with which we were negotiating. For example, talks would draw free-trade arrangements with free-trade economies, managed-trade agreements with managed-trade economies, and appropriately tailored, mixed agreements with those economic systems in between. At the same time, there are some crosscutting issues, such as improved protection of intellectual property rights, that need to be negotiated across the five economic systems in either a plurilateral or multilateral forum. . . .

Top priority should go to the most pressing trade issues. Almost two-thirds of the U.S. trade deficit in recent years has been with Canada, Japan, South Korea, Taiwan, and Germany. It is only common sense that we seek bilateral negotiations with these countries. Rather than wait for cumbersome multilateral talks to grind forward, the United States should quickly seek direct negotiations aimed at reducing current imbalances. The Canadian pact shows that this approach will work. And it should show the other countries that agreement has benefits.

While the goal of a tailored-trade strategy will always remain the same—to expand trade—the focus and negotiating tactics will vary from one economic system to the next. . . .

Future of GATT

Tailored-trade agreements need to be supplemented by negotiations on crosscutting issues, problems that are part of the current global economy regardless of economic system. Counterfeiting, for instance, concerns several advanced industrial nations, including Britain, Japan, and Sweden, each of which operates with a different system. Another worry is the burgeoning number of offset requirements—arrangements that vary in complexity from barter requirements to complicated coproduction and technology transfer requirements. Plurilateral negotiations are best for addressing such issues.

If there is a future for the GATT, it is as a second-tier forum in which to resolve issues like these. There will always be problems of definition—what constitutes a government subsidy, for example—which can be tossed to the GATT to handle. But the United States ought not to deceive itself about the future role of the GATT or the best way to represent America's interests in the global economy. A tailored-trade strategy can give America the means and flexibility to expand commerce with other nations by bridging economic differences and making U.S. trade policy far less ideological and far more practical.

"We should not be distracted by current tensions into wrecking the multilateral trade system. "

The U.S. Should Strengthen the General Agreement on Tariffs and Trade

Robert E. Litan and Peter O. Suchman

Robert E. Litan is a senior fellow in the Economic Studies Program in the Brookings Institute, a liberal Washington, D.C. think tank. Peter O. Suchman is an attorney specializing in international trade law. In the following viewpoint, they argue that the U.S. should maintain its historical commitment to the General Agreement on Tariffs and Trade (GATT). Litan and Suchman refute the argument that U.S. trade policy no longer fits world economic realities, and assert that U.S. leadership in world trade is more necessary today than ever.

As you read, consider the following questions:

1. What principles have formed the basis of international trading success, according to Litan and Suchman?
2. What factors have led to doubts over U.S. trade policy, according to the authors?
3. What problems do Litan and Suchman see with bilateral trade arrangements?

Robert E. Litan and Peter O. Suchman, "U.S. Trade Policy at a Crossroads," *Science*, vol. 247, (5 January 1990), pp. 33-38. Copyright 1990 American Association for the Advancement of Science. Reprinted with permission.

Since the end of World War II the United States has been perhaps the leading advocate among industrialized nations of liberalized international trade. It was the motivating force behind the General Agreement on Trade and Tariffs (GATT), the seven major trade negotiations pursued under its auspices, and the significant reductions in tariffs that these negotiations have produced.

Tariff liberalization, quite predictably, has promoted both trade and interdependence. The ratio of world exports to gross national product (GNP) has climbed throughout the postwar era, especially in the last two decades. This is a healthy development. It implies that nations increasingly have found it cheaper to buy their goods abroad than to produce them at home, affording consumers around the world a wider choice of goods at less cost than if nations had continued to hide behind the high tariffs that they introduced in the 1930s.

Two Principles

Two principles underlie this success. First, the widespread reductions in tariff barriers were made possible only through multilateral bargaining. The industrialized countries formed GATT largely because of the economies in negotiation that could be purchased if a large number of countries reduced their trade barriers simultaneously rather than successively on a bilateral basis over a long period of time. Second, the GATT members agreed on the rules that should govern trade rather than on the results—import and export levels and balances of trade—that individual countries might find desirable or appropriate. In addition, the GATT parties agreed on a framework for resolving bilateral disputes over particular rules.

In the last few years, however, many in the U.S. academic, business, and policy-making communities have raised significant questions about each of these principles. The critics argue that the GATT multilateral framework is no longer viable: it is unsuited for reducing nontariff barriers, it lacks an effective enforcement mechanism, and the members themselves have lost interest in continued negotiations. One prominent economist, Lester Thurow, has even pronounced the GATT to be dead. The preferred alternative is bilateral or regional trade negotiations or even "free trade arrangements" (FTAs), such as those the United States completed with Israel and Canada.

Thurow and other critics go one step further. In their view, the new less-than-multilateral negotiations should specify outcomes. Unlike tariffs, which are easily observable and readily monitored, many nontariff barriers can be invisible and inherently difficult, if not impossible, to negotiate away. Results rather than rules should therefore become the centerpiece of trade negotiations.

216

There are many indications that support within the United States for the rules-oriented, multilateral approach to freer trade is rapidly eroding and that U.S. trade is indeed at a critical crossroad. In this article, we discuss the reasons for this trend, distinguishing along the way fact from myth. We then outline the major shifts in trade policy that critics of the old regime have advanced. We conclude that the critics are wrong. It is in the interest of the United States to vigorously renew its commitment to reducing trade barriers on a multilateral basis without specifying trade outcomes. But this country is unlikely to be successful unless it also undertakes certain measures at home to attack the major sources of current trade tensions.

Growth of World Trade

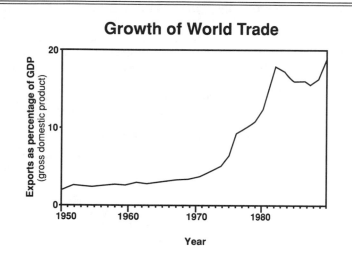

International Monetary Fund, *International Financial Statistics*, 1989.

[Several] key factors have been undermining the commitment of U.S. policy-makers and business leaders to the GATT framework.

The trade deficit. The dominant influence, unrelated to the operation of the GATT, is the dramatic deterioration in U.S. trade performance. From a positive $7 billion balance in 1981, the U.S. current account (which includes trade in both goods and services) fell to a deficit of $154 billion only 6 years later, before improving modestly in 1988 to $144 billion. . . .

The Cold War and Trade

A multipolar world. Perhaps no event in the 1980s has been more unexpected than the significant easing of East-West tensions. At the same time, U.S. economic hegemony has disappeared. The United States is now a net debtor nation, owing increasing sums to Japan, the FRG [Federal Republic of Germany], Taiwan, and other nations with large trade surpluses. In short, in both economic and political spheres the bipolar world that we lived in before 1980 has been replaced by a world increasingly governed by multiple centers of economic and political strength.

Paradoxically, the emergence of a multipolar world may be weakening commitments to the system of multilateral trade rules and negotiations. The GATT was formed in 1948 very much as the free world economic counterpart to the formal and informal political-military alliances formed between the United States and many other countries after World War II. In particular, at least in its early stages, the GATT was dominated by the United States and was seen in a bipolar context. The Soviet Union was not a founding member and still does not belong today, although recently it has expressed interest in joining. . . .

Weaknesses in the GATT. Finally, the GATT itself has weaknesses. These have existed since the GATT was formed, but they have been seen as more irritating as tariff barriers have been reduced and as other trade tensions have surfaced.

No Enforcement Mechanism

First, the GATT lacks an effective enforcement mechanism. Ironically, it was the U.S. Congress that was primarily responsible for this defect when it rejected the formation of a multilateral enforcement arm for GATT, the International Trade Organization. Second, the GATT fails to cover large areas of trade: agricultural products, services, and textiles (governed by a multicountry system of quotas arranged under the Multi-Fiber Arrangement).

Third, and perhaps most important, an increasing share of trade within the industrialized countries is being burdened by nontariff trade barriers, especially so-called "voluntary restraint agreements" (VRAs) designed to circumvent the letter of the GATT. VRAs are technically legal because they are negotiated "voluntarily" between importing countries, such as the United States (one of the worst offenders in the 1980s, with restrictions on imports of steel and automobiles), and their exporting trading partners. But the "voluntariness" of VRAs is clearly a fiction, and it is widely understood that they run afoul of the spirit of the GATT.

To many, the weaknesses in the GATT highlight the futility of the organization and the multilateral process of negotiation that it represents and encourages. To others, the missing links in the GATT, much like the nuclear weapons stockpiles of the major military powers, represent challenges for future negotiators to overcome. . . .

The factors weakening the U.S. commitment to the postwar multilateral, rules-oriented trade regime have prompted a vigorous debate within the political and academic communities in this country about what principles should govern U.S. trade policy in the future. Three schools of thought, somewhat overlapping, have emerged.

The first, and least revolutionary of the alternatives, advocates that the United States itself fill the enforcement void in the GATT by playing the role of "super-cop." The United States has already embarked down this path, not only in adopting the new Super 301 provisions of the 1988 Trade Act, but in President George Bush's decision in May 1989 under those provisions to single out Japan, Brazil, and India as countries engaged in discriminatory practices and thus "priority" targets for our retaliation if those practices are not soon ended.

The second alternative also focuses on rules, but it advocates bilateral FTAs with other like-minded countries—Mexico, South Korea, Taiwan, and even Japan—modeled on the FTAs the United States negotiated with Canada and Israel, as well as the more ambitious integration effort now under way in Europe. The FTA policy model, which urges the bilateral negotiation of new rules on many subjects not covered or imperfectly covered by GATT (including investment, services, and agriculture), is thus more forward looking than the "super-cop" approach, which seeks unilateral enforcement of existing rules (that the United States sets) on a case-by-case basis. . . .

The third trade policy alternative would jettison not only the emphasis on multilateral action but on rules as well. Instead, it would "manage trade" by having the United States set bilateral trade targets with our trading partners. The targets could cover only our exports to them or our overall trade balance (as the Gephardt amendment advocated). Similarly, the targets could be set for individual products or industry sectors or could cover all trade.

A Critique of the Critics

Each of the suggested alternatives to the traditional multilateral, rules-based trade policy followed by the United States has its appeal. But each also holds dangers that we think outweigh any benefits they may achieve.

The least risky, but also least promising, alternative is the United States as super-cop. As President Bush's decision under the Super 301 provision demonstrated, there will always be competing foreign policy objectives that any chief executive must take into account in deciding whether to single out individual countries as "unfair traders." It is widely assumed, for example, that the Administration exempted the European Community nations from the priority list primarily in order to avoid exacerbating then-worrisome tensions within the North Atlantic Treaty Organization over an appropriate response to the Soviet Union's nuclear arms reduction proposals.

GATT's Success

It is ironic that GATT is increasingly viewed as outmoded. In fact, GATT has been a great success; since World War II, tariff rates have been cut by over 75 percent through successive GATT "rounds" of trade negotiations. . . .

GATT aside, U.S. access to foreign markets is growing in a practical, measurable sense. U.S. exports are booming.

Kenneth W. Dam, *The American Enterprise,* July/August 1990.

But even President Bush's minimalist 301 effort has its risks. Several of the practices targeted by the President, notably India's trade-related investment measures and its insurance practices, are not covered by the GATT. If, therefore, we retaliate against these measures, our actions would violate the GATT and entitle the targeted countries lawfully to retaliate against us. Critics also have been too quick to dismiss the efficacy of the GATT enforcement mechanism. Of the 75 disputes brought before the GATT through September 1985, 88% were settled or dropped by the complaining country. By circumventing the GATT dispute resolution mechanism, we weaken the commitment of other nations to lawful settlement of trade disputes.

Free Trade Agreements

Bilateral or regional FTAs do not offer a much better solution, and conceivably, could produce a worse one. The premise underpinning the case for more FTAs—that GATT negotiations take too long—is questionable. In fact, once the parties in the Tokyo Round got down to hard bargaining, agreement was reached in only 18 months, about the same time that was consumed in the United States-Canada talks. Similarly, the tough negotiating in the Uruguay Round did not really begin until President Bush assumed office, and even if completed late, in 1991 for example, would take less than 3 years—a major accomplishment given the round's ambitious objectives.

Moreover, as pioneering as they were, the FTAs with Canada and Israel were relatively limited in scope. Neither dealt with the highly controversial issues that are now being discussed in the Uruguay Round, including agricultural subsidies, protection of intellectual property rights, and restrictions on services and investment, or the subjects that inevitably would be on the table in future FTA discussions with other countries. Indeed, if the advocates are right that many restrictions against imports are extralegal and thus not amenable to international agreement—such as the complex Japanese distribution system, for example—then FTAs could disadvantage the United States; we would further open our market without meaningful reciprocal concessions.

More FTAs could actually harm world trade. In purely economic terms, such arrangements have two offsetting effects: although they may promote more efficient location of production within the areas covered by the agreements and thus enhance trade and consumer welfare, they may also divert trade from other countries outside the agreement to those inside. Although the net effect of these two tendencies will differ in different cases, it is noteworthy that three of the recent advocates of more bilateral arrangements have also estimated that the 1992 integration effort with the European Community will divert more trade than it creates.

Undermining GATT

More fundamentally, however, further movement by the United States—the leader of multilateral trade liberalization efforts since the end of World War II—toward bilateral or regional pacts runs a serious risk of undermining, if not unraveling, the GATT. Indeed, given the current inward-looking focus of the Europeans and Canada's new-found partnership with the United States, who would be left to lead the liberalizing process in the GATT if we, too, abandon our commitment to multilateralism? The answer is no one.

Instead, nations would quickly enter a free-for-all to obtain from each other the best deal each could. The world trading system would thus degenerate into a complicated maze of discriminatory bilateral and regional arrangements. Frictions would dramatically increase over "rules of origin" because it would then become all-important to know from which country imports and exports had "originated." In a world of multinational enterprises that often manufacture products in multiple locations, disputes about rules of origin could lead to serious trade rifts and would lead to substantially more red tape and uncertainty for all those involved in international trade. . . .

In any event, the setting of trade targets would be counterproductive. If the targets were bilateral trade balances, it is more than likely that foreign countries would be happy to comply by restricting their exports to the United States rather than liberalizing imports. Like the VRAs that have limited the exports of Japanese cars and steel, these new restrictions would simply raise the price of goods exported to the United States and increase the profits of the foreign producers. Meanwhile, forcing foreign consumers to buy U.S. products they have not voluntarily chosen to purchase can hardly enhance the attractiveness of American goods overseas. . . .

The Best Approach

In our view, the best approach lies not in abandoning the rules-oriented, multilateral strategy that the United States has pioneered since World War II, but instead in reaffirming the commitment to that strategy and enlisting the vigorous participation of our trading partners. At a purely political level, we think that other countries that maintain trade barriers are more likely to lower them in response to international pressure, lawfully applied through the GATT, then solely in response to U.S. complaints. Indeed, our "lone ranger" attitude toward other nations' trade barriers runs a severe risk of tarnishing our broader political influence. For example, U.S. relations with both Japan and South Korea have already been severely strained as a result of our constant pressure on particular trade issues. Resentment builds, meanwhile, as the United States continues to demonstrate an inability to significantly reduce its national overspending, which other countries think, quite correctly, is the overwhelming reason for their trade surpluses with us.

The United States even runs broader geopolitical risks if it abandons its mantle of leadership on multilateral trade liberalization. It is fitting to recall the history of the period between the two major world wars of this century, when the rise of rival trading blocs contributed significantly to the tensions that led to World War II. Similar tensions led to repeated conflicts in the 17th and 18th centuries. Only when Great Britain, espousing the free trade principles of Adam Smith and David Ricardo, emerged as the dominant world power in the 19th century did these conflicts abate. The United States assumed this mantle of leadership toward free trade after World War II and until now has promoted increased liberalization, more trade, and improvements in living standards around the world.

It would be a severe mistake for the United States to abandon its leadership role simply because of its inability to address the root causes of trade difficulties abroad and its economic weaknesses at home. In the long run, we should realize that trade is still a positive sum game, not the zero sum game some have now contended. We should not be distracted by current tensions into wrecking the multilateral trade system that has helped bring all of the nations that participate in it to unprecedented levels of economic well-being.

"A world of superblocs could be increasingly mercantilistic and protectionist. "

Trading Blocs Will Harm the World Trading System

Jeffrey E. Garten

The rise of Japan as an economic superpower, the 1992 economic unification of Europe, and the U.S.-Canada trade agreement have led some observers to predict that the world trading system will be divided into three trading blocs dominated by Japan, Europe, and the United States. In the following viewpoint, Jeffrey E. Garten argues that such a course in world trade would be harmful to the U.S. and to the world economy. He calls for policies to try to stop or slow the rise of trading blocs. Garten is an investment banker in New York, and held government positions during the Nixon, Ford, and Carter administrations.

As you read, consider the following questions:

1. What are some of the trade statistics Garten believes indicate the rise of trading blocs?
2. What are some of the harmful effects of trading blocs, according to the author?
3. According to Garten, what should the U.S. do with regard to international trade?

Jeffrey E. Garten, "Trading Blocs and the Evolving World Economy," *Current History,* January 1989. Reprinted with permission from *Current History* magazine, © 1989 Current History Inc.

In the late twentieth century, there is a strong tendency for three major parts of the world to form regional economic blocs—superblocs. There is one forming in West Europe, one in North America (including Mexico and the Caribbean), and one in East Asia. This tendency may well create centrifugal forces in the Western alliance (the United States, West Europe, and Japan) and may cause serious problems for American influence and interests around the world.

Europe 1992

West Europe provides the clearest case of a group of sovereign nations moving deliberately to form a closer union. This is not a new development. Thirty years ago, the Treaty of Rome established the European Common Market. Since then, West European nations have cooperated extensively in many areas, including agriculture, steel and exchange rates. But something far more ambitious is happening: a quantum leap in economic integration. There is no fuzzy futuristic deadline: the goal is a single European market in 1992, and on many different levels, both official and private, there is an expectation—and a policy calculation on the part of businesses and governments—that the deadline will be met.

In the last years of the twentieth century, the remaining trade barriers among the members of the European Community may be eliminated, leading to freedom of capital movements and easier mobility of labor. West German banks should be able to service the everyday needs of Belgians; engineers from the Netherlands should be automatically licensed in Italy; construction crews from Great Britain ought to be able to work on French projects outside Paris.

West European companies are restructuring themselves furiously to take advantage of a new enlarged market; insurance companies, banks, food conglomerates and other industries are all merging. Currency coordination is getting tighter. There is increasing talk of some type of European Central Bank. The European Currency Unit (ECU)—the currency cocktail that is part German mark, part French franc, part Italian lira, and so on—is being used more widely.

North America

The second superbloc is forming in North America including Canada, the United States, Mexico and the Caribbean Basin (e.g., Central America and the islands). Close economic relations between the United States and the Basin did not begin yesterday, but the momentum for broader and deeper integration is growing rapidly.

In the early 1980's, Washington designed and supported a

"Caribbean Basin Initiative" that provided unprecedented trade and investment concessions to Central America and the Caribbean islands. The impact was to link these nations with the United States by giving them greater access to United States markets and by providing American investors with new incentives. It was an innovative plan. No American initiative had ever combined so integrally trade and investment incentives. And none in recent memory had so blatantly excluded West Europe and Japan.

© Harris/Rothco. Reprinted with permission.

The United States-Canadian free trade agreement would result in major reductions in trade barriers and accelerate the integration of Canadian and American industries—from banking to energy to transportation. The treaty would be the first to guarantee that Canadian companies will be treated exactly like American companies in the event of new United States trade barriers, American retaliation against foreign companies, new restrictions on foreign investment, embargoes, and so on. It would intertwine the two countries at every level in an irrevocable way.

And low-key discussions have begun between Washington and

Mexico City about a more formal framework for United States-Mexican relations. Any new President will probably find ways to further ties to get a stronger handle on the related problems of trade, debt, immigration, energy and drug traffic. The large loan made by Washington in October 1988—some $3.5 billion—to Mexico was a clear sign of vital American interests in Mexico.

East Asia

The third superbloc is forming across the Pacific in East Asia. From Melbourne to Seoul, intraregional trade and investment are expanding. There is rapid growth in virtually every country on the Pacific Rim, but the dynamo that is propelling economic integration is Japan. The instrument is the strong yen. Again, this development may seem familiar but few would have predicted the strength and depth of the new Japanese economic empire a few years ago.

The real turning point came in 1985 when the yen started to soar. Japan's economic and business establishment recognized that a major restructuring of the Japanese economy and a reordering of economic strategy in Asia would be required. The strong yen began to draw in relatively cheaper imports from Hong Kong, South Korea and Thailand. It also encouraged a massive wave of new Japanese investment in East Asia, where labor and materials were cheaper. From there it was a short step to a division of labor in which labor-intensive manufacturing moved from Japan to neighboring countries, and more technologically driven industry stayed near Tokyo and Osaka to be used locally and for export. This transformation is not complete, of course, but it is being orchestrated by Tokyo.

Trading Bloc Trends

Regardless of the stage of development of the superblocs, fundamental forces pushing for regional consolidation are clear. Recent trends show that both economics and technology are leading to closer ties across adjacent borders:

• Intra-European trade now dwarfs trans-Atlantic trade.

• Studies predict that within ten years in East Asia, North-South trade will be larger than trans-Pacific commerce.

• Long before the United States-Canadian free-trade agreement was written, the cat was out of the bag: today one-third of all United States investment abroad is in Canada; the United States trades more with the province of Ontario than with Japan; much of New York's skyline is owned by Olympia and York.

There are also political and psychological reasons for the emergence of superblocs:

• West Europeans are cooperating more closely because they believe this is the only way to compete with the United States and Japan in the race for commercial technology.

• Both West Europe and Japan are worried about American policy that may become protectionist and formulated with less and less regard for international rules or the impact on other nations. Their best hedge is to ensure that they have their backyards secured.

• Both West Europe and Japan have grown economically more powerful in the last quarter of a century, and this is being reflected in a desire to act more independently, a great temptation, particularly when United States leadership is not inspired.

• And in the United States, despite a lot of bravado talk, there is a mood to lessen the burdens of international leadership, to ask others to accept more responsibility for military security, foreign aid, and support for international organizations. It is only a short step from this attitude to isolationism.

The three superblocs are not airtight. There is much evidence of global interdependence; international trade of all types continues to grow. Big multinationals are roaming every corner of the globe. Mergers between Bridgestone and Firestone or between Credit Suisse and First Boston are occurring with increasing frequency. Hughes Aircraft builds satellites for Australia to mount on Chinese rockets and there are many more examples of the spaghetti-like structure of the world economy.

But there are other equally powerful and fundamental forces. Interdependence within regions will grow faster. And although American firms may operate in West Europe, there is no evidence that they will serve United States interests more than those of the host country; in fact, for practical purposes, they may well be card-carrying members of the European bloc. Governments can still set the tone for future trade and investment patterns and, economic interdependence notwithstanding, a political bloc mentality may still take a toll.

Why Care?

There are several causes for concern because of the growth of the regional superblocs. A world of superblocs could be increasingly mercantilistic and protectionist. In West Europe, for example, Americans should worry about the way economic consolidation is achieved and try to make sure that it is not achieved at the expense of foreign investment or exports to West Europe. Already West European officials are using code words to put Americans on notice that their own industries may have to be given preference over foreigners in their evolving market. When these officials use such euphemisms as "transitional arrangements," "nurturing industries" or "reciprocity," for example, Americans ought to pay close attention.

American trade policy has some worrisome aspects, too. The fact that it will take a swing of some $200 billion in the United

States trade balance over the next few years to keep the foreign debt from soaring will tempt Americans to resort to extremes to increase exports or reduce imports. This is all the more worrisome because the United States now has a trade bill that gives the government license to take unilateral protective action or to retaliate, with far less international justification than ever before. A ready-made excuse could be found to keep out Asian producers and look to Mexico as a substitute. If economic pressures south of the border increase, as may well happen, or if there are intractable problems persuading South Korea, Taiwan and others in East Asia to take more American goods (as well may be the case) the stage will be set for an inward-looking North American strategy not conducive to freer trade with the rest of the world.

Fragmentation

Unless some initiative is taken, the international economy, which contributed so greatly to world economic growth in the decades after World War II, could conceivably become fragmented into trading blocs. Such an event would represent a sizable economic loss for the United States, and an even bigger political loss.

Anne O. Krueger, *An American Trade Strategy,* 1990.

As for the Pacific bloc, a tightly woven industrial structure—built around Japanese and South Korean notions about state-dominated economic growth and all that the concept entails—would not lead to an easily penetrable market.

Other Problems

Beyond protectionism, there are other problems in the evolution of superblocs. A world of mercantilistic superblocs will create major strains in the Western Alliance and in Japan. . . .

In a world of superblocs, nonalignment would not have the cold war connotation of refraining from entanglements with the United States or with the Soviet Union. The poles will be the three superblocs. And the new nonaligned group may be the Soviet Union, China, Poland, Brazil and India, which could be the battleground for mercantilist scrambles.

Finally, there is the question of global approaches to the awesome international problems of our age. Superblocs are likely to put more emphasis on regional policies and organizations. This will ensure fragmented efforts in place of broader coordination. On drugs, on terrorism, on the environment, on economic development—it is difficult to see how superblocs, acting on their own, can do anything but retard what progress could otherwise have been made.

The trends are there, unfortunately, in the increasing ineffectiveness of the World Bank, the International Monetary Fund (IMF) and some of the United Nations agencies. Americans should care about this breakdown not only out of concern for solving problems that affect their lives, but also out of recognition that the best chance for Americans to influence these problems is to be primus-interpares in a global institution.

What Should Be Done

The United States administration will not find it easy to harness the centrifugal forces of the emerging regional superblocs. But it ought to try.

The first imperative is to recognize the trends. The issue of superblocs and all they represent is particularly timely. European officials are deciding on their external trade strategy. The Japanese government is considering its position in East Asia and asking what role South Korea and Thailand should play in economic and foreign policy aims. And Washington must consider what happens when the United States-Canadian free trade agreement goes into effect, and particularly how to deal with Mexico in the framework of a North American community. Moreover, the race among American allies for concessions from Gorbachev—going on right now—will create new problems if there is no agreed Western framework for dealing with the Soviets.

Washington itself needs some framework for dealing with the superblocs. In the cold war years, it was the Communists versus the West and the watchword was "containment.". . .

The superblocs need to stimulate a new way of thinking about the purpose of foreign policy beyond the givens of promoting peace, prosperity and human rights. In the world of superblocs, the objective should be to promote outward-looking blocs in a framework of cooperative allied relations. This is something between balance-of-power politics and United States hegemony. The starting points are strong American leadership that emphasizes multilateral diplomacy and integration of policymaking in the economic and national security arenas.

American leadership is indispensable. The natural tendency and, indeed, the existing momentum in Europe is to turn inward. Japan is almost certainly going to key its policies to the United States.

"Trading blocs. . .need not be economic or military disasters."

Trading Blocs Will Not Harm the World Trading System

Lester Thurow

Lester Thurow is a well-known economist and author, and is dean of the Sloan School of Management at the Massachusetts Institute of Technology in Cambridge, Massachusetts. In the following viewpoint, he argues that the evolution of three main trading blocs featuring the U.S., Japan, and Europe could be beneficial to world trade. He recommends that the U.S. should make plans to adjust to the reality of trading blocs.

As you read, consider the following questions:

1. Why does Thurow argue that GATT is dead?
2. How will the economic unification of Europe affect the world trading system, according to the author?
3. What U.S. policies does Thurow recommend?

Lester Thurow, address before the World Economic Forum, Davos, Switzerland, January 1988. Reprinted with permission of the author.

Since 1945 the world has been slowly but persistently moving towards an ever more open integrated world economy. The very success of this trend, however, has undermined its continuation. Success has replaced a single polar world economy centered around the United States with a multi-polar economic world where Europe, Japan, and the United States are rough economic peers.

Many of the institutions and practices that worked in a single polar world, however, do not work in a multi-polar world. The major players in the world economy could build a new set of institutions and practices that would keep the world evolving on the trajectory of the past 45 years, but no country wants to make the necessary changes. To make an open integrated multi-polar world work, the major countries (the United States, Germany, and Japan) would have to tightly coordinate their monetary and fiscal policies. Put bluntly, no one is prepared to do what they would have to do. No one is prepared to yield the economic sovereignty that would have to be yielded.

The macro-economic problems of coordination are tough, but the micro-economic problems of harmonization are even tougher. To make an open world economy work, everyone must feel that they have an equal chance to win—what is known as 'a level playing field' in America, 'reciprocity' in Europe, 'equal opportunity not equal outcomes' in Japan. If the economic game is to be seen as fair, there must be broadly similar tax and regulatory policies and broadly similar private modes of operation. What I will call 'economic lifestyle variables' must be harmonized. As with macro-economic coordination, however, no one is prepared to make the changes that would be required to create a level playing field, reciprocity, or equal opportunity.

Prospects for Trade

As a consequence, in the next decade the undercurrents that are today moving the world very rapidly toward trading blocks will become obvious. Within each block trade will become freer but between the blocks trade will be increasingly managed in the next decade.

To use the words 'trading blocks' is to instantly be accused of predicting disaster, but it need not be so. The negative connotation of trading blocks springs from our experiences in the 1930s when the world split into trading blocks centered around Britain, France, Germany, Japan, the United States, and the Soviet Union. Each block aimed at reducing imports from the other blocks to the lowest possible level and eventually the different blocks formed the basis for choosing up sides to fight World War II.

Trading blocks, however, need not be economic or military disasters. If the situation is managed in the right way, no one will aim for zero trade or even less trade. The blocks may in fact be a vehicle for making the world grow faster than it is now growing. They may even be a necessary intermediate step on the way to truly integrated open world economy at a later date.

Trade and GATT

Theoretically one can argue that it would be better to continue on the trajectory set by the basic philosophical principle underlying the General Agreement on Tariffs and Trade—whatever special deals are given to any one country will be given to all others—but in practice it is always better to face up to reality rather than live in a dream world. The circumstances that led to GATT's birth and permitted it to prosper have changed.

Trade Strategy

A good trade policy should be active and directed toward opening the economy on the import side while creating more and better export opportunities. A trade bloc approach would seem a fruitful strategy to give a new life to a strategy of freer trade.

Rudiger W. Dornbusch, *An American Trade Strategy*, 1990.

GATT IS DEAD!

The Montreal GATT meetings ended in total failure. Future meetings will also end in failure. The agenda guarantees it. What is now being negotiated cannot be negotiated.

In the agricultural area the world faces an unsolvable problem. The world's temperate farmers can produce much more than those who can pay for food want to eat. Therefore millions of farmers somewhere must go out of business. But what government is going to sign a treaty that forces their farmers to go out of business?

In services the problems are equally unsolvable. If one examines real service exports and imports (American statistics include many items that are not services such as earnings on foreign assets) services trade is small and is not going to become large. Most services simply have to be produced where they are used. . . .

The Canadian-American trade agreement and the integration of Europe in 1992 also fundamentally violate the spirit, but not the legal letter, of GATT. In neither case do insiders plan to give outsiders the same rights and privileges that are given to insiders. Bilateral agreements are the wave of the future.

GATT's corpse will be propped up. The diplomatic activity necessary to deny GATT's death are already underway. But

GATT cannot be resurrected. No one in the near future is going to find a path that leads to significant multilateral reductions in trade barriers.

Given this reality it is far better to channel what is, I believe, an irresistible movement toward trading blocks in a benign direction rather than refusing to face up to reality until that reality has in fact created the very monster that everyone wants to avoid. Pretending that what will happen won't happen is not the route to success. . . .

Europe 1992

The integration of the EEC [European Economic Community] in 1992 will be the event that visibly destroys the post-World War II GATT era, but it should be seen as a precipitating and not a causal event. It will just make visible and speed up what would have occurred anyway.

In 1992 Europe must harmonize its non-tariff barriers. In the process it is going to become a much more restrictive market.

Consider the market for automobiles. The French strictly limit, the Italians essentially prohibit, and the Dutch freely permit the sale of Japanese cars. What are to be the common limits on Japanese cars after 1992? The rules will not be the Dutch rules, the average of the Dutch and Italian rules, or even the French rules. They will be the Italian rules. The Italians will insist. And everyone else will explicitly or implicitly support their stubbornness. . . .

When foreigners charge 'Fortress Europe', Europeans counter with the argument that they are only interested in 'reciprocity'. It is important to understand that although the two terms sound very different, they are in fact identical.

Consider the ability of foreign banks to enter the Common Market. Under the doctrine of reciprocity Europe can keep American banks out of Europe or stop those that are already in Europe from expanding on the grounds that many American states do not permit interstate banking. If a European bank does not have access to all of America, then an American bank cannot have access to all of Europe. Similarly America does not allow banks to own shares in industrial firms. If European banks are not to have that privilege in America, then American banks cannot come to Europe where banks do have such rights. . . .

What makes a firm a European firm? Is it ownership, management, R&D [research and development], production, local content? All of these questions can be answered in ways that keep the rest of the world out of Europe after 1992.

Reciprocity could mean an open market but it probably means a closed market. Repeatedly in my trips to Europe I hear over and over again from private businessmen and public officials the phrase "We are not going to let the Japanese do in Europe what they have already done in the United States." The goal may be to restrict the Japanese and not the Americans, but as the automobile industry illustrates, separating the treatment of Japan from that of the United States is not going to be easy. One cannot keep out Japanese products without keeping out Japanese-American products.

Europe does not want to operate under the harsh dictates of factor price equalization. It does not want to give up its economic way of life—its long vacations, its high minimum wages, its generous social welfare system. Given these desires, it has no choice but to isolate itself and not give to outsiders what it gives to insiders. Harmony within Europe is going to be difficult enough without worrying about outsiders.

Europe will be blamed for destroying GATT but in fact no one on either side of the Atlantic or Pacific is willing to do what would have to be done—change a majority of their standard operating procedures to bring them into harmony with the other two great polar blocks. Given the reality of three roughly equal regions, no one should expect to play their traditional economic game more than one-third of the time. Everyone should be prepared to give up two-thirds of their economic way of life. Unfortunately no one is prepared to do so.

Possible Advantages

To speak of trading blocks is to be accused of being a pessimist. They need not be a disaster if we prepare for them. Inter-block trade will be managed by governments, but management is not a synonym for elimination. There are real comparative advantages to be taken advantage of between the blocks that do not require changes in lifestyles. Effective management can capture those gains.

The economic losses from forgoing some of the advantages of comparative advantage are also much smaller than economic descriptions would lead one to believe. The axiomatic advantages of free trade flow from the assumption that human welfare is dependent upon one and only one variable—the consumption of goods and services. In fact many other economic factors, such as the nature of one's job, contribute to human welfare. Man is a producing as well as a consuming animal. Maximum consumption is quite rationally occasionally sacrificed to raise production welfare or to achieve other goals such as a more egalitarian society than the market would by itself generate.

The axiomatic advantages of free trade also assume that full employment can at all points be maintained and that transition costs do not exist. In fact few countries have successfully maintained full employment in recent years, and the transition costs of moving human and physical resources from one industry to another in response to the vagaries of world trade are often enormous.

The importance of man-made comparative advantage—the dominant form of comparative advantage in the modern technological age—also changes the conclusions of classical free trade. The man-made comparative advantages constructed by any one set of humans can presumably be duplicated by any other set. As a result, restrictions on trade that interfere with man-made comparative advantages need not lead to large loss in consumption.

Bilateral Trade with Latin America

Multilateral free trade is a thing of the past. Japan doesn't want it because it would bring access to its home market. Canada can't have it because trade with the United States is too important in terms of employment, taxes, and capital investment. The Europeans choose to perfect their common market and tie others to the European Community in bilateral trading arrangements. . . .

It's time the United States offered . . . a bilateral trading arrangement to one or more Latin American countries. Such agreements with Mexico, Brazil, Argentina, and Venezuela will create more intraregional trade between them and the United States, expand local employment, the tax base, and domestic capital formation, and help these countries reduce their debt.

Douglas F. Lamont, *Forcing Our Hand,* 1986.

If interblock trade is managed even half intelligently, the comparative advantages that automatically flow from differences in natural resource endowments can be maintained. The other classic source of comparative advantage, differences in factor endowments, can be eliminated with free capital markets. Open world capital markets are perfectly consistent with restricted trading markets and even quite likely, given electronic funds transfer. Technology has simply made capital controls impossible in most countries.

If each block manages its macro-economic coordination better than the world is now managing it, then faster growth within the blocks may lead to more trade and swamp the hypothetical gains that form an integrated open but slower growing world economy. Germany might worry more about European growth if it knew that the United States was not worrying about European growth. The US might be much more willing to do something about Latin American debt if it saw Latin America as part of its trading block. What happens outside of Europe is not clear. Ex-ambassador Mike Mansfield has publicly called for a US-Japan common market. Given great differences in economic lifestyle variables between these two countries make the establishment of a common market difficult.

If the world splits into three blocks, the nature of the split is not obvious. Economic geography may dominate physical geography. Korea and Taiwan are much more integrated with the United States than they are with Japan. There are lots of potential opportunities for creative or surprising alliances.

An optimist might also say that regional (block) free trade is a necessary first step to world free trade. To try to harmonize economic practices on a world-wide basis is to attempt too much. Harmonize regionally and then later on harmonize world-wide.

Rather than quarreling about which region of the world is now the most restrictive (and hence causing the world to move toward trading blocks) it is far better to accept the reality of trading blocks and get on with the job of understanding how we might manage trade between the blocks so that it doesn't deteriorate into the negative-sum games of the 1930s.

Broad Categories of Products

What needs to be done is clear. A range of permissible management techniques should be defined so that block managers focus on broad categories of products rather than highly specific products. Blocks might be required to keep imports growing at least as rapidly as their GNPs [gross national products]. GATT is dead but some system of international rules is not beyond our capacity.

The world of the first best may be a world of free trade with macro-coordination and macro-harmonization. But when the first best is both impossible to obtain and not obviously that much better, the first best should never stand in the way of the second best.

"Businessmen, politicians and bureaucrats see a unified Europe as a way of 'getting tough' with exporters from the rest of the world through Europe-wide protectionism."

A Unified Europe May Threaten the World Trading System

Wendell H. McCulloch Jr.

An important issue in world trade is the future of Europe. The twelve members of the European Economic Community (EEC), including France, Germany, and Great Britain, have made continuing progress to unite their economies into a single market with no trade barriers. Many observers have wondered whether such unification, while promoting free trade within the EEC, might result in more trade barriers aimed to limit imports from non-European countries, including the U.S. In the following viewpoint, Wendell H. McCulloch Jr. argues that this is a strong possibility. McCulloch is a professor of international finance at California State University at Long Beach.

As you read, consider the following questions:

1. What significant event occurred in 1985, according to McCulloch?
2. Why might Europeans turn to protectionism, according to the author?
3. What examples of European protectionism does McCulloch describe?

Wendell H. McCulloch Jr., "'Europe 1992': Ensuring a Fair Deal for the U.S.," The Heritage Foundation *Backgrounder*, May 5, 1989. Reprinted with permission.

American policy makers focus considerable attention on trade with Asian countries—especially with Japan. Yet United States trade with the twelve countries of the European Economic Community (EEC), which has a combined gross national product second only to the U.S., actually exceeds its trade with either Canada or Japan. Moreover, some 40 percent of U.S. overseas investment is located in the EEC, while European investment in the U.S. is substantial and growing fast.

Fundamental changes now taking place in Europe will have a major impact on Europe's economic relationships with the U.S. By the end of 1992, the EEC countries are scheduled to remove the remaining barriers to each other's trade, investment, and movement of labor, creating a true common market of 320 million people. Discrimination against other EEC countries in procurement policies by European governments is to be abolished, and the structure of value-added taxes—a form of sales tax used by EEC countries—is to be standardized.

There is concern in the U.S. that this liberalization of trade between EEC countries will be accompanied by higher protectionist trade barriers against the goods and services from countries outside the EEC. Another fear is that as a European trade bloc emerges, competing blocs of trading nations also will emerge, undermining the efforts of the General Agreement on Tariffs and Trade (GATT) to maintain and improve a global trading system. . . .

How the EEC Was Developed

After World War II the countries of Western Europe saw the need for closer economic and political ties to promote economic recovery, reduce the risk of a future European war, and to face the growing Soviet threat. U.S. recovery assistance under the Marshall Plan, moreover, required that the West Europeans seek economic cooperation among themselves. America understood that trade liberalization would promote economic growth. A result of this early cooperation was the 1952 European Coal and Steel Community, initially between France and Germany and later incorporated into the EEC.

These early efforts culminated in the Treaty of Rome, signed on March 25, 1957, by Belgium, France, Italy, Luxembourg, the Netherlands and West Germany. This established a European Economic Community—or Common Market. Today this organization, since expanded, is known as the European Community. This latter designation implies both economic and political forms of cooperation.

In any such common market, countries remove trade barriers, such as tariffs and quotas, between member states and establish common tariffs towards nonmember countries. This differs from a free trade area, in which member states retain control over their trade policy to nonmember countries. In addition, a common market can allow the free movement of labor, capital and other factors of production between the member countries.

Toles. © 1989 *The Buffalo News.* Reprinted with permission of Universal Press Syndicate. All rights reserved.

The EEC has expanded since its inception. In 1973, Denmark, Britain and Ireland joined the community. But further progress toward European integration slowed dramatically in the 1970s, due to worldwide economic problems. By the early 1980s, however, progress toward a more unified market again began to accelerate. Three new members were added—Greece in 1981, Portugal and Spain in 1986.

The Brussels-based EEC Commission, the policy-making body whose members are appointed by the EEC governments, developed some 300 directives in 1985 in a document called "Completing the Internal Market." Referred to as the "White Paper," these directives, if enacted by the member governments, will harmonize technical standards for production of goods, eliminate long delays for cargo shipments at frontier crossings, remove barriers to trade within the EEC of such services as banking and transportation, and eliminate restrictions against bids for government purchases and contracts by businesses residing in a different EEC country. It is the planned enactment of the White Paper directives that will achieve full EEC economic integration by the end of 1992—if indeed they are enacted by that time.

What the White Paper Does Not Do

The arrangement in 1992 would not eliminate every barrier to free markets and economic growth. The directives will not, for instance, remove barriers to competition from other countries. Example: import quota restrictions on automobiles, textiles, footwear and electronics will remain. The White Paper also is virtually silent on steps to introduce non-EEC foreign competition into government procurement—which accounts for about 15 percent of the EEC's gross national product. Only 2 percent of procurement by EEC governments currently is produced by foreign companies.

There is little indication, moreover, that the EEC intends to abolish internal government subsidies to agriculture, fisheries, steel and textiles. The EECs notorious Common Agricultural Policy has created "mountains" of butter and "lakes" of wine at the expense of European taxpayers and consumers. Further, such crucial sectors as energy, some modes of transportation, water supplies and telecommunications have been exempted from broad 1992 reforms.

Also not addressed in the plan for 1992 are economic and industrial policies that have contributed to relatively slow growth and job creation in Europe. Example: high unemployment benefits and social insurance taxes that discourage employment; rigid curbs on plant closings and layoffs, which discourage entrepreneurs. Similarly, the White Paper contains no plans for a substantial reduction in government ownership of industries, which usually are a drag on the economy—although some member countries, most notably Britain, are "privatizing" state-owned corporations. . . .

Protectionist Pressure

Many Europeans argue that they and the rest of the world face economic domination by America and Japan unless Europeans stick together. Indicative of this mood in Europe was a 1987 television commercial, sponsored by the French government, showing a skinny French boxer squaring off in a one-sided, evidently unfair, battle with a giant American football player and an equally menacing Japanese sumo wrestler. Eventually, eleven other boxers, representing the EEC countries, rushed to the boxer's rescue and the "bullies" turned away.

Crude though such a commercial may seem to Americans and their lawmakers, it captures the tone of Europe and explains a major part of the impetus for European economic integration. On one level, Europe's politicians and businessmen proclaim the benefits that will flow from the single EEC market in 1992. But on another level, businessmen, politicians and bureaucrats see a unified Europe as a way of "getting tough" with exporters from the rest of the world through Europe-wide protectionism.

Many European policy makers invoke the buzz words of protectionists in the U.S.—"reciprocity," "level playing field" and "fair trade." In light of the trade restrictions enacted by the U.S. in recent years, and still threatened by Congress, it is likely that the pressure for protectionist reciprocity will grow in Europe as 1992 nears. Though Sir Roy Denman of Britain, the EEC representative to the U.S., says there is nothing to worry about, many Americans rightly remain concerned.

Actions by the EEC have done little to quell U.S. fears. In 1988, for instance, the EEC imposed anti-dumping duties on such Japanese products as typewriters assembled in Taiwan. Further, the American subsidiary of Japan's Ricoh Co., Ltd. is the subject of a case in an EEC customs advisory committee.The EEC will decide on whether to accept a U.S. certificate of origin granted to California-made Ricoh photocopiers. When the EEC imposed a 20 percent anti-dumping duty on Ricoh copiers imported directly from Japan, production at Ricoh's Irvine, California, plant was doubled to 4,000 copiers per month, many of which were shipped to the EEC. The EEC has no firm rules to determine whether the percentage of Japanese-made parts is "too high" for the assembled product to be considered of U.S. origin. The EEC committee's decision is awaited with keen interest by American and Japanese authorities and companies.

Restricting U.S. Firms

The standardization of EEC product specifications could be another obstacle to the entry of the U.S. products into the EEC market after 1992—despite the general assumption that they will make marketing in Europe much simpler for U.S. firms. The EEC harmonization directives for such standards easily could be framed to limit American manufacturers' ability to meet the EEC specifications. This would restrict the ability of U.S. firms to sell in the huge EEC market. U.S. companies will not be given the opportunity to review and comment on proposed EEC standards and directives during this crucial development phase. And when directives are published in final form, usually there is little chance for changes.

Further, an EEC policy of trade "reciprocity" would mean that a country seeking to sell in the EEC would be subject to the same restrictions that the country maintains against EEC products coming into its market. This is the "mirror" approach to trade rules. Sometimes reciprocity involves a "market-share" or "managed trade" policy, in which one country guarantees a certain percentage of its market to another country in return for a percentage of its market.

A Poor Record

Countries outside of Europe, especially Japan and the United States, are watching Europe, suspicious that the free trade ideas of 1992 will be kept within boundaries, behind a wall of protectionism to exclude everybody else. The EEC does have a poor record of protectionism, one that is hard to escape. Onlookers are also disturbed by talk of a "reciprocity clause," proposed by the European Commission as a control on competition for 1992. This clause would make admittance of a foreign competitor depend upon mutual openness: before an American bank would be allowed to open a branch in Europe, the Community members would have to be satisfied that a European bank would have the same access to the U.S. banking market.

Nick Elliott, *The Freeman*, March 1989.

Such mirror legislation by the EEC could be especially harmful to U.S. banking. For example, it would lead to demands for EEC-based banks to have the right to operate in the U.S. across state lines—a right not fully accorded American banks. Failure by the U.S. to guarantee this for European banks could lead to tight limits on the right of U.S. banks to conduct business across EEC borders, while European banks and institutions from most other countries would be free to compete. One positive sign is that the EEC Commission has decided so far not to seek retroactive reciprocity on foreign banks already inside the Community. The opportunities for new U.S. bank ventures in Europe, however, are questionable. . . .

EEC and Protectionism

If the EEC follows a protectionist trade policy, the greatest danger to the U.S. probably will be an economically weak Europe. Gains in EEC economic efficiency and output could be offset in the long run by the adverse effects on its economy of trade protection. Combined with the high taxes and overregulation now typical of almost all EEC countries, this could cause economic stagnation. The EEC would be less able to purchase U.S. goods and services due to its protectionism and resulting lower incomes. . . .

EEC 1992 will not see a United States of Europe. There are too many obstacles, cultural and institutional as well as economic, to overcome in too short a period. Indeed, there are doubts whether the EEC will reach even its limited goal of integration by 1992.

A More Open Market

However, the EEC in 1992 will be a different, more cohesive place, and probably will be on the path toward closer union and a more open internal market. As the EEC moves toward this, Washington must bargain for U.S.-based companies to be permitted to function in the immense, rich EEC 1992 market.

The growth of U.S. trade protectionism and a protectionist EEC could endanger international economic growth as protectionism did in the Great Depression of the 1930s. Yet the U.S. should use European integration as an opportunity to promote further trade liberalization. The removal of trade barriers, whether between the EEC countries themselves or between the U.S. and its free trade area partner, Canada, benefits all countries involved.

The desire for higher economic productivity, more consumer choice, lower prices and greater access to foreign markets in part has motivated Europe to seek integration and the U.S. to seek FTAs [free-trade agreements]. If the U.S. and the EEC approach one another in this spirit, their interests need not conflict, but will allow both to achieve these goals through mutual trade liberalization.

"A lot of the anxiety and paranoia is based not on facts and figures, but on the hype of self-proclaimed expert consultants drumming up business."

A Unified Europe Will Not Threaten the World Trading System

Klaus Burmeister

Klaus Burmeister is an attorney living in San Francisco, California, who specializes in Europe-U.S. trade. In the following viewpoint, he argues that predictions of a protectionist Europe that severely restricts global trade are erroneous. European unification, he writes, will lead to expanding global trade and new opportunities for U.S. business. Complaints about protectionism are unfounded, he argues.

As you read, consider the following questions:

1. How have Japan and the U.S. differed in their reactions to European unity, according to Burmeister?
2. What kinds of barriers between nations is Europe eliminating, according to the author?
3. Why does Burmeister argue that complaints about Europe's trade practices have been blown out of proportion?

Klaus Burmeister, "Europe 1992: Getting Set to Flex Its Collective Muscle." Reprinted, with permission, from *USA Today* magazine, January copyright 1990 by the Society for the Advancement of Education.

The term "Europe 1992" stands for one of the most ambitious programs of deregulation ever undertaken anywhere in the world. By 1992, the 12 member states of the European Community (EC)—Belgium, Denmark, France, West Germany, Greece, Ireland, Italy, Luxembourg, the Netherlands, Portugal, Spain, and the United Kingdom—intend to create a single European market of more than 320,000,000 consumers by removing the physical, technical, and fiscal barriers currently existing between them.

In the 1985 White Paper on completing the Internal Market, the Commission of the European Community identified and proposed to adopt, change, or abolish 279 legislative or regulatory measures in order to achieve a truly integrated market. Once these changes are implemented, border controls no longer will exist in the European Community. Technical standards and approval certificates issued for a product in one member state will be accepted in all others if the goods meet agreed-upon essential requirements. Governmental and semi-public agencies in all member states will be required to follow non-discriminatory procedures in procuring goods and services, fully disclosing them to all potential bidders. The liberalization of capital movements, banking, and investment services will reduce the costs of financing businesses.

Economic Benefits

The economic benefits expected from Europe 1992 are staggering. The Cecchini report commissioned by the EC Commission predicts costs savings of more than $220,000,000,000. The integration of the European market will result in an increase of 4.5% in the gross domestic product (GDP) of the European Community and a real deflation of 6.1% of consumer prices, as well as boosting employment by creating 1,800,000 new jobs.

Although the national governments are dragging their feet on the politically more sensitive parts of the Europe 1992 program, the project has gained a self-carrying momentum and the progress made is believed to be irreversible. By June, 1989, 127 of the proposed 279 legislative measures had been adopted by the Council of Ministers; 97 additional measures were still under discussion by the Council—the main source of delay—while 48 measures had yet to be tabled by the EC Commission.

Foreign reactions have differed greatly. Japanese companies were among the first to adopt a pro-active approach in order to take advantage of the integrated European market. Japanese investment in the European Community has increased dramatically in the last few years, and further plans to build or enlarge Japanese-owned manufacturing facilities in Europe are announced on a daily basis. In the U.S., there has been a lot of talk about "Fortress Europe," and action mostly has been limited to complaints about potential trade restrictions. If American businesses fail to recognize the dynamics of the European integration, they risk becoming the biggest loser in the EC.

If the individual measures identified in the 1985 White Paper are analyzed in the appropriate context, Europe 1992 loses much of its mystique. Indeed, when looking at the bottom line, the removal of the targeted physical, technical, and fiscal barriers will benefit U.S. businesses, unless deliberately implemented in a discriminatory fashion.

U.S-European Community Merchandise Trade

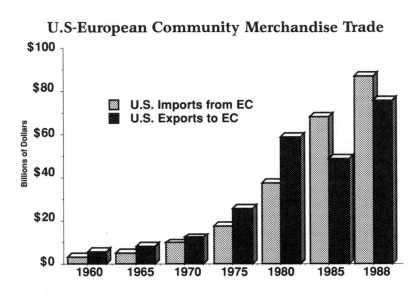

Sources: *Economic Report of the President,* January 1989; *Statistical Abstract of the United States,* U.S. Census Bureau; and *United States Performance in 1988,* U.S. International Trade Administration.

Physical barriers are the customs and immigration posts at the borders between Germany and France, Spain and Portugal, etc. Currently, the shipment of goods is interrupted at the border to allow checks in order to enforce national trade quotas; collect value-added and excise taxes; carry out health, safety, road transport, and similar controls; compile trade statistics; and implement EC agricultural policy. In addition, individuals are checked for immigration, taxation, and law enforcement purposes. Due to the uniform external customs regime of the European Community, customs posts are used for the collection of duties only when goods are imported from non-EC countries.

Europe 1992 proposes the elimination of all systematic controls at frontiers within the European Community. It has brought forth the Single Administrative Document, which replaces about 70 different customs and border control forms with a single one. As a consequence of the elimination of the customs posts as an enforcement mechanism, national trade quotas which prevent the free movement of goods within the European Community will be abolished gradually and a new mechanism for the collection of value-added taxes on cross-border transactions will have to be devised.

Technical barriers targeted include a variety of legal or regulatory measures which currently prevent the free movement of goods, labor, skilled professionals, services, and capital within the EC or restrict competition in public procurement and create obstacles to industrial cooperation.

The Free Movement of Goods

One of the fundamental principles of the European Community is the free movement of goods if they are produced in the EC or have been imported legally and put into circulation anywhere in the Community. However, a multitude of laws, regulations, and/or industrial norms has prevented or inhibited the intra-Community trade in goods. A prominent example is the West German beer purity law that prevented foreign beer manufacturers from selling their beer in that nation if it contained any ingredient other than barley, hops, yeast, and water. The European Court of Justice ultimately prohibited Germany from using this statute to prevent the importation of beer lawfully marketed in another member state of the European Community.

Currently, equipment and machinery may have to meet very different technical specifications or standards, depending on the member state in which they are sold. Testing and certification procedures often have to be duplicated. In the past, many attempts to harmonize the national standards applicable to certain products have failed because it required a detailed discussion of technical aspects at a ministerial level and the unanimous approval by the delegates of the member states.

The 1992 program proposes a radical new approach: only essential health and safety as well as consumer and environmental protection requirements will be harmonized. These new uniform requirements will be set out in general terms, whereas the detailed specifications will be drafted by several European standards organizations, such as the Comite Europeen de Normalisation or the Comite Europeen de Normalisation Electrotechnique. With respect to non-essential requirements, the member states mutually have agreed to recognize each other's standards and approval certificates. . . .

The free movement provisions will allow companies to offer

their services throughout the EC in areas such as banking, insurance, and securities transactions. The legislative initiatives include such revolutionary concepts as a single banking license, which will authorize banks to render financial services in any member state. No local approval will be required, and the bank's home country authorities will be responsible for the supervision of the financial institution's foreign activities. In addition, air, road, and water transportation will be liberalized, and new rules will be provided for advanced technology services such as television, telecommunications, information processing, home videotext, and electronic banking. . . .

A Significant Impact

While the 1985 White Paper focuses on the completion of the internal market, rather than the external relations of the European Community, the program will have a significant impact on foreign companies wishing to do business in Europe. In order to assess this impact, it is important to be aware of what the Europe 1992 program can not be expected to achieve.

Although the declared purpose of Europe 1992 is the creation of one single, truly integrated European market, the EC and the rest of Europe are not, and for a long time will not be, one single market that can be penetrated successfully by applying a uniform marketing strategy. The major obstacle is the cultural diversity in the particular European countries, reflected by the lack of a common language, the difference in commercial attitudes and philosophies, and the socio-political background of European business partners and consumers. This diversity will not cease as a result of Europe 1992. Investment, marketing, and sales decisions must continue to be based on the anticipated requirements of capital, manpower, and experience, and the expected rate of return. Individual national data will determine whether to focus on certain parts of the EC, go direct, join forces with another company, or use independent marketing intermediaries in a particular country.

U.S. businesses also must assess the likelihood of increased competitiveness of European companies, which is one of the key objectives of Europe 1992. According to the studies commissioned by the EC, the removal of the physical, technical, and fiscal barriers will strengthen European businesses by providing significant reductions in administrative and other costs, economies of scale, and increased industrial cooperation. While increased competition on the European market may seem bad enough for a U.S. exporter, a factor often overlooked is that European businesses, being the world's largest exporters (EC, 20%; U.S., 15%; and Japan, nine percent), may be more competitive on foreign markets as well. In other words, U.S. businesses should make sure they will be able to compete domestically against more competitive European companies. . . .

While cultural diversity, increased competitiveness, stricter enforcement of antitrust rules, and higher technical standards present challenges to all companies doing business in Europe, things could turn "ugly" if discriminatory measures are implemented against foreign companies. A number of proposals made in connection with the Europe 1992 program have caused great irritation in the U.S., and the "Fortress Europe" buzzword is heard more frequently these days than the term "Eurosclerosis" was used in the U.S. a few years ago.

The Hype of Experts

A lot of the anxiety and paranoia is based not on facts and figures, but on the hype of self-proclaimed expert consultants drumming up business. Representatives of the U.S. government and EC officials have contributed to the confusion by engaging in shadow-boxing, presumably to improve their bargaining position for upcoming bilateral and multilateral trade negotiations. Skeptical assessments by the U.S. Commerce Department of the Europe 1992 program have been countered with critical reports by the EC Commission concerning American trade barriers. Vague and ambiguous concepts such as "reciprocity" are thrown into the discussion without definition or explanation, then construed as protectionist measures.

Faith in the Free Market

Europe is today—and I believe will remain—the freest economic region in the world. Let us not forget that 45 percent of American capital currently invested overseas is in equity ownership within Europe. It is a very strange fortress indeed that welcomes its "enemies" to buy parts of its fortifications. The creation of a united Europe was inspired by a faith in the benefits of a free market. To close it off would defeat our main purpose: remaining in the vanguard of industry and technological innovation.

Giovanni Agnelli, *Foreign Affairs*, Fall 1989.

A prime example is the recent uproar about the European Community's adoption of a product-specific rule of origin for integrated circuits. The regulation provides that a semiconductor chip originates in the country where the chips are diffused, rather than where the wafers are cut or the chips assembled, tested, and packaged. Diffusion is the technical process by which the integrated circuit is given all its functional capabilities. Considering the technical and economic aspects of the overall manufacturing process, it should not have come as a surprise that the EC considered the diffusion to be the last substantial operation in producing the chips.

Rules Help Interpret Laws

A number of journalists falsely have characterized the rule as a local content requirement preventing U.S. suppliers from selling their chips in the European Community and forcing them to open expensive and otherwise unneeded manufacturing facilities in Europe. U.S. Trade Representative Carla Hills has suggested that the EC may be "manipulating" the rules of origin to use them in an "exclusionary way." These rules do not create any direct legal obligations or restrictions, however. Instead, they are used to interpret and implement other laws or regulations which, in turn, impose legal prohibitions or grant legal privileges. Consequently, depending upon the nature and contents of the law or regulation that incorporates the rules of origin, they may cut either way.

In the European Community, rules of origin play a crucial part in determining whether imported goods are eligible for preferential rates of duty for customs purposes, and whether specific goods may be imported into the EC or into any particular member state under quantitative, external, or intra-Community import restrictions. They further may disqualify goods under the proposed public procurement directives that give a preference to European-origin bids and may determine whether anti-dumping duties can be imposed against certain goods assembled in the European Community. Finally, they establish whether the goods must be marked physically or certified as having a European or a foreign origin.

The 279 legislative or regulatory measures identified in the Europe 1992 program do not include any initiative to introduce a general local content requirement that legally would impede or prevent the importation of non-European goods into the EC. Clearly, rules of origin do not establish such a requirement. . . .

U.S. industry stands to gain a lot from the integration of the EC, if proper attention is paid to the business opportunities evolving in Europe. . . . While misconceptions about the scope of the regulatory program and an unsubstantiated fear of protectionist measures would be the wrong reasons for a U.S. company to go to Europe, the changes in the business environment and the reaction of European and Japanese competitors may not leave American companies a choice.

Understanding Words in Context

Readers occasionally come across words they do not recognize. And frequently, because they do not know a word or words, they will not fully understand the passage being read. Obviously, the reader can look up an unfamiliar word in a dictionary. However, by carefully examining the word in the context in which it is used, the word's meaning can often be determined. A careful reader may find clues to the meaning of the word in surrounding words, ideas, and attitudes.

Below are excerpts from the viewpoints in this chapter. In each excerpt, one word is printed in italicized capital letters. Try to determine the meaning of each word by reading the excerpt. Under each excerpt you will find four definitions for the italicized word. Choose the one that is closest to your understanding of the word.

Finally, use a dictionary to see how well you have understood the words in context. It will be helpful to discuss with others the clues which helped you decide on each word's meaning.

1. Free trade advocates have contributed to America's economic decline by *EXACERBATING* the nation's trade problems.

   EXACERBATING means:

   a) reducing   c) helping
   b) worsening   d) solving

2. In recent years, trade officials have been overwhelmed by the *BURGEONING* number of complaints about unfair trade practices.

   BURGEONING means:

   a) strange   c) small
   b) shrinking   d) growing

3. The once-powerful United States has seen its economic *HEGEMONY* disappear as Japan's trading power and leadership have increased.

   HEGEMONY means:

   a) decline   c) weakness
   b) dominance   d) problems

4. If negotiations fail to provide solutions, free trade may be severely damaged by *INTRACTABLE* problems arising between the United States and its major trading partners.

   INTRACTABLE means:

   a) common   c) unmanageable
   b) minor   d) age-old

5. The major players in the world economy could continue past practices and keep the world evolving on the same *TRAJECTORY* it has followed for the past 45 years.

   TRAJECTORY means:

   a) rocket   c) mission
   b) path   d) comet

6. U.S. prosperity will not be harmed if we channel the movement toward trading blocs in a *BENIGN* direction.

   BENIGN means:

   a) strange   c) westerly
   b) negative   d) favorable

7. So far, the EEC [European Economic Community] Commission has looked only toward the future, and has decided not to seek *RETROACTIVE* benefits from foreign banks already inside Europe.

   RETROACTIVE means:

   a) nuclear   c) relating to the past
   b) money   d) unemployment

8. A united Europe was created to overcome the technological backwardness of the past and to once again place Europe in the *VANGUARD* of industrial and technological innovation.

   VANGUARD means:

   a) army   c) middle
   b) forefront   d) pursuit

Periodical Bibliography

The following articles have been selected to supplement the diverse views presented in this chapter.

Giovanni Agnelli	"The Europe of 1992," *Foreign Affairs*, Fall 1989.
Peter Brimelow	"The Dark Side of 1992," *Forbes*, January 22, 1990.
Susan Dentzer	"The Coming Global Boom," *U.S. News & World Report*, July 16, 1990.
Department of State Bulletin	"U.S.-Canada Free Trade Agreement, October 1989.
Michael Elliott	"EC, Phone Home," *The New Republic*, March 27, 1989.
Robert P. Forrestal	"Europe's Economic Integration in 1992," *Vital Speeches of the Day*, August 1, 1989.
Jeffrey E. Garten	"Japan and Germany: American Concerns," *Foreign Affairs*, Winter 1989/1990.
Fred Gluck	"Europe, Japan Would Lose Trade War," *The Wall Street Journal*, December 10, 1990.
Hans J. Halbheer	"The Integrated European Market 1992—A Swiss Perspective," *Vital Speeches of the Day*, May 15, 1990.
Gary Hufbauer	"Beyond GATT," *Foreign Policy*, Winter 1988/1989.
Robert Kuttner	"Bloc That Trade," *The New Republic*, April 17, 1989.
John Marcom Jr.	"The Unacceptable Face of Protectionism," *Forbes*, November 12, 1990.
Walter Russell Mead	"On the Road to Ruin," *Harper's Magazine*, March 1990.
Robert A. Pastor	"Salinas Takes a Gamble," *The New Republic*, September 10-17, 1990.
Robert J. Samuelson	"World Trade on the Brink," *Newsweek*, December 10, 1990.
Lee Smith	"What's at Stake in the Trade Talks," *Fortune*, August 27, 1990.
Irwin M. Stelzer	"How to Save Free Trade—And Still Trade with Japan," *Commentary*, July 1990.
Preston Townley	"Going Global in the 1990s—The Case for Trading Blocks," *Vital Speeches of the Day*, July 15, 1990.

Glossary of Terms

balance of payments the ratio between a country's income (from exports, loans, etc.) and its outflow of payments (from imports, debt repayment, etc.).

bilateral trade agreements trade agreements between two countries.

Common Market see **EEC/EC**

COCOM Coordinating Committee for Multilateral Export Controls; organization of the United States and its allies created to prevent the export of sensitive technologies to enemy countries.

EEC/EC European Economic Community/European Community; twelve European countries that seek to establish monetary and economic union.

free trade trade based on unrestricted international exchange of goods with little or no governmental restrictions; opposite of **protectionism**.

FTA free trade agreement; usually a **bilateral** agreement to eliminate trade barriers and tariffs between countries; examples of FTAs include those between the U.S. and Canada, and the U.S. and Israel.

GATT General Agreement on Tariffs and Trade; a set of multilateral agreements that aims to reduce restrictions on world trade; member countries work together to reduce tariffs and other barriers to international trade.

mercantilism economic theories prevailing from the sixteenth to eighteenth centuries, in which major trading countries used trade regulations to encourage exports and restrict imports; Adam Smith's attack on mercantilism in 1776 is considered one of the earliest arguments for **free trade**.

MFN most-favored nation clause; a trade agreement clause that requires one member of a trade agreement to extend equal trade benefits to all other members of the agreement; the underlying principle of **GATT**.

multilateral trade agreements trade agreements involving more than two countries; an example is the General Agreement on Tariffs and Trade (**GATT**).

NTM non-tariff barrier; term used to describe **subsidies** and other forms of **protectionism** that are usually less direct and less obvious than **tariffs**.

protectionism policies designed to protect a country's industries from foreign competition; might include import **tariffs** or **quotas**, **subsidies** for domestic products, and other kinds of support for domestic industries.

quota assigned limit on the quantity of a particular good to be imported from a particular country.

Smoot-Hawley Tariff Act passed by the Congress in 1930, bringing tariff levels to their highest point in U.S. history; the Act resulted in a decline of U.S. foreign trade.

subsidy government support, usually financial, for a certain company or industry, often used to help the beneficiary compete with foreign businesses; many countries, for example, subsidize farmers by buying surplus produce at guaranteed prices.

tariff tax on imported goods and services and, more rarely, exports; often designed to protect domestic industries from foreign competition.

trade deficit when a country imports more goods than it exports.

UNCTAD United Nations Conference on Trade and Development; established in 1962 to represent the interests of Third World nations not included in the **GATT**.

Organizations to Contact

The editors have compiled the following list of organizations that are concerned with the issues debated in this book. All of them have publications or information available for interested readers. The descriptions are derived from materials provided by the organizations. This list was compiled upon the date of publication. Names and phone numbers of organizations are subject to change.

American Enterprise Institute
1150 17th St. NW
Washington, DC 20036
(202) 862-5800

The Institute sponsors research on a wide range of national and international issues. It generally takes a stance supporting free trade and opposing protectionism between nations. The Institute publishes the bimonthly journal *American Enterprise.*

American Federation of Labor/Congress of Industrial Organizations (AFL/CIO)
815 16th St. NW
Washington, DC 20006
(202) 637-5000

The AFL/CIO is made up of ninety labor unions with fourteen million total members, and is the largest federation of its kind. It believes the U.S. should take protectionist measures to protect U.S. industries and jobs. It publishes reports and position papers on trade and other labor issues.

The Brookings Institution
1775 Massachusetts Ave. NW
Washington, DC 20036
(202) 797-6220

The Institution, founded in 1927, is a liberal research and education organization that publishes material in the fields of economics, government, and foreign policy. It generally supports free trade and opposes protectionism. The Institution publishes the quarterly *Brookings Review* and various books and reports, including *An American Trade Strategy.*

CATO Institute
224 Second St.
Washington, DC 20003
(202) 546-0200

The Institute is a libertarian public policy research organization that generally opposes government regulations restricting trade. The Institute publishes the *CATO Journal* and various books and reports, including *The Perils of Managed Trade.*

The Commission of the European Communities
2100 M St. NW, Suite 707
Washington, DC 20037
(202) 862-9500

The Commission provides information about the European Community. The EC consists of twelve European countries scheduled for economic unification in 1992. The Commission publishes the magazine *Europe* and provides reports and figures pertaining to trade between the EC and the world. Publications include *Report on United States Trade Barriers and Unfair Trade Practices.*

The Committee for Economic Development (CED)
477 Madison Ave.
New York, NY 10022
(212) 688-2063

The Committee is a research and education organization whose goal is to study and seek solutions to social and economic issues that affect the long-term health of the U.S. economy. Composed of business and academic leaders, it publishes reports and statements on the U.S. economy. Its 1990 report *Breaking New Ground in U.S. Trade Policy* calls for continued U.S. support of free trade and for various U.S. government actions to open foreign markets.

Economic Policy Institute (EPI)
1730 Rhode Island Ave. NW, Suite 200
Washington, DC 20036
(202) 775-8810

EPI is a liberal think tank that conducts research on economics. It advocates strategic trade policies to protect U.S. jobs and to develop U.S. industries. It publishes position papers and reports including *Beyond Free Trade and Protectionism* and *Getting Rid of the Trade Deficit.*

Economic Strategy Institute (ESI)
1100 Connecticut Ave. NW
Suite 1300
Washington, DC 20036
(202) 728-0993

The Institute is a research center that focuses on the links between economic policies, global security, and international trade. It argues that the U.S. needs a national trade and economic strategy to lower America's trade deficit and maintain U.S. technological leadership and economic strength. It publishes *ESI News* and reports including *Looking to the Twenty-first Century.*

Essential Information (EI)
PO Box 19405
Washington, DC 20036
(202) 387-8030

EI is a center for investigative journalism and public education on social, corporate, and global affairs. It publishes *Multinational Monitor*, a monthly magazine which examines multinational corporations and their role in trade and the world economy.

The Foundation for Economic Education, Inc. (FEE)
Irvington-on-Hudson, NY 10533
(914) 591-7230

FEE publishes information and commentary in support of private property, the free market, and limited government. It frequently publishes articles on trade in its monthly magazine *The Freeman*, and has also published the book *Free Trade: The Necessary Foundation for World Peace.*

Institute for International Economics
11 Dupont Cir. NW
Washington, DC 20036
(202) 328-9000

The Institute is a research organization that focuses on trade and other international economic issues. It has published many books and monographs on trade, including *Free Trade Areas and U.S. Trade Policy* and *World Agriculture Trade: Building a Consensus.*

Institute for Local Self-Reliance (ILSR)
2425 18th St. NW
Washington, DC 20009
(202) 232-4108

ILSR promotes the economic self-reliance of cities and communities. It believes that countries and communities should produce their own goods and services rather than trade for them, and opposes efforts to liberalize international trade. The Institute publishes books, pamphlets, and technical reports.

Reason Foundation
2716 Ocean Park Blvd., Suite 1062
Santa Monica, CA 90405
(213) 392-0443

The Foundation promotes individual freedoms and free-market principles. It frequently publishes articles supporting free trade and opposing protectionist policies in its monthly magazine *Reason.*

Retail Industry Trade Action Coalition (RITAC)
701 Pennsylvania Ave. NW, Suite 710
Washington, DC 20004
(202) 662-8744

RITAC is a national association of retail chains and department stores. The Coalition opposes protectionism and import quotas, which it believes lead to higher costs for consumers. It publishes reports on trade legislation.

United States Business and Industrial Council (USBIC)
220 National Press Building
529 14th St. NW
Washington, DC 20045
(202) 662-8744

The Council is a conservative organization which supports trade restrictions when necessary to support U.S. national security and economic strength. It publishes research papers on trade, and several newsletters including *Bulletin.*

United States International Trade Commission (USITC)
500 E St. SW
Washington, DC 20436
(202) 252-1000

USITC is an independent agency which conducts research on foreign trade and how it affects U.S. employment and commerce. It investigates allegations of unfair trade practices, and is responsible for providing trade figures and analysis for the U.S. government. The Commission's numerous reports on U.S. trade are available free to the public.

Bibliography of Books

Donald Altschiller, ed.
Free Trade vs. Protectionism. New York: The H.W. Wilson Company, 1988.

Annelise Anderson and Dennis L. Bark
Thinking About America. Stanford, CA: Hoover Institution Press, 1988.

Robert E. Baldwin
Trade Policy in a Changing World Economy. New York: Harvester Wheatsheaf, 1988.

Jagdish Bhagwati
Protectionism. Cambridge, MA: The MIT Press, 1988.

Don Bonker
America's Trade Crisis. Boston: Houghton Mifflin Co., 1988.

William E. Brock and Robert D. Hormats, eds.
The Global Economy: America's Role in the Decade Ahead. New York: W.W. Norton & Co., 1989.

S. Tamer Cavusgil and Michael R. Czinkota, eds.
International Perspectives on Trade Promotion and Assistance. Westport, CT: Quorum Books, 1990.

Pat Choate and J.K. Linger
The High-Flex Society. New York: Alfred A. Knopf, 1986.

John M. Culbertson
The Trade Threat and U.S. Trade Policy. Madison, WI: 21st Century Press, 1989.

Detlev Chr. Dicke and Ernest Ulrich Petersmann, eds.
Foreign Trade in the Present and New International Economic Order. Boulder, CO: Westview Press, 1988.

Khosrow Fateni, ed.
International Trade. New York: Taylor & Francis, 1989.

Douglas Frantz and Catherine Collins
Selling Out: How We Are Letting Japan Buy Our Land, Our Industries, Our Financial Institutions, and Our Future. Chicago: Contemporary Books, 1990.

Antonio Furino, ed.
Cooperation and Competition in the Global Economy. Cambridge, MA: Ballinger Publishing Company, 1988.

William J. Gill
Trade Wars Against America. New York: Praeger, 1990.

David Greenaway, ed.
Economic Development and International Trade. London: Macmillan Education Ltd., 1988.

Grant T. Hammond
Countertrade, Offsets, and Barter in International Political Economy. London: Pinter Publishers, 1990.

Kichiro Hayashi, ed.
The U.S.-Japanese Economic Relationship: Can It Be Improved? New York: New York University Press, 1989.

Elhanan Helpman and Paul Krugman
Trade Policy and Market Structure. Cambridge, MA: The MIT Press, 1989.

Gary Clyde Hufbauer, ed.
Europe 1992: An American Perspective. Washington, DC: The Brookings Institution, 1990.

John H. Jackson
The World Trading System: Law and Policy of International Relations. Cambridge, MA: The MIT Press, 1989.

C.J. Jepma, ed.
North-South Co-operation in Retrospect and Prospect. New York: Routledge, 1988.

Ronald W. Jones and Anne O. Krueger, eds.
The Political Economy of International Trade. Cambridge, MA: Basil Blackwell, 1990.

Margaret Kelly et al.
Issues and Developments in International Trade Policy. Washington, DC: International Monetary Fund, 1988.

Anne O. Krueger	*Perspectives on Trade and Development.* New York: Harvester Wheatsheaf, 1990.
Paul R. Krugman	*Rethinking International Trade.* Cambridge, MA: The MIT Press, 1990.
Robert Z. Lawrence and Charles L. Schultze, eds.	*An American Trade Strategy, Options for the 1990s.* Washington, DC: The Brookings Institution, 1990.
Edward J. Lincoln	*Japan's Unequal Trade.* Washington, DC: The Brookings Institution, 1990.
Robert Emmet Long, ed.	*Japan and the U.S.* New York: The H.W. Wilson Company, 1990.
William J. Long	*U.S. Export Control Policy.* New York: Columbia University Press, 1989.
Frank. J. Macchiarola, ed.	*International Trade: The Changing Role of the United States.* New York: The Academy of Political Science, 1990.
Ira C. Magaziner	*The Silent War.* New York: Random House, 1988.
Syed Javed Maswood	*Japan and Protection.* New York: Routledge, 1989.
Kenichi Ohmae	*The Borderless World.* New York: Harper Business, 1990.
Richard Pomfret	*Unequal Trade: The Economics of Discriminatory International Trade Policies.* New York: Basil Blackwell, 1988.
Michael E. Porter	*The Competitive Advantage of Nations.* New York: The Free Press, 1990.
Ernest H. Preeg	*The American Challenge in World Trade.* Washington, DC: The Center for Strategic and International Studies, 1989.
Clyde V. Prestowitz Jr.	*Trading Places: How We Allowed Japan to Take the Lead.* New York: Basic Books, 1988.
Matt Schaffer	*Winning the Countertrade War.* New York: John Wiley & Sons, 1989.
Jeffrey J. Schott	*The Global Trade Negotiations: What Can Be Achieved?* Washington, DC: Institute for International Economics, 1990.
Joan Kennedy Taylor, ed.	*Free Trade: The Necessary Foundation for World Peace.* New York: The Foundation for Economic Education, Inc., 1986.
George Vargish	*What's Made in the U.S.A.?* New Brunswick, NJ: Transaction Books, 1988.
Raymond Vernon and Debra L. Spar	*Beyond Globalism: Remaking American Foreign Economic Policy.* New York: The Free Press, 1989.
John Whalley, ed.	*Developing Countries and the Global Trading System.* Ann Arbor: The University of Michigan Press, 1989.
John Yochelson, ed.	*Keeping Pace: U.S. Policies and Global Economic Change.* Cambridge, MA: Ballinger Publishing Company, 1988.

Index